DIGITAL @ SCALE

DIGITAL @ SCALE

*How you can lead your business
to the future with Digital@Scale*

ANAND SWAMINATHAN
JÜRGEN MEFFERT

WILEY

CONTENTS

PREAMBLE: THINKING DIGITAL

THE DIGITAL REVOLUTION *is here, and no industry is immune from its impact. The good news: all companies—big or small—can benefit. German booksellers have grasped their opportunity against a seemingly unassailable opponent.*

For 550 years, everything was fine: Ever since Johannes Gutenberg founded printing with movable letters in 1450, the retail book industry largely remained unchanged. The print shop produced the books and delivered them to the store; customers visited the store, browsed through the selection, and bought their reading material. With the dawn of the new millennium, however, a new upstart turned all the rules upside down. It wasn't enough that the online retailer Amazon grew to become the largest bookseller around the world; with its Kindle device, it introduced a reader for electronic books that quickly became popular.

Pure fear gripped booksellers and the management of big bookstore chains throughout the world. They were faced with a disruptive technology and revolutionary change that was upending the old business model. Digitization had reached their industry, and if they weren't to be ejected from the market like photography specialist Kodak years earlier, or like mail-order catalog retailers, as well as several travel agencies and newspapers, then something had to be done. Large bookstore chains like Borders in the United States and Waterstones in England had already fallen victim to the Amazon infiltration: they ignored the threat for too long, and then reacted too slowly and halfheartedly.

But it was a crisis with a happy ending for German booksellers. Faced with the pressure of rapid change, the bookstore chains Thalia with Michael

Busch, Hugendubel with Maximilian Hugendubel, and Weltbild with Carel Halff, as well as the book clubs of media giant Bertelsmann with Niklas Darijtschuk, had a meeting. According to coinitiator Michael Busch, CEO of Thalia: "We needed to establish strong marketing power in the German-speaking area." And since Thalia as well as Hugendubel and Weltbild had been unable to successfully market their own electronic readers in previous attempts, the book retailers now sought the services of Deutsche Telekom as a technology partner. "We wanted to build a value chain in which all partners were playing at Champions League level," according to Busch. Together, they developed the Tolino e-reader as a rival to Amazon's Kindle, created a Tolino app for mobile devices, and invested in an Internet campaign to market the electronic offering.

Tolino—Alliance of German book retailers with 1,800 stores combined and Deutsche Telekom

Source: http://mytolino.de/shops/

WHY, WHAT, AND HOW? THE KEY QUESTIONS BEFORE ANY DIGITAL TRANSFORMATION

The book retailers and Deutsche Telekom followed a strict strategy based on the overriding sense of urgency that the retailers needed to understand precisely why they needed to act. That is, if they didn't tackle the challenge of digitization, their core business would be threatened. "Fear spurs you on," as Michael Busch puts it.

So what was to be done? The partners needed a concept to conquer the e-reader and e-book market with the ambitious aim of becoming market leaders. And since customers in the digital world wanted stable and above all, simple processes, Tolino needed to offer a customer experience similar to Apple: that is, intuitive to grasp and with an animated and captivating customer journey across all contact points from first contact to purchase.

How could Tolino meet these ambitious targets? The way not to do it quickly became clear: with existing corporate structures, large committees, and elaborate meeting agendas. Instead, a small core team was given extensive authority and decision-making powers. The most important developments were started at the same time and were based on a two-speed information technology (IT) architecture. A traditional IT structure ensured the stability of all the usual processes and the integrity of important data, while another group was organized in the manner of a start-up company, allowing fast and flexible processing of the many tests, learning steps, and corrections that digital product innovations inevitably entail. Deutsche Telekom, meanwhile, designed the hardware, the actual e-reader. At the market launch in 2013, an advertising campaign ran across all digital channels, focusing on television and social media.

Who would have bet on the success of Tolino? In one corner, a group of traditional medium-sized companies and a former state-owned company, and in the other corner, one of the leading global success stories of the digital age. Everything pointed to Amazon. However, the smart approach of the latecomers paid off. In 2015, Tolino pulled level with Amazon in Germany with a market share of between 40 and 45 percent, depending on the counting method.

The key to its success was a specific advantage that traditional retailers have: bricks and mortar. They were able to combine their high-street stores and their online business into an omnichannel concept with 60 million people in Germany visiting a bookstore each year. And since the Tolino partners consistently aligned their marketing mix across all channels, they secured a structural competitive advantage over Amazon: the Americans still had no physical presence in Germany. The Tolino campaign also brought new customers into the brick-and-mortar stores. "Naturally, we sold most of our e-readers in our bookstores," says Michael Busch. This was a major success, but not grounds for relaxing. The battle for superiority is far from decided: market and customer needs are still developing, placing high demands on agility and innovation.

At the beginning of 2017, Deutsche Telekom sold its share in Tolino to the Japanese-Canadian group Kobo, the third-largest online retailer in the world after Amazon and Alibaba. The move further strengthens the Tolino alliance because Kobo has its own generation of e-readers and e-books. Unlike Deutsche Telekom, Kobo, a subsidiary of Rakuten, has global reach, and is therefore an ideal partner for the Tolino alliance in its rivalry with Amazon's Kindle.

TOLINO IS NOW PRESENT IN MORE THAN 1,800 GERMAN BOOKSTORES

The success has not helped all Tolino partners. Weltbild applied for insolvency, and Bertelsmann ended its book clubs in late 2015. However, the media group is still on board with Tolino Media, the wholesaler for e-books, and new partners have joined. For example, the wholesaler Libri brought with it 1,300 bookstores, and with two strong regional groups, a further 70. Today, the Tolino can be bought in more than 1,800 out of a total of 6,000 German bookstores, and the open system has even expanded to Belgium, Italy, Holland, Austria, and Switzerland.

Furthermore, the success of Tolino and the associated prospects for booksellers is likely to have contributed to Thalia being sold for a nine-figure sum in 2016. One of the new owners is CEO Michael Busch. He expects further double-digit growth in e-book commerce with nine million Germans using e-readers by 2020. The Thalia boss sees them as good customers. If they like an e-book, they often also buy the print copy because they still want to flip through an actual book.

The Tolino adventure has taught Busch something: "It doesn't matter where you come from or how big or small your company is. If you have enough imagination and strong willpower, you can achieve just as much with digitization as the giants in Silicon Valley."

The Tolino success can therefore serve as a blueprint for all those companies whose business models are threatened by digitization. The answers to three questions provide a model for digital transformations—including for your company:

1. *Why* does a company need to change in light of the digital challenge, and how critical is the topic of digital for the company's business?
2. *What* precisely needs to change—from the overall business model and the central elements of value creation such as product development, marketing, and the supply chain, through to basic functions such as technology, organization, and corporate culture?
3. *How* will the company organize the digital transformation and change structures, processes, IT, and management instruments?

This book provides concrete answers to these questions, and includes numerous success stories, putting you and your business on the path to a successful digital future.

□–□–1–□–□
DIGITAL IS CHANGING OUR WORLD, QUICKLY AND IRREVERSIBLY

FROM CUSTOMER RELATIONSHIPS *and production control to communication with suppliers: In the digital age, companies need to rethink their entire business models. Those who don't risk failure and extinction.*

The successful battle of the traditional booksellers and their Tolino e-reader with the Internet giant Amazon and its Kindle device not only inspires courage, but is also rich in lessons. Even the most cursory of analyses is enough to dispel a widely held belief that, contrary to popular opinion, digitization is not primarily an information technology (IT) issue. Effective IT is just the foundation on which the digitization of the entire company is built. It's about far more than simply implementing digital technologies—the ultimate goal is to develop completely new business models. This takes us to the heart of the issue: digitization starts with the CEO.

1.1 WHAT IS A DIGITAL TRANSFORMATION?
A digital transformation leverages the opportunities presented by technology—from IT to advanced analytics, sensors, robotics, and 3D printing—to drive business forward. The entire ecosystem of the company is affected, including employees, customers, suppliers, and partners. Companies that want to digitize successfully can either improve their current business model and processes, add new sources of revenue to their business model, or replace their old business model with a new superior model. In doing so, companies realize new customer experiences, generate new value propositions, and raise the organization to new levels of effectiveness and efficiency. Digitization thus changes structures, processes, and IT, as well as the people who live and work in this new reality.

Digital Players Conquer and Disrupt All Industries

However, this wonderful new world has a dark side: those who refuse to change, lose. Digitization triggers creative destruction, a term popularized by economist Joseph Schumpeter. The new combination of production factors ousts and destroys old structures and traditional business models.

Digitization is fundamentally changing the world

	Market leader	Attacker
Computers	COMPAQ	DELL
Video rental	BLOCKBUSTER	NETFLIX
Books	BORDERS	amazon
Mobility	TAXI	⚠ UBER
Automakers	⛽ 🚗	⚠ TESLA

Digitization claimed its first prominent victim when the Internet was still in its infancy, when smartphones belonged to the realm of science fiction and apps were still unheard-of: Compaq was the undisputed global leader in personal computer (PC) and server sales in 1996, with a market share of more than 50 percent in the business customer segment. Compaq built its computers in the old-fashioned way, and delivered them to distribution partners for sale in their stores. That same year, the then 31-year-old Michael Dell launched direct sales of his Dell PCs via the Internet without the need for brick-and-mortar stores. And it wasn't just the order process that was revolutionary: Dell's customers were able to assemble their own customized PCs using a kit on the website. Thus, computers were no longer built according to the Compaq principle of "build to stock," but rather "build to order," and were tailored to the needs of the individual customer.

Although not immediately apparent to its competitors, Dell's business model was superior to the business model of Compaq and the rest of the industry. Online sales and lean mass production according to the build-to-order principle made the difference between earning and losing money in this hard-fought market with tight margins. Compaq didn't dare to change its business model because it feared a channel conflict, and ultimately stayed true to its existing model. In 1997, Compaq was acquired by Hewlett-Packard, and Dell rose to become the world market leader.

Since Dell's digital revolution of the PC industry, many industries have had their foundations shaken. Video libraries, CD stores, travel agents, and local banks are just some of the endangered species in a world where we now stream our movies and music via Netflix and Spotify, book our flights and accommodations via portals like Expedia and Airbnb, manage our bank accounts online, and can even secure classic banking services like loans via crowdfunding sites like Prosper.

Digitization Is Relevant for All Industries—Only Scale and Speed Will Vary

Anyone who hopes one's own industry will not be affected by digitization and chooses to continue along as before in blissful oblivion is making a risky assumption. Essentially, all sectors are affected; the only difference is the severity and length of time until the old business model is rendered obsolete.

Digitization affects all industries—with varying speed and scale

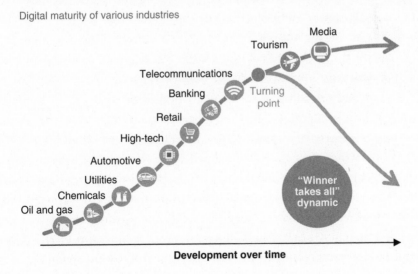

Digital maturity of various industries

Companies face dramatic challenges in many industries. Who is to say that tomorrow's driverless cars will still be built by Ford, BMW, Toyota, and the like, and not by Tesla, Google, or Apple? And in a few years, who will equip our smart homes with Internet-connected robot vacuum cleaners and ovens? Who will deliver the groceries that our smart refrigerators automatically order online? Kroger or Amazon?

Naturally, the topic of digitization is on the agenda of most companies. Many companies have started digital initiatives, for example in customer communications, in production, or in supplier interaction. However, most CEOs currently admit they do not have an overarching digital strategy. Their ideal transformation toward becoming a digital company often lacks definition, and all too often they have too narrow an understanding of the term *digitization*. It is not just IT and technology. These are only the foundation. Rather, it is about transforming the entire company—redefining customer value propositions, value-added processes, and people's working methods.

It has radically changed consumer behavior and expectations, destroyed traditional business models, and redefined industries. It revolutionizes production—think Industry 4.0—and rocks entire business sectors. Retail faces challenges from digital competitors like Amazon and Alibaba, the banking industry is threatened by lucrative fintech segments, travel portals like Expedia and Priceline are shaking up the tourism industry, and the traditional business models of the advertising industry are being rocked by a variety of digital channels. Digitization is even creating new markets, for example the so-called sharing economy where urban hipsters dispense with owning a car in favor of Uber or Zipcar.

Companies operating in the analog world must not let it get too late before they join the digital mix. Start-ups that tap into a customer need sometimes experience explosive growth. In China, for example, Tencent, whose WhatsApp-equivalent QQ is used by 900 million Chinese customers, saw its revenues increase a hundredfold in 10 years to around €14 billion in 2015. Tencent states that one in two employees works in research and development. And Chinese Uber rival Didi Chuxing, which dominates the taxi and limousine market in the country, more than tripled its company value in 18 months from around $6 billion in 2015 to some $20 billion.

New Business Models Follow a Classic Pattern

The business ideas triggered by digitization can be grouped across two dimensions depending on whether they are driven by the supply side or the demand side and whether they lead to extended or improved or even completely new business models. An example of a new offering leading to an extended business model is Kayak. The company has digitized the classic travel agency business, allowing users to search for flights, hotels, and rental cars online. The business model itself is still based on a classic system where providers pay a commission to Kayak.

Other digital companies' offerings tap into a demand that it was previously not possible to service. One example of this is Spotify, whose streaming service provides customers with access to its entire library of music. Rather than paying to listen to individual songs, users pay a subscription. This completely new business model revolutionized the music market and fundamentally turned the industry on its head. By comparison, Apple's iTunes music store appears conventional.

An example of a demand-driven revolution is the Dollar Shave Club. The company, which was recently bought by Unilever for $1 billion, offers razors and shaving accessories for men in return for a membership fee. By subscribing, members receive a monthly package containing the necessary blades and shaving foam, which saves a trip to the drugstore.

Nike iD is a demand-driven extension of a business model. Customers can individually design their sports shoes online, customizing the shape, material, and color, and even add a monogram.

Consumer Behavior Has Dramatically Changed in Recent Years

The McKinsey long-term study "TMT Digital Insights" tracks changes in consumer behavior in the most important global markets and segments, and has revealed dramatic changes in US consumer behavior. Here are two examples:

Consumers want everything, anywhere, anytime: In 2016, 83 percent of consumers possessed a smartphone—the same number as those who own a home PC. Even tablets, which first became a mass phenomenon in 2010 with Apple's iPad, are now owned by two-thirds of consumers. This has key consequences for user behavior: US consumers now spend more time on

Digitization enables new business models

Expansion of previous business model

Demand

Supply

New business model

their smartphones and tablets than they do on the PC. Mobile consumers expect answers immediately when researching products and prices on the move or when they want to order something. Smartphones and tablets have become personal command centers. Companies that do not adjust their online presence to service the mobile "anytime, anywhere" mentality may lose ground to their competitors.

Increasing relevance of visual media: The medium of video has become significantly more important. Consumers now spend more time watching videos than before—often at the same time as other (often also digital) activities. So-called over-the-top (OTT) video content published directly online is threatening traditional linear TV and pay-per-view models. To remain attractive to customers, companies need to supplement their traditional text-intensive communications with videos. For a long time now, consumer fascination with the virtual world has impacted the real world economy: advertising budgets have shifted dramatically—from TV and print to mobile providers. And now video content is conquering the small screen: series are now optimized for smartphone screens in terms of time and image composition.

Retailers, service providers, and consumer goods companies are also feeling the pressure to digitize their processes and offerings, driven by customers whose research and buying behavior has drastically changed in the past decade. Consumers browse online forums to find out about a product's quality, they check value for money on comparison sites, and they use Twitter, Instagram, and the like to post their opinions. And even when shopping in a store, they're happy to check their smartphones to see if a product they like is available for a lower price from an online retailer or a local rival.

1.2 ESTABLISHED MARKET DEFINITIONS DON'T APPLY ANYMORE

At the same time, managers find that the established definitions of their markets no longer apply—new challenges lurk everywhere. The networking of previously unconnected devices with online data sources—the Internet of Things—has dissolved traditional industry boundaries. Take the health care sector as an example: suddenly, technology firms with their apps and fitness bands have entered their industry, using the data leveraged from their customers to develop completely new business models. Even the old classification of companies that sell to business customers (B2B), and those that deliver to end customers (B2C) is becoming blurred—suddenly we see the term B2B2C. Even an industrial company like Alcoa might now like to know what the end customer does with its aluminum.

Naturally, as digital pushes through, the frequency of channel conflicts that need to be managed increases. The accumulated data needs to be professionally analyzed, which requires new talent in the company. The result of all these factors is increased pressure on management.

Innovations Arise at Industry Boundaries

Previously, the business world was transparent: everyone knew who their competitors were, and surprises from outside the industry were rare. This fine sense of certainty has gone; digitization has made transgressions easy. For example, Amazon with its Amazon Web Services (AWS) is now the world's leading provider of cloud services. Microsoft and IBM, which might have been expected to occupy this position as the top dogs in the IT industry, are positioned on the next rung down by some distance—they never reckoned with this competitor. Originally, Amazon had only intended to better utilize the capacities of its huge data centers. In the meantime, IT companies yet again find themselves wrangling with another intruder:

General Electric (GE), whose subsidiary Predix offers a cloud-based platform for analyzing data sent from industrial machines—a cornerstone of Industry 4.0 applications.

Even traditional machinery manufacturers are now crossing industrial boundaries. John Deere, for example, one of the giants in agricultural machinery and tractor manufacturing, offers software and data-based services. These services process highly detailed weather forecasts with data on soil conditions, the specific properties of the seed used, and a wide range of additional information to provide recommendations to farmers to help them increase their yields. It also helps save fuel, reduce repair cycles, and ensure optimum use of the vehicle fleet. Sensors installed in the vehicles send on-site data to the Deere data center, and farmers can access their information via the MyJohnDeere.com platform or view it on their smartphone or tablet via the Mobile Farm Manager app.

The chemicals group Monsanto is pushing into the agricultural world from a different direction. In 2012, the seed specialist bought Precision Planting, a manufacturer of hardware and software, whose products help farmers during sowing to optimize seed depth, distances, and conditions to ensure the best roots. It's the same customer base as Monsanto's core business and the same value proposition—more yield in the field—and yet a completely different technical approach. Monsanto has harmoniously expanded its business model, while at the same time breaking down industry boundaries.

Blurring Boundaries between B2B and B2C: B2B Becomes B2B2C

Previously, these worlds were strictly separated. When addressing end consumers, the pitch focused on emotion, enjoyment, and, above all, simplicity: the choice had to be made simple for consumers. Business customers, on the other hand, wanted to know the details; they demanded facts and rationality.

This distinction, however, is now obsolete due to digitization. Once business clients experienced how easy orders were with Amazon or Google as private consumers, how simple it was to search for products, and how quickly items could be delivered, they naturally transferred these expectations to the B2B segment. Why should an order for machine spare parts be more complicated than ordering a book from Amazon? Why does the delivery take weeks instead of one day? Why is the manual written in technical jargon and not simple to understand? Why is the supplier's website so difficult to search? And why doesn't the supplier respond immediately to a complaint?

And it's not just customer relationships in the B2B segment that are increasingly mirroring those in the consumer sector. Thanks to digitization, many B2B providers are expanding their business model and also addressing end customers: B2B2C. Take Craftzilla as an example: the Indian e-commerce platform connects small-scale home decor manufacturers and artisans, who previously sold their products through specialty retailers, directly to the end customers. Craftzilla doesn't hold any inventory—the company connects sellers with customers and takes a commission from sales made on its website.

Fitness band manufacturer Fitbit applies the B2B2C concept by establishing company fitness programs with companies like BP and Adobe to promote employee health: the contract partner is the company—B2B—and the employees are the consumers—B2B2C. Panasonic and Allianz also collaborate in the same manner to make houses and apartments more secure. Panasonic installs its monitoring and control systems at the customer's home, while Allianz Global Assistance, a subsidiary service provider of Allianz, is alerted in the event of a serious incident so that emergency services are dispatched.

Managing Channel Conflicts

Digitization is revolutionizing customer contact, and not just in the end consumer segment. New rules also apply in B2B, often based on the B2C model. German heating system manufacturers, for example, previously marketed their products primarily via the installers. Companies such as Buderus, Viessmann, Vaillant, Wolf, and Junkers all cultivated their heating installers, who in turn brought in customers.

A Berlin-based start-up, Thermondo, however, disrupted this model by creating a platform to connect the various decentralized service and installation teams that supply customers with heating systems across Germany. The portal was founded in 2012. As early as 2015, the company was achieving an annual growth rate of 864 percent. A customer searching the portal can choose from numerous brands, and is given a tailored fixed price that includes installation. Thermondo even gives advice on applying for funding.

Manufacturers and tradespeople now have a problem: their old business model is under threat. The problem sounds familiar—think back to the Compaq example. And just like in the Compaq case, the problem doesn't simply go away. An approach now needs to be developed governing how, for example, heating system manufacturers, installers, Thermondo, and the other market players work together in the new ecosystem. What is needed is omnichannel management.

Thermondo is revolutionizing the heating industry, providing customers an end-to-end offering of installation and assembly

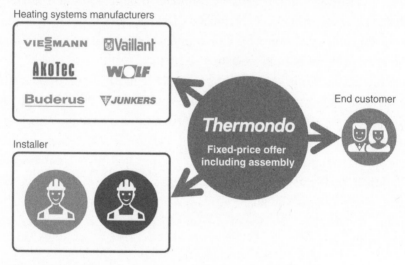

Source: Company websites

Software and Analytics Competencies Becoming
Increasingly Important

"Data is the new oil" is a popular saying. Data forms the raw material for any digitization initiative. According to a McKinsey study, in 2015 international flows of data contributed more to global economic growth than classic trading of goods. Companies receive or procure huge amounts of data that can be translated into large sums of money with smart analytics.

Thus, online retailers like Amazon or Overstock use dynamic pricing systems that allow them to make second-specific price adjustments for the several million items in their ranges. To this end, they constantly retrieve information about competitors' prices, and process this along with data about current sales promotions. Using time series and big data analyses, they then calculate new inverse demand curves for all their items in hourly cycles.

The Battle for Digital Talent

Although digitization opens up countless opportunities, large companies with a traditional structure and strong division of labor from production through to sales find it difficult to grasp them. The fact that they don't have enough digital talent on board and therefore have to compete in the labor market for the scarce resources of new IT and software experts is just part of the problem. Even if these companies already had such talent, they could not achieve much as an isolated department. There needs to be a basic understanding throughout management of the possibilities and limitations of digitization.

This includes the observation that nothing is to be gained with classic departmental thinking, and that cross-functional teams need to take control of projects. Whoever wants to win the battle for digital talent needs to start here. This is particularly difficult for traditional companies: after all, specialization and a strong division of labor were for a long time considered factors of success.

1.3 THE PACE OF CHANGE IS INCREASING EXPONENTIALLY

A further obstacle on the path toward becoming a digital company lies in a deeply human weakness: we are accustomed to thinking linearly, and highly disruptive change makes us uneasy. According to the futurist and Google director of engineering, Ray Kurzweil, this is why we tend to smooth exponential functions back toward a linear curve by mapping them on a logarithmic scale. However, this is fatal when it comes to mental processing of the changes involved in digitization, because they develop according to an exponential function and at an increasingly rapid pace.

In his essay *The Law of Accelerating Returns* Kurzweil impressively describes the exponential dynamics of technological progress throughout human history when correctly mapped on a linear scale, and not on a distorting logarithmic scale. He surmises that people intuitively gravitate to this distorting perspective, and thus—against their better judgment—significantly underestimate the speed and extent of future developments. He predicts rapid progress for the twenty-first century because we are currently in the advanced section of the exponential curve.

In an interview, he explained the fundamental dynamics of exponential growth: "If I take 30 steps in a linear manner—1, 2, 3, 4, 5—I get to 30. If I take 30 steps in an exponential manner, I go 2, 4, 8, 16, and get to a billion." It's fascinating logic and one that can't be refuted—and yet it's so hard to believe, the mind blocks it out. "Today, everyone expects continuous, linear development in technical advances, but the future will surprise us far more dramatically than most observers believe," Kurzweil says. "Very few understand what it will mean for the pace of change to accelerate even faster."

Ray Kurzweil's *Law of Accelerating Returns* describes the exponential dynamics of technological progress

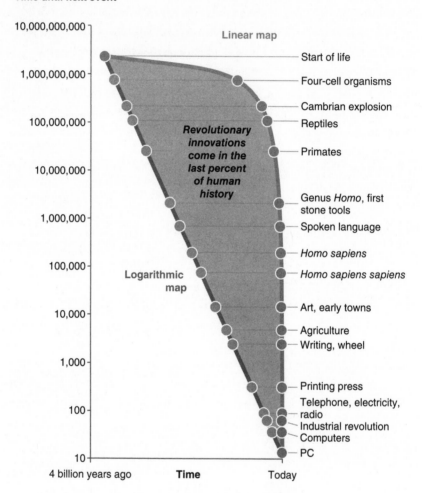

Source: Ray Kurzweil

Progress and Moore's Law

Two examples corroborate Kurzweil's theory of the logarithmic development of progress. The best-known is Moore's law. Gordon Moore, cofounder of Intel, formulated his theory in 1965 in the journal *Electronics*. He noted that the number of circuit components in an integrated circuit doubles each year, and predicted that this will continue. To this day, he has been proved right—processing power has doubled every year. Chips have become smaller and smaller. Today, a standard smartphone has 120 times the processing power of the control computer of NASA's Apollo moon program, and is four times that of an IBM mainframe from 1998—which was the size of a refrigerator. And an iPad 2 would have been one of the world's fastest supercomputers in 1994.

Further support for Kurzweil's theory is the fact that new technologies are adopted increasingly quickly. Following the invention of the radio, it was another 38 years before 50 million devices were in use around the world. The TV needed 13 years to be welcomed into 50 million living rooms. The Internet boasted that many users after just three years. Facebook needed one year to reach this figure, and Twitter just nine months. In 2016, the hype surrounding Pokémon Go heralded a new record: the game was downloaded to the smartphones of 50 million fans in just 19 days. New products and services are being developed and distributed at an unprecedented pace. Managers around the world still struggle to anticipate such rapid change.

1.4 THOSE WHO TURN A BLIND EYE TO DIGITAL RISK FAILURE AND EXTINCTION

Even though no one expects managers to develop psychic powers, the example of the erstwhile global brand Kodak shows what happens when the company's management refuses to accept digital change. Blessed with creative developers, Kodak Labs presented the world's first digital camera as far back as 1975. However, the management put the brakes on the project, fearing that this novelty might adversely affect the highly profitable business with Kodak films. Instead, rivals from Japan did so in the 1980s. When Kodak finally started making digital cameras, it was too late and their early advantage was lost. By 2012, Kodak was bankrupt and its market value of $35 billion was gone.

New technologies spread ever faster
Years to first 50 million users

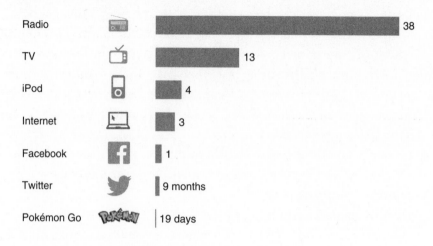

Radio		38
TV		13
iPod		4
Internet		3
Facebook		1
Twitter		9 months
Pokémon Go		19 days

Source: Company reports; McKinsey Global Institute

In the meantime, even the market for digital cameras has become a niche market, but who knows, had Kodak taken the bold step into the digital age in 1975, maybe a learning curve like that of Apple would have been possible. Perhaps then the first iPhone would have been built by camera manufacturer Kodak and not by the computer manufacturer Apple.

QUESTIONS MANAGERS SHOULD ASK THEMSELVES: WHERE ARE YOU?

- What is the phase and degree of digitization in your industry?
- Where is your business model most vulnerable?
- How quickly do changes take place, and how big are they?
- How do you react to these changes—with a lot of small, short-term initiatives or with larger, long-term initiatives?
- Do you know which digital investment(s) deliver the greatest benefit in your industry?
- How much change do you need to survive?
- What are you doing yourself? Where do you need partners or acquisitions?

□-□-②-□-□
DIGITIZATION REQUIRES FUNDAMENTAL RENEWAL: DIGITAL@SCALE

WHY? WHAT? HOW? *The concept for a successful transformation into a digital company is based on the answers to these three questions.*

For a hundred years, Henry Ford defined our image of business: highly specialized assembly line production with a clear division of labor producing mass scale products ("You can have the Ford Model T in any color as long as it's black"). The Taylorist system that focuses entirely on specialization and efficiency has given us affordable cars, washing machines, and holiday travel.

And it is this very model of success from the twentieth century that has now become the obstacle to the successful digital transformation of companies. Indeed, organizations that are built for efficiency fear that change brings disorder, and instead tend toward incremental adoption of innovation in tightly defined niche projects so as not to halt the well-oiled corporate machine. All economists know the S curve concept that defines the performance of a technology as a function of the funds invested for research and development. As such, the transition to a new superior technology—the leap to the next S curve—is initially always met with a loss in efficiency.

Unfortunately, those who hesitate to take this leap will lose in the long term. Although efficiency increases only slowly in the lower curve of the new S, the curve suddenly rises very sharply and is ultimately catapulted far beyond the level of the old technology. But this doesn't help us: those who want to successfully lead their companies into the new digital age need to rethink all structures, processes, and products at scale across the board—that is, Digital@Scale.

It's easy to build an app. A digital transformation is a much harder task. To ensure that the transformation doesn't founder on good intentions and unfinished business, digitization needs to follow a clearly defined concept. To start, we need to leave aside catchphrases like Industry 4.0 in order to prepare for fundamental renewal. Three simple questions point the way forward: Why? What? How?

Digital@Scale—The transformation framework

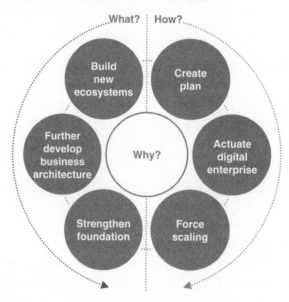

2.1 WHY? THINGS ARE GOING WELL, SO WHY DO WE NEED TO CHANGE?

Companies that are doing good business find it very difficult to suddenly reinvent themselves in order to ensure sales and profit tomorrow. Early indicators of change are often overlooked or seen as unimportant. Even today we still see experiences with the digital revolution like that of Blockbuster, Inc.

In 2004, Blockbuster was the largest video rental company in the United States with 8,000 stores and revenues of $6 billion. No one on the board of the powerful market leader took Netflix seriously, the rival company formed just a few years before where customers could rent DVDs online and receive them in the mail, with attractive subscription models. With no sense of urgency, the Blockbuster engineers worked on a system for online orders. In 2007, Netflix took a huge leap forward by offering video on demand—movies that could be streamed directly via the Internet. The DVD was obsolete. Customers swarmed to Netflix in droves thanks to its attractive offering: no waiting times for mail delivery, no returns to mail, immediate enjoyment.

Only then did Blockbuster react, and developed its own video-on-demand system, but it was too late and of poor quality. Netflix had already gained significant market share, and Blockbuster did not offer any innovative new features that might have won customers back—and to top it all, Blockbuster's level of service and delivery was worse than that of Netflix. Netflix had immediately won over the Internet-savvy, mostly young customer base. And in just a few years, the vast majority of movie fans discovered just how easy it was to enjoy a pleasant evening with Netflix. Today, Netflix is the market leader, while Blockbuster filed for bankruptcy in 2010.

Netflix replaced DVD rental with a consistent digital online offering—despite all its efforts, market leader Blockbuster was unable to survive

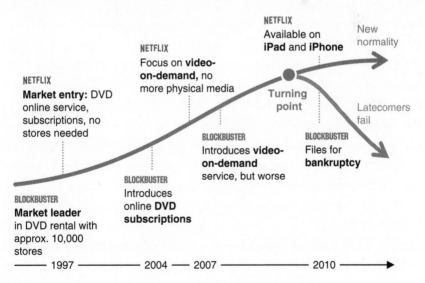

The lesson from this example is clear: regardless of how well positioned a company is, if the management underestimates the potential for change that digitization poses to its business model, it runs the ultimate risk. And those who see the change but delay their response so as not to jeopardize their current revenues are taking a virtually suicidal stance.

Creating a Sense of Urgency: The Key Challenge

Fundamental renewal demands strength, conviction, and, in most cases, a trigger. A little fear—even existential fear—is a good thing. Fear spurs you on. In established companies, it creates the pressure to act and the willingness to embrace innovation—crucial for digitization. After all, it's about developing new products, services, and processes that enable attractive prices—in short, a completely new value proposition. Those who fail to implement the transformation across the board (@Scale) will fall behind. It is simply fatal to underestimate the extent of the impending change.

Bosch CEO Volkmar Denner put it like this: "There are many things that just make it easier to order a pizza or call a taxi. But don't underestimate the influence of such solutions on society; people are changing their consumer behavior. Suddenly others are earning the money." Without a sense of urgency, nothing is possible; we are only too happy to look the other way.

Determining the Nature of the Change Requirements

We've already discovered that digitization affects everyone, just not necessarily to the same degree. The question that CEOs should ask themselves is: is our current business model obsolete, or will targeted changes suffice?

Usually, if the change requirements are high, the business model will look completely different post-transformation. As Jeffrey Immelt, CEO of industry giant General Electric, put it in the summer of 2016: "We need to become a software company in *all* divisions of GE." In addition to selling machines and equipment as well as maintaining them, software for the networked world of the Internet of Things (IoT) is to become a new business area for the company.

Radical change is also underway. For example, the Chinese iron and steel giant Baosteel has established an open online marketplace called Ouyeel. While initial versions of the e-commerce website allowed Baosteel to offer its products on a new channel, it has since expanded significantly to include competitor products and adjacent offerings such as financing, logistics, data, and technical services. Ouyeel is also supported by a massive analytics engine that provides pricing and analytics insights. Between 2013 and 2015, revenue from digital activities for Baosteel grew at more than 300 percent per annum. By the end of 2015, Baosteel's digital activities contributed more than $800 million to the top line.[1]

Digitization has also reached manual trades. For example, at elevator maker Schindler, over 50 percent of the staff work in field services. This staff performs activities that are largely manual and heavily reliant on expertise. In the past, the time to resolve an issue was often impacted by the fact that the field service staff had limited information on the issue prior to the site visit, and therefore might not have the required tools and/or parts on hand. Finally, part reorders created extra costs and revisits. Schindler was able to simplify this whole process by automating diagnostics, applying predictive analytics to preemptively address issues and order parts in advance, and the company enabled field services staff with iPhones and supporting apps to help simplify in-field activities. All this has helped significantly improve service efficiency, as well as customer and employee satisfaction.[2]

Identifying Barriers to Change Early

Traditional organizations have high levels of inertia. When business is going well, managers and employees generally only pay lip service to change requirements. Any manager who still wants the company to change therefore needs to analyze and eliminate the barriers.

Efficient organizations in particular tend to prove especially resistant to change. They follow their own logic: any change to the existing system would create efficiency costs and must therefore be avoided. The most successful managers often slow down transformation efforts behind the scenes. They calculate that they have little to win personally, but much to lose. They are often the opinion leaders and belong to the inner circle—making change twice as difficult. After all, doesn't the team still need these managers? Perhaps not.

[1] McKinsey; www.ouyeel.cn/aboutus.html
[2] www.apple.com/business/success-stories/

Identifying Relevant Assets and Setting the Aspiration Level

Those who want to propel their company from the analog present to the digital future should first focus on the strengths: What sets the company apart from the competition? The technology in the product or service? The strong customer loyalty? The attractiveness of the brand? All of these strengths also count in the digital world. And while they may count differently, whoever retains them will have an advantage.

Without a clearly defined objective, the journey into the digital world can easily become an odyssey. The company management should therefore formulate its quantitative or qualitative objective, and communicate this to the employees. Interim goals—depending on whether and how they are achieved—are also helpful in determining whether the project is on track.

In all of these points, from generating awareness of the need for action, determining the change requirements, and identifying the greatest obstacles and the greatest strengths, through to formulating objectives, responsibility rests with the company management. Chapter 3 deals with how to respond to employees who ask why change is necessary, and how to respond in such a way that they are happy to embark on the digital transformation.

2.2 WHAT? WHAT DOES DIGITIZATION MEAN FOR MY COMPANY, AND WHAT PRIORITIES ARE DERIVED?

Digitization means different things to different people. We need a structure and a plan. To answer the "What?" question, it is helpful to build a three-stage structure that can be used to prioritize the strategic and operational tasks.

Building New Ecosystems

At the first level, New Ecosystems, strategic thinking is needed. Innovations arise at industry boundaries. This is all about the new markets that emerge as a result of the technological possibilities. In this book, we select nine of the most important new ecosystems. In Chapter 4, we discuss how digitization is changing mobility, how smart our homes will become, what will happen to commerce, what banks need to focus on, what will change in public administration, what digital health care will look like, the threats to telecommunications groups, how drastically logistics is changing, and how even old technologies like electricity grids are being revolutionized by digitization.

These are the strategic questions all managers need to ask themselves: are competitors attacking our business with new technologies? Are we grasping the opportunities of digitization and actively developing new value propositions? Are new profit pools emerging at the boundaries between traditional industries? The more unsettling the answers, the greater the willingness to revise the current business model and to accept cannibalization of revenues. A new vision for the company is needed with a convincing value proposition that takes into account the disruptive force of change.

Developing Business Architecture

The second level, Business Architecture, deals with operational questions: Are we using the opportunities of the digital world and reaching our customers at all contact points—both traditional and new? Are we leveraging all the advantages that digitization and new analysis methods offer? And how is digitization changing our management and administrative processes?

In Chapter 5, we describe how digitization is changing the business architecture, focusing on three areas: the customer experience, product innovation, and value added. The challenge is significant: digital attackers are strongest when it comes to the customer experience. With simple and reliable processes, they seamlessly shape the entire journey from first contact to completed order, often making traditional companies appear outdated. Many new players also benefit from open platforms for developments, thus increasing the innovation pace of their products. Billing, support, data analysis—the best attackers have digitized the entire value chain. However, digitization doesn't just affect production areas; it also fundamentally changes management and administrative functions. These new players set the example for all companies that intend to take up the challenge.

Strengthening the Foundation

The third level, Foundation, deals with the technological and organizational frameworks. Typical questions include: are we employing state-of-the-art technology in our company? How can we make our company agile without taking on too many risks? How can we attract digital talent and build targeted partnerships?

In Chapter 6, we discuss the challenges for the foundation, and focus on two areas: technology as well as culture and organization. We start with a practical problem: an existing IT system cannot be replaced overnight if completely new skills are required for digital projects. Thus the company also needs a second pillar, an agile and fast separate IT system. To operate it, the best new digital talent may need to be hired—talent that expects flat hierarchies and cross-functional working. In short, both the culture and the organization need to be overhauled.

2.3 HOW? HOW DO I MANAGE THE TASKS RESULTING FROM A DIGITAL TRANSFORMATION?

The answers to the What question resulted in a list of priorities to be addressed on the road to the digital transformation. Now it's time for the How. Successful transformations require profound changes to structures, processes, management instruments, and IT. Again, a three-stage structure is needed, which sorts the relevant points by priority.

Create a Plan

At the top of the list is a road map to the digital future: calibrate people and processes for the digital world. Second, it's always about the customer—digitize all contact points that customers have with the company according to importance. And to ensure we find the digital solutions, we radically abolish the functional silos in the company, and form overarching teams supplemented with digital talent.

The plan outlines the direction and priority, and is often the cornerstone of a transformation program that almost always lasts years. Chapter 7 describes how companies can meet the requirements of the plan.

Ramping Up the Digital Company

The next level down defines the elements of the digital company. This is where companies need to optimize their development according to the motto "Pace before perfection" in a culture of testing and learning.

New products and services are quickly tested in the market; the results are measured, and then further optimized if necessary. Budgets are tied to the achievement of interim targets, progress is analyzed in fixed cycles, and projects are immediately canceled if necessary—in short, the digital operating system. Chapter 8 explains how this works.

Consistent Scaling

The third level deals with consistent implementation, focusing on scaling and rolling out the transformation process to the entire company and its ecosystem. A twin-track IT structure is needed: day-to-day business where all the sensitive data is handled in the stable structures as usual, and agile IT systems for the fast-developing new projects. The biggest challenge at this level, however, is the rapid, company-wide installation of solutions tested in pilots—Digital@Scale, as explained in Chapter 9.

Digitization begins with the strengths of the company. Companies that build their business models on outstanding customer service need to consider which new service offerings are made possible by digital technology. Companies that process large volumes of data each day should first look for big data solutions that allow them to offer new services to their customer base. For example, a networked health care model combines tried-and-tested communications technologies with new IT concepts. It's a combination that's already demonstrating its potentials. Thanks to big data, treatment paths can be personalized, while the smart evaluation of data enables predictive diagnostics, benefiting both physicians and patients.

And companies such as discount retailers that focus on the efficiency of their processes have much to gain from the digitization of the supply chain. For example, sensors can be fitted to transported goods, and the generated data can be analyzed to help develop improved routes and more efficient supply chains.

2.4 CARGO CULTS DON'T WORK

The considerations sound simple. However, treacherous traps lurk in practice that are best illustrated using the example of the "cargo cult." The term was coined by the recipient of the 1965 Nobel Prize for physics, Richard Feynman, to describe poor scientific method. He told his students an anecdote from the island of Samoa.

During World War II, US aircraft regularly landed in Samoa, and the airmen would often share with the indigenous locals the glorious gifts of western civilization: Coca-Cola, Camel cigarettes, and Cadbury chocolates. Following the end of the war, the flights stopped, and the disappointed Samoans called for the return of the flights and their beloved cargo in what quickly developed into a cult. They built wooden aircraft and wore bamboo headphones to simulate radio traffic. However, it was all in vain, as Coca-Cola and the rest of the treasured cargo never returned. Although the islanders had recognized the phenomenon—the aircraft brought their coveted products—they had drawn the wrong conclusions.

Many companies respond to the digital challenge in a similar way. They recognize the phenomenon, but react wrongly. These are our top three cargo cults of the digital world:

1. *Digital start-ups:* Cosmetic exercises such as these are seen quite often. A digital start-up is founded a long way from the company's head offices with a small budget and a couple of young employees. However, these halfhearted efforts are rarely able to have any influence on the established business model. This isn't to say that we shouldn't still learn and actively employ such structures. Just don't expect start-ups like these to solve your digitization challenges for you.

2. *Digital sugar-coating:* Another unsuitable method is to bolt a digital process onto any opportunity that seems to appear. There are plenty of examples of teams of interns being asked to look after social media communications. Another example is that companies often understand the value of their data, be it data about customers, suppliers, or the value chain, and they begin to collect this data systematically. However, the will to use this collected knowledge in all processes is often lacking, and big-data islands emerge.

3. *Efficiency traps:* Another trap emerges from the legacy of Taylorist efficiency methods. For example, when it comes to digitization, management concentrates entirely on automation, rather than thinking at scale and looking for opportunities to increase value across all processes.

The CEO Must Take the Lead

And once again, everything depends on the CEO. Only if change is demonstrated and exemplified by the top management will the necessary changes to structures, processes, and management instruments, as well as the establishment of new skills and new IT systems, be successful. No one is saying that this is easy. "We don't go to bed one night and say: when we wake up, we don't want to be an industrial company anymore; we want to work like Oracle or Microsoft instead," says Jeffrey Immelt, the CEO of General Electric.

Six years ago, Immelt ushered in a digital transformation at the 120-year-old industrial corporation. It was a laborious process during which GE studied elements of the digital economy—for example, abolishing hierarchies and bureaucracy—while at the same time reactivating proven methods such as lean production and streamlined development. Immelt also hired digital talent in the thousands, and with Predix now offers an open platform for controlling Industry 4.0 processes on which not only GE apps can run, but also those of external developers. Software has now become its own division at GE, and yet the digital transformation is far from over—this is a journey that never ends.

Thus, the fate of traditional companies depends on the attitude of the CEO. Will he or she recognize the signs, and plot an early course toward digitization like Jeffrey Immelt? Or will the CEO read events like the last German kaiser read the emergence of the automobile—as a passing trend ("I believe in the horse," said Wilhelm II).

$$\square - \square - \boxed{3} - \square - \square$$

WHY? THE CLOCK IS TICKING

LEADERSHIP IS NEEDED: *Only CEOs can explain to employees the need for digital change, define the scope and direction needed, and overcome the forces of inertia in the company. Only then can the march toward to the digital future begin.*

When the Springer publishing house sent the editor-in-chief of its *Bild* newspaper and the director of marketing to Silicon Valley for nine months in 2012, there was much amusement within German management circles—more so when *Bild* helmsman Kai Diekmann immediately assimilated and grew a hipster beard and started wearing a hoodie like a true West Coast native. Since then, the publishing house's example has become the norm—Springer is regarded as one of the pioneers in German business when it comes to digital transformations. CEOs around the world have since started taking study trips to Silicon Valley, often taking their entire executive teams along.

For a long time, the biggest tech companies have been inundated with visitors. Everyone wants to know the secret of the Big Five of Apple, Facebook, Google, Amazon, and Uber. They go in search of stimulation and ideas, hoping to be inspired in this world of innovation. At Google, there is a dinosaur skeleton in the foyer that states: "Big is nothing. You can still die out." This point must be top of the list when CEOs explain the need for a digital transformation to their employees and try to impart a sense of urgency.

How dangerous is the current situation? How far-reaching are the necessary changes in the company? What is stopping the transformation?

What strengths should we build on? And where will the journey take us? Answering the 15 questions on these five topics in the graphic will give you a good sense of where your company stands and how it needs to move forward.

Why? Key questions for management

Sense of urgency	1 Have we identified the threats and potentials of digitization?	2 Have we engaged in frank and honest stocktaking?	3 Have we experienced digitization at first hand?
Type of change	4 Can our current business survive in the digital world?	5 Are targeted interventions enough?	6 Do we have the new talent for the digital change?
Barriers to change	7 Are owners, employees, and managers suffering extreme stress?	8 Are the best and most successful managers supporting the change?	9 Are our organizational silos standing in the way of change?
Relevant assets	10 What are our key assets—customers, products, technologies?	11 Which of these assets are still relevant in the digital age?	12 How can we successfully transform these assets for the digital age?
Ambition	13 Is the CEO personally driving change?	14 How high should we aim, and how fast should we act?	15 Are our employees on board?

3.1 CREATING A SENSE OF URGENCY: HOW URGENT IS DIGITIZATION?

The observation that change is needed is one thing—but the actual trigger to embark on a transformation often arises in emotionally charged moments following meetings and experiences. Book retailer Michael Busch, CEO of Thalia, had such a moment when he contacted Apple to discuss whether there was any possibility of collaborating on e-books, and was met with complete disinterest. For Busch, the answer was clear: the company needed its own solution. He soon set about bringing together collaboration partners for the Tolino system.

Markus Langes-Swarovski, CEO of crystal emporium Swarovski, shocked his family business partners in 2012 by drawing parallels with the recently bankrupted Kodak, a firm that was founded in 1888, seven years before Swarovski. Both companies were market leaders and successful for decades—until Kodak was felled by digitization. At supervisory board meetings, just as at family meals, family get-togethers, and festive events, Langes-Swarovski always imparted the same message to his relatives: if the company is to remain highly successful, it needs to transform into a technology company. And progress, he cunningly argued, was in the genes of the family and the company that their great-grandfather, a gifted engineer, turned into an unrivaled leader with his ideas on glass processing. Langes-Swarovski convinced the partners, and the company now enjoys successful online sales, and boasts modern production techniques using the latest robotics and 3D printers; it has its own start-up laboratory in the Inn valley, a wealth of innovative products, and much more. Close and professional customer support throughout the customer journey coupled with the ability to also manufacture cost-effectively in small runs have today been shown to be important and effective tools, even against low-cost offerings from China that flood the market.

The alarm bells sounded for Martin Viessmann, CEO of the heating, cooling, and energy systems company of the same name, in 2014 when Google bought the start-up Nest, a developer of smart, self-learning heating and cooling thermostats. "When the world's biggest Internet company starts looking at a small manufacturer of thermostats, it's clear where the journey's headed," he said. According to Viessmann: "If we don't want to end up as an extended workbench of U.S. technology giants, we also need to get involved in the battle for platforms, software, and data." Since then, Viessmann has transformed his company. Instead of continuing to concentrate predominantly on equipment sales, the 100-year-old family business is developing more and more software services, from remote control of heating and air-conditioning systems via a smartphone app to automatic meter reading and self-regulating systems. "Those who don't take digitization seriously are risking extinction," says Martin Viessmann. In mid-2016, he stood down from the operational leadership of the business and took a backseat as president of the board of directors. His successor as CEO was the former CDO—the chief digital officer.

Jeffrey Immelt, CEO of General Electric, remembers precisely the day in June 2009 when his developers came to him and presented a new jet turbine full of sensors that could send back a stream of data about any flight. Immelt noticed two things. First, this data could actually be just as valuable as the turbines themselves. Second, GE wouldn't be able to do anything with it, because the company lacked the software expertise. Immelt poured his energies into bringing about a digital transformation, including in the mind-sets of his employees. Instead of thinking of their primary competitors as companies like Siemens, they needed to start focusing on Amazon or IBM instead. "We act. We learn. We get better" was his interim conclusion in the 2015 annual report.

As the GE example shows, the start of a successful digital transformation requires more than the CEO simply having a eureka moment. The CEO must shape this moment of enlightenment and make it intuitively clear, at least to the top management, that the company needs to take the path toward the digital future.

It is often easier to convince the board members in smaller companies—the most successful of which tend to have an inherent survival instinct—than those of large, listed corporations. The governance structures in these companies often act as a brake; works councils and supervisory boards tend not to welcome profound change, and very few of their members would be classified as digital natives. Following their revelatory moment, the top managers must then act as multipliers to spread the message throughout the company that digital transformation is urgently required. These, then, are the most important tasks that management must perform to motivate the entire workforce and sensitize all employees to the idea of digitization.

Taking Leadership in Hand

The top management must overcome mental barriers in the company such as "not relevant to us" or "we've done that for a long time anyway." To do so, strong arguments are combined with entrepreneurial vision to inform, convince, inspire, and motivate all stakeholders. There will always be resistance and concerns in certain groups. Owners (particularly in family businesses) or active investors, employees, and managers, but also sales partners and suppliers need to get involved from their current starting positions. Each of these groups can either act as a catalyst for the transformation or become an obstacle. It is crucial to capture the heart and mind: the mind through convincing business logic, new best practice examples, tools, and methods; the heart through success stories, tales of heroism, and even personal experience.

Benchmarking to Assess Starting Position

To determine the degree of urgency for digitization, substantive and objective stocktaking is in order. To this end, the management should answer 10 critical questions on the current strategy of the company:

1. Are we anticipating the impact of the digital revolution on our business model and revenues?
2. Are we actively creating an ecosystem of partners, customers, and suppliers that will last into the digital world?
3. Are we allowing room for a digital strategy that may even cannibalize current revenues?
4. Are we assessing whether we can use our strengths and the new business model to penetrate completely new industries within the current rules?
5. Do we intend to spin off currently valuable areas of the portfolio because they have too little potential for the digital future?
6. Does our current strategy reflect the high pace and uncertainty of the digital age?
7. Are we taking into consideration the force with which future technological developments may impact our business?
8. Are we using our best talent in our digitization teams?
9. Are we prioritizing and allocating capital, talent, and management capacity in accordance with our digital strategy?
10. Have we defined a feasible time scale and meaningful key performance indicators (KPIs) to reliably measure success or failure?

The answers to these questions, which are drawn from McKinsey's Digital Quotient (DQ) diagnostics, allow very reliable stocktaking. If you are interested, and would like to know where your own company stands and how a benchmarking can be taken, find out more at: www.mckinsey.com/business-functions/digital-mckinsey/how-we-help-clients/digital-quotient.

Experiencing Digital Live

The Bible states: "Blessed are those that have not seen, and yet have believed." In the real world, however, only real experiences count. The situation today is a reminder of a time 25 years ago when, once again, there was a key moment. Toyota ran a two-page advertisement: on the left, an S-class Mercedes; on the right, two Lexus S 400s plus a flight ticket to New York on the Concorde—for the same price. In the early 1990s, costs were important. Leading companies around the world promptly made a pilgrimage to Japan, and returned with lean production and Six Sigma. Spurred on by Toyota, Honda, and Sony, they tried to recapture their international competitiveness.

And it's exactly the same when it comes to digital, as the examples at the beginning of this book show. But it doesn't always have to be Silicon Valley—a walk through New York's Silicon Alley and the start-up scene in Austin, London, and Singapore, to name a few, is also insightful. Investments are manageable, and the benefits are huge. For a real eye-opener, though, just pay a visit to the digital scene in China—particularly Shanghai, Hangzhou, and Beijing.

Sampling Digital at a Hackathon

To emphasize the urgency of digital change in the workforce, it can help to borrow a tried-and-tested tool from the digital natives: the hackathon. This portmanteau of hacking and marathon refers to creative sessions where small, cross-functional groups of tech-savvy innovators work locked away together until they find an ingenious solution to a particular problem. Working according to the motto "build, test, refine," the teams—which largely have a free hand—focus on pace and pragmatism. Facebook, for example, developed its "Like" button in this way. Companies in many industries now use this fast and cost-saving method.

The benefits are clear: long-winded meetings, steering committees, and working groups are no longer necessary to provide smaller, market-ready products and services.

Large companies now even use hackathons to have external experts analyze problems. Consumer goods group Unilever, for example, launched a hackathon competition in which the teams were asked to develop original ideas as to how the company could influence the purchase decision of consumers in favor of its brands before they visit the supermarket. The winning team would win a prize of £30,000 and a long-term partnership with the group.

In 2015, supermarket group Sainsbury's invited all of its 161,000 employees to submit ideas as to how technology could make the lives of its customers and employees easier. The best six ideas were made into prototypes in just 24 hours in a hackathon in the Sainsbury's digital laboratory in London. The topic was so important to the executive management that both the CEO and the chairman took part.

To enable companies to tap into the hackathon as a source of innovation, a scene of specialist providers has now emerged: Hacker League, for example, has organized more than 600 of these creative sessions since 2011, and was taken over by Intel in 2013. AngelHack, founded in 2011, boasts a network of 97,000 developers, designers, and entrepreneurs. The Angels organize public hackathon events around the world where thousands of developers take part. However, they also organize private hackathons for customers including Comcast, MasterCard, Hearst, HP, Hasbro, and UBS.

Mobilizing Your Employees to Uncover Weaknesses

Most CEOs, however, rely on their own employees. Bosch CEO Volker Denner, for example, asked his workforce to form "disruption discovery teams." The teams were to asked consider which digital strategies could be used to attack the Bosch business model—according to the motto: "Better that we find our weaknesses than allow others to." In just six weeks, employees had submitted 1,800 ideas. Denner and his management team selected the most interesting, and then released those teams from their daily duties for eight weeks. During this time, they were able to work on their ideas, and either develop ideas for new business models or at least highlight the weaknesses of the current models.

As with all projects that fundamentally change a company, the digital transformation must also be triggered and driven forward by the person in charge—either the CEO or the owner. Employees need an example to emulate. Business leaders can find inspiration in the legendary speech of U.S. President John F. Kennedy in September 1962 in which he announced his plans to put a man on the moon before the end of the decade. His justification for setting such an ambitious target was interesting: "We choose to go to the moon not because it is easy, but because it is hard; because that goal will serve to organize and measure the best of our energies and skills." The attempt to reach the stars brings out the best in teams, and that's excellent advice for business leaders.

3.2 DETERMINING THE KIND OF CHANGE REQUIRED

All companies need to act, but not necessarily in the same way. First and foremost, it is imperative to understand the urgency of the situation. A glance at the extent of digital penetration in the company's own industry reveals the first insight—B2C already tends to be more affected by digitization than B2B. Another important aspect is the extent to which assets are utilized. Whereas in retail comparatively few assets are needed (asset light), it is completely different in chemicals and mining (asset heavy).

The type of change can be broken down into four archetypes

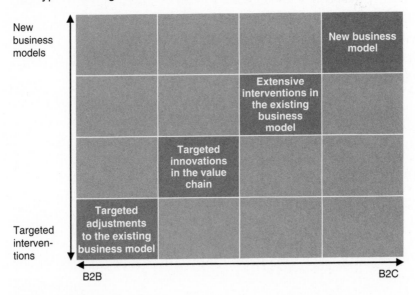

The position of the company's own industry determines the nature and pace of the response. For example, industries that so far have barely been affected by digitization such as the oil and gas industry or the chemicals industry are typically able to manage with a few functional interventions. The greater the extent of digital penetration, the more urgent the need for change. And once past the turning point, generally only those companies that completely revise their business model will survive.

Those at the Top Right Need an Entirely New Business Model

An example of this is the former publishing house Axel Springer. CEO Mathias Döpfner realized early on that the revenue base for the newspaper business was breaking up, starting with classified ads for cars, property, and jobs. He anticipated that while digitization would on the one hand change the reading habits of his customers, on the other hand it would also grow into an attractive medium for advertising, thus further eroding the foundations of the old business model of the newspaper and magazine group.

However, the publisher still enjoyed high returns, and as early as the turn of the new millennium, Döpfner began decisively investing this money in digital. Some of this was in the form of acquisitions, including online portals that are now flourishing businesses with real estate advertising (Immowelt) and job boards (StepStone). Continuing with its ambitious plans, Springer also founded its own digital company. Even though the CEO is rarely seen without a tie, he called for a digital culture to be established throughout the group, and ensured that the start-up mentality remained strong in the acquired and recently founded companies, with flat hierarchies and fast decision making.

Döpfner sacrificed tradition in order to usher in the digital transformation of the company. In 2014, he sold a whole range of titles that included not only the TV listings guide *Hörzu*, which was once the foundation for founder Axel Springer's fairy-tale rise to becoming the most powerful newspaper mogul in Europe, but also *Hamburger Abendblatt*, the first daily newspaper that Springer founded. Publishing group Funke Mediengruppe took over the portfolio of print products, which were still entirely profitable. Springer, meanwhile, now makes more money than ever: in the 2015 financial year, around 70 percent of its earnings before interest, taxes, depreciation, and amortization (EBITDA) were generated in digital.

Extensive Interventions in the Existing Business Model

The fashion industry is also high up on the digital penetration curve. Change at the venerable U.S. fashion house Nordstrom—founded in 1901—began with a realization. "In our industry, most growth will be seen in e-commerce in future," noted Blake Nordstrom, CEO of the family business, back in 2003. "This is the field on which our battle will be won or lost." As a result, he instigated far-reaching changes to the old business model.

Nordstrom gradually introduced an online store, and right from the outset ensured a consistent crossover of sales channels. Soon, customers were able to collect the goods they had ordered online in the local stores. Conversely, the stores also had an online connection to the warehouse, and if a customer was unable to find an item in the right size or color, the store could immediately check its availability and organize delivery.

It was clear that the customer experience must always be at the heart of the process. For example, it was important that the sales assistant didn't scuttle off to a back room to check availability on an arcane inventory management system, but instead showed the customer the ordered item on the attractive layout of an iPad.

In the battle with online-only retailers, Nordstrom relies on a solid advantage: the shopping experience in brick-and-mortar stores. Customers are given the red carpet treatment in stores, where they can view, touch, and try on the items. The chain deliberately sets out to ascertain buyers' needs: for customers uncertain of their fashion choices, they offer the Nordstrom Trunk Club, which uses an online survey to identify preferences, and then suggests and sends suitable items. Nordstrom Rack offers online and offline discount bargains.

All Nordstrom formats run on the same technology, but deliver the customer completely different offerings. The strategy targets attractive multichannel shoppers. According to market research, this group spends three to four times as much money as customers who shop only in-store or online. Delivering a seamless service in both worlds hasn't come cheaply for Nordstrom: by 2020, the U.S. outfit intends to invest $1.5 billion in its technology platform.

Targeted Innovations in the Value Chain

Unlike Nordstrom, U.S. airlines are not yet ushering in a new business model, but rather making do with a few extensive interventions in their value chain when it comes to digitization. Primarily, these relate to processes governing customer information, bookings, and check-in and boarding. These are areas where digitization has made significant inroads. The airline websites and apps have long taken the place of travel agents. Passengers who don't already have their boarding card electronically on their smartphone can print it themselves. And the staff aren't even needed at boarding anymore: a scanner at the gate reads the QR code on the boarding card or smartphone and allows the passenger to pass. Even the reading material has gone digital. The passenger can download the latest newspapers and magazines before takeoff. After this, it's back to analog. As yet, there's no transporter that can beam us to our destination. We still need an airplane and pilot.

Targeted Additions to the Existing Business Model

Industries that primarily operate at a B2B level, and for which key assets such as patents, brands, customer relationships, or market understanding are critical to success, currently have relatively stable business models. However, digitization is also generating considerable pressure on the cost position. This is why companies in this position are typically using digitization to further improve their efficiency, as the example of a multinational oil group shows.

The purchasing department awards hundreds of thousands of contracts each year, from procuring parts for drill rigs to servicing work performed on oil fields across every continent. However, it was always impossible for buyers to create price transparency, because there were simply too many variables in too many countries. In one case, for example, costs for drilling into shale varied enormously. The company put together a data team that gathered information from the company's own finance department, from operational departments, from competitor and investor presentations, and from published reports. A software program then processed the millions of items of data, adapted the data, and looked for price correlations and probabilities. A team of engineers and buyers then analyzed the results, and made suggestions as to how the design of the boring tubes should be adjusted, and how the procurement and selection of the drill crew should change. As a result, the company saved $700,000 per drill hole. With 1,300 drill holes, that's almost a billion dollars, all thanks to the intelligent evaluation of large data volumes, or big data.

Naturally, there are far simpler examples. Rio Tinto is replacing the drivers in its Australian mines with autonomous wagons. Caterpillar is increasing equipment utilization with predictive maintenance based on the operating data permanently transmitted by its machines. As a result, Caterpillar has increased utilization by 30 to 40 percent: a significant impact with relatively little cost.

Those Who Know the Roadblocks Overcome Them More Easily

Once the company has realized that something needs to change, and once the management has identified the extent of change needed, there is still one more step before the transformation can begin. It is vital to discover as soon as possible which hurdles may cause the digitization project to fail. Three insights reveal the biggest obstacles. Companies that anticipate these stand the best chance of a successful transformation:

1. *Efficient organizations often slow down the necessary change.* When business is going well, the company lacks the sense of urgency; specialization and a strong division of labor are barriers to the necessary cross-functional approach for a digital transformation.

2. *Ironically, it is often the best and most efficient managers who stand in the way of the project.* And it's hardly any wonder—they're being asked to give up much of what made them and their company successful. The transformation needs to start with the person at the top, and it's often those who have grown accustomed to success who find it most difficult to change course.

3. *Deep-rooted mind-sets and working methods in functional silos are also a barrier.* A successful digital transformation focuses the attention of all employees on the customer, the benefits for the customer, and the customer journey. This view extends across all contact points, from first contact through to repairs and spare parts services long after the purchase.

How can the brakes be released? With convincing leadership and communication. John Chambers, executive chairman of Cisco Systems: "At least 40% of all businesses will die in the next 10 years . . . if they don't figure out how to change their entire company to accommodate new technologies."[1]

3.3 IDENTIFYING RELEVANT ASSETS

Where to start? First and foremost, it's about the core of the business—the benefit to the customer. What are the relevant assets, the company strengths that must be transferred over to the digital world? Which can be left behind? A self-developed technology or technological expertise?

[1] http://robllewellyn.com/digital-transformation-quotes/

Customer relationships or a strong brand? Products? Services? Or detailed customer or product data? What really counts? Once this is clear, the threat becomes an opportunity. After all, established companies do not necessarily have poorer prospects than start-ups or industry outsiders—quite the opposite in fact. On no account does everything suddenly need to be jettisoned. Companies that transfer their strengths to the digital world will retain their lead. It's about recognizing where the new technology can help the company the most, and how it will help to renew the company.

What it's not about is a patchwork project—something that many associate with digitization. "We don't just program apps, but build solutions around our products that our customers should desire," according to Bosch CEO Volkmar Denner. This is something that the company is increasingly succeeding in doing. Take domestic products, for example: "We are the Apple of the heating systems industry; we've turned heaters into design objects."

Powerful Brand

Markus Lange-Swarovski of Austrian crystal specialists Swarovski is also relying on the greatest strength of his company in the digital future: the radiance of the brand. In addition to a website, he has also set up a sales platform that offers products from other luxury manufacturers that contain Swarovski crystal. The allure of the Swarovski brand draws customers to the website, and if they order something from the Oscar de la Renta, Stuart Weitzman, or Escada collections, Swarovski receives a commission.

Strong Customer Relationship

Even Disney has firmly staked its digital future on its greatest strength: knowing what Disney customers really want, and having the ability to deliver it. As the message of the theme parks states, "Making memories to last a lifetime." Disney uses digital technology to make everything as easy and pleasant as possible for the customer from initial contact to making memories—from planning the trip and staying at the theme park, right through to departure and beyond. Using the My Disney Experience website and app, customers can plan a trip, make reservations for specific attractions and restaurants, check information, and purchase photos after their visit.

The MagicBand is a waterproof plastic wristband that provides access to all the reservations made in My Disney Experience. It acts as an entrance card for entering the theme park and even as a door key in the Disney Resort Hotel. It stores restaurant reservations, and allows wearers to use the "fast lane" to skip the long lines at popular attractions. At the same time, Disney also collects data about customer behavior, which it uses to offer even more tailored recommendations to further increase customer satisfaction.

Extensive Installed Base

Caterpillar, the world leader in construction machinery and other heavy equipment, wants to tap new revenue sources using a specific advantage that many other machinery manufacturers also have: an installed base of machines in use by customers around the world. Of the three million active Caterpillar vehicles, around 400,000 have numerous sensors built in. These transmit vast amounts of data to Caterpillar's Vital Information Management System (VIMS) platform, allowing data-driven monitoring (e.g., protection against theft), control (vehicle deployment planning), and optimization (avoiding unplanned downtimes by monitoring vital elements like the gearbox and engine).

Volume of data is the key, which is an advantage for the manufacturer given its large installed base. Older models and even vehicles of other manufacturers can be fitted with cost-effective sensor kits. Caterpillar leases software-as-a-service packages to its customers to manage their vehicle fleets and increase productivity.

Deep Customer Insights

John Deere, the manufacturer of agricultural machinery introduced in Chapter 1, has even gone a step further. Deere not only ensures longer life cyles for its machines—as does Caterpillar—but has also transferred an old strength to the digital world. Deere has always helped its customers achieve greater yield in their fields, but now the farmers are sent sowing and fertilizing recommendations directly to their tractors via a John Deere app. The recommendations are based on the specific soil data and highly detailed weather forecasts.

Emotional Ties

Lego customers often form an emotional relationship with the brand, and Lego uses this to interact with fans across various channels. Lego Ideas allowed children and adults to submit new ideas for building kits. These were assessed by other members of the community, and Lego then brought the most popular ideas to market.

Beer drinkers, too, develop emotional ties to their favorite brands. Heineken relies on this, and thanks to its entertainment offerings and interactive games, the drinks company has managed to acquire more than 20 million likes on Facebook, several times more than its competitors.

Even more successful than Lego and Heineken, however, a 2,000-year-old organization has translated the appeal of its global brand into social media success: the Catholic church. More than 10 million people follow Pope Francis on Twitter, where he posts brief messages to his followers around the world.

3.4 DETERMINING THE ASPIRATION LEVEL FOR THE TRANSFORMATION

Identify and communicate: first, the management needs to be clear about the objective of the transformation, and formulate it articulately. The managers must then consider and describe the scope and impact of the changes. Next comes the difficult part: the aim of the changes must be communicated to the team, while at the same time creating enthusiasm and enjoyment for the upcoming work.

Once again, a specific example may help. In 2009, Mathias Döpfner, CEO of Axel Springer, announced that within the next 10 years, half of the company's revenues and profit should come from digital. He delivered: in 2015, 62 percent of revenues and 70 percent of EBITDA were generated in digital activities.

Jeffrey Immelt of General Electric, on the other hand, verbalized his aim, albeit a very ambitious one, rather than quantifying it: GE must become the world's leading digital industrial company. In its business report, the company already describes itself as "The Digital Industrial."

QUESTIONS MANAGERS SHOULD ASK THEMSELVES: WHERE ARE YOU?

If even the pope has gone digital, there can no longer be any doubt: the clock is ticking. CEOs and managers need to tackle the challenges of digitization. As ever, the transformation begins with an honest self-assessment. Where do we stand, on which strengths can we build, and what roadblocks can be expected? This stocktaking exercise helps to answer the key questions that we posed at the introduction to this chapter.

Why? Key self-appraisal questions for management

Level of agreement from 1 (very low) to 5 (very high)

		1 2 3 4 5
Sense of urgency	1 Have we identified the threats and potentials of digitization?	
	2 Have we engaged in frank and honest stocktaking?	
	3 Have we experienced digitization at first hand?	
Type of change	4 Can our current business survive in the digital world?	
	5 Are targeted interventions enough?	
	6 Do we have the new talent for the digital change?	
Barriers to change	7 Are owners, employees, and managers suffering extreme stress?	
	8 Are the best and most successful managers supporting the change?	
	9 Are our organizational silos standing in the way of change?	
Relevant assets	10 What are our key assets—customers, products, technologies?	
	11 Which of these assets are still relevant in the digital age?	
	12 How can we successfully transform these assets for the digital age?	
Ambition	13 Is the CEO personally driving change?	
	14 How high should we aim, and how fast should we act?	
	15 Are our employees on board?	

CONCLUSION: BRING ON THE NEW ECOSYSTEMS

This chapter outlined why companies need to embark on the journey to the digital world. The following chapters explain the new industries and ecosystems in which they can find their future path, how digitization is changing every function in the company, and how the foundations must be built on technology and organization for the new age. New ecosystems are breaking down boundaries across all industries, from automotive to banking, retail to construction, and bringing in competition between competitors that previously had nothing to do with each other.

□-□-④-□-□

WHAT? DOING THE RIGHT THINGS INTELLIGENTLY

DIGITIZATION IS A *very broad term, but a program needs structure. It's about new ecosystems, further development of the business model, and acquiring fundamental skills.*

When managers today talk about the challenges of digitization, they encounter countless definitions and completely different worldviews, and some struggle with adapting their business model. They wonder if their market will still exist tomorrow, or if they are destined to go the same way as Kodak. Others are highly focused on their business system, and wonder how IT can improve the supply chain or help them better understand their customers. Others again wonder if their IT is even capable of handling the new data streams. To develop a viable strategy, we need a common language, a common understanding, and a structure supported by all.

To this end, we introduce three levels in this book. The first level is about our future market. Are new competitors disrupting our current business model with innovative technologies? Are they upending once-irrefutable paradigms?

The second level is about whether our business model is capable of meeting the challenges. Are we grasping digital opportunities to fundamentally improve the customer experience? Are we decisively leveraging dormant efficiency potentials with digital and advanced analytics?

The third level concerns the foundation—the IT technology and the organization. Are we using state-of-the-art technologies? Are we an attractive company for new digital talent, and are we building targeted partnerships?

What? Key questions for management

Building new ecosystems	1 Are competitors attacking our business model with new technologies?	2 Are we leveraging the potentials of digital technologies to reinvent ourselves?	3 Are new profit pools emerging at the boundaries between traditional industries?
Developing the business architecture	4 Are we fully grasping digitization to fundamentally improve the customer experience?	5 Are we developing new products quickly and radically enough to get ahead?	6 Are we fully leveraging the efficiency potentials of digitization and advanced analytics?
Strengthening the foundation	7 Are we using state-of-the-art technologies and IT?	8 Do we have an agile and flat organization, and do we promote entrepreneurial thinking?	9 Are we attracting new talent to our company, and are we building targeted partnerships?

At each of these three levels, companies will face specific challenges on the road to the digital future. When it comes to new ecosystems, it's about companies finding their place in the emerging markets. The business architecture needs to be rebuilt to work successfully in new ecosystems, and the foundation of technology, organization, and culture must in turn create the conditions for the new business architecture to function.

Management faces key questions at each of the three levels. At the level of the new ecosystems, the threat to the company's business model by competitors with advanced technologies must be assessed, while, on the other hand, the opportunities presented by this very same technology must be considered. In evaluating the business architecture, the company must analyze the extent to which it already leverages the potentials that digital offers in marketing, innovation, and value added. And in terms of the foundation, it's about how suitable the company's technology, processes, and culture are for the challenges of the digital world.

The New Ecosystems, the Business Architecture, and the Foundation
Industry boundaries belonged to the old economy, and the digital revolution has swept them away. Entirely new ecosystems of companies are

What? New ecosystems, business architecture, and foundation

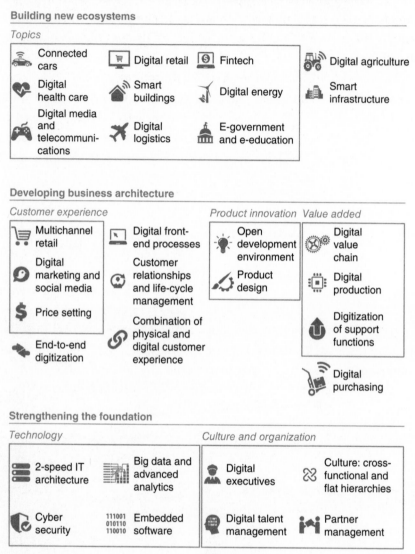

Building new ecosystems

Topics

- Connected cars
- Digital retail
- Fintech
- Digital agriculture
- Digital health care
- Smart buildings
- Digital energy
- Smart infrastructure
- Digital media and telecommunications
- Digital logistics
- E-government and e-education

Developing business architecture

Customer experience

- Multichannel retail
- Digital front-end processes
- Digital marketing and social media
- Customer relationships and life-cycle management
- Price setting
- Combination of physical and digital customer experience
- End-to-end digitization

Product innovation

- Open development environment
- Product design

Value added

- Digital value chain
- Digital production
- Digitization of support functions
- Digital purchasing

Strengthening the foundation

Technology

- 2-speed IT architecture
- Big data and advanced analytics
- Cyber security
- Embedded software

Culture and organization

- Digital executives
- Culture: cross-functional and flat hierarchies
- Digital talent management
- Partner management

- Connectivity
- Agility

emerging to meet demand. Who will build the fully connected autonomous cars of tomorrow? Will banks still be needed for the financial transactions of the future? Will the equipment for smart homes come from the heating suppliers of today, or will completely different companies tap the added value? Digitization brings us entirely *new economic ecosystems* that will create redistribution of market shares. This is the focus of Chapter 4, in which we discuss the most exciting developments.

However, digitization is also changing the internal *business architecture* of companies—from the way marketing is done to the organization of the value chain. Chapter 5 discusses how the company's functions need to change. Chapter 6 looks at the new demands that digitization places on the *foundations* on which companies work, from the IT architecture to the digital culture.

What: Building new ecosystems

The most spectacular developments are in the new ecosystems, where everything is at stake for the traditional market leaders. Industry boundaries are being redrawn, old strengths suddenly count for less, and unexpected symbiotic alliances are being formed. In this chapter, we look at the most exciting ecosystems that are currently emerging. They concern mobility and smart buildings, online retail and digitized utilities, logistics, finance, health, media, and public administration.

4.1 ALWAYS ONLINE, GLADLY ELECTRIC, OFTEN ON AUTOPILOT: MOBILITY IN THE DIGITAL AGE

Aamer Baig and Gianluca Camplone on the future of motoring.

The headlines for the first mass-produced autonomous (driverless) car to drive on public roads weren't in celebration of General Motors or Mercedes, or even Toyota or Audi. Instead, the plaudits were for Silicon Valley–based electric car manufacturer Tesla. A few accidents later, and it's clear this is more about public relations (PR) than a technological breakthrough. The Tesla has a built-in autopilot classified as Level 3, which means autonomous driving is possible in some situations, but continuous monitoring is required. Only at Level 5 can the redundant drivers turn their attention to other distractions. So the race is still on, and even though Silicon Valley giants like Tesla are working hard, it's a little premature to lower the final curtain on the car industry in the rest of the world.

However, as of April 2018, Tesla's market capitalization is $51 billion, and it has surpassed Ford, Chrysler, and General Motors to become America's most valuable carmaker. That despite losing more than $700 million in 2016 and Ford making $11 billion in profits. Investors are expecting Tesla to dominate the new autonomy space, similarly to how Amazon has dominated retailing. Additionally, Tesla is investing in solar and battery technology, and building an ecosystem in the process.

Everyone agrees that the automotive industry will change fundamentally. Experts expect the kind of revolution that the smartphone brought to our day-to-day lives to occur within the automotive industry in the next few years. Soon, the car will be electric and driverless, won't belong to us anymore, and will be used only as required; we'll make it available to others when we don't need it. The revolution raises a lot of unanswered questions: (1) What will happen to the hundreds of thousands of workers who build the internal combustion engines and transmissions of today? Especially when electric powertrains are much simpler to build and do not require a transmission system. (2) In the further future, what will happen to the automotive supply chain? The whole supply chain and manufacturing process is getting digitized, and it is not hard to fathom a future with almost "lights-out factories" that automatically produce cars that are made to order. (3) How will the aftermarket repair and servicing industry be affected? The ecosystem present today will not go away, but demand will lessen significantly, as electric vehicles will not require maintenance as frequently as today's vehicles. (4) Will we see the end of urbanization? Will we prefer to move back to the country if we can work on the way to the office instead of having to sit at the wheel and steer the car? What will the public transport of tomorrow look like? Will normal buses and rail be replaced by driverless minibuses that pick up passengers who entered similar destinations into an app, and later drop them off at their doorsteps? Additionally, there are other technology questions that remain: for example, how will cyber security risks be addressed—not just loss of data but the threat of actually taking control of the car while driving.

Managers in the executive levels of the auto industry are braced for change. Bill Ford, chairman of Ford Motor Company, referred to the feared disruption as early as 2014, describing the revolution of the business model as happening "from every angle: from the type of powertrain in our cars to the ownership model and sharing." Dieter Zetsche, CEO of Daimler, expects the reinvention of the automobile in the next few years. Eighty-eight percent of the managers McKinsey surveyed expect some of the established automakers and suppliers of today to have disappeared by 2030. And 75 percent are sure that new competitors like Google and Uber will by then have gained a significant share of total revenues in the industry.

The sense of urgency that is the primary prerequisite in any digital transformation has been well and truly awoken among the traditional car manufacturers. The fight is worth it. According to a McKinsey study, global revenues in the auto industry will grow at an annual rate of 4.4 percent to around $6.7 trillion by 2030. Although classic vehicle sales are stagnating in established markets like Europe and North America, they have grown in Asia to 75 million vehicles annually, 28 million more than in 2015. In addition to sales proceeds and revenues from customer service and repairs, regularly recurring revenues are also experiencing rapid growth: customers pay $1.5 trillion each year for all digital services related to cars.

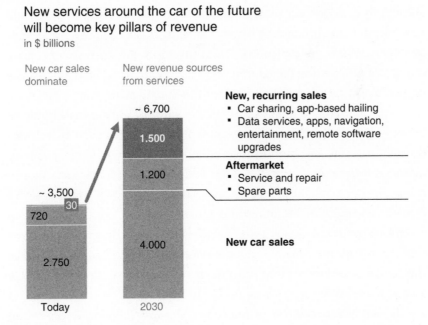

New services around the car of the future will become key pillars of revenue
in $ billions

New car sales dominate

New revenue sources from services

~ 6,700

1.500

1.200

~ 3,500

30

720

4.000

2.750

Today

2030

New, recurring sales
- Car sharing, app-based hailing
- Data services, apps, navigation, entertainment, remote software upgrades

Aftermarket
- Service and repair
- Spare parts

New car sales

It's not just a digital revolution that the industry faces. In the analog world, too, little will remain as is. The study predicts that by 2030, the market share of cars with electric motors could grow from the current 2 percent to 65 percent, driven primarily by the rapidly growing demand for hybrid vehicles.

Automakers need to build an entirely new ecosystem based around the electric powertrain. Who will build the powerful and fast-charging batteries that will be needed in fully electric vehicles? These batteries represent a significant proportion of the car of tomorrow's added value. Who will deliver the charging infrastructure that electric cars rely on? Tesla already has a network of 5,000-plus charging stations across the United States. And how will sports car manufacturers, whose customers covet the distinctive sound of a powerful engine, react to these almost silent electric motors?

Connectivity Will Define the Fate of the Industry

The fate of the established automakers and many suppliers will be decided on the digital battlefield. Connectivity, where the car constantly measures and sends a range of data, is an increasingly important topic for consumers. In 2014, 20 percent of car buyers indicated they would switch to a new brand if that model had better connectivity. In 2015, this figure rose to 37 percent. While data protection advocates predicted that consumers might worry about the digital trail they leave behind, 76 percent of drivers surveyed said they had no problem with their data being shared.

In the future, then, software will become the differentiating factor between car models. Even today, the control software used in vehicles comprises on average around 100 million lines of code. By 2030, this is expected to rise to 300 million lines, which means the traditional automakers need to establish greater software competence. Manufacturers typically leverage only around 30 percent of the value that the software in a vehicle represents. Competitors like Tesla and newcomer Google, however, handle all the software development in-house. All automakers face the challenge of establishing ecosystems of external developers to create an in-car app store.

The fully connected car of the future will install an entire ecosystem around itself, connecting in-vehicle sensors and microchips directly to the

Internet and offering a seamless user experience. Part of the task is to fully integrate this in the digital ecosystems of the buyers and their passengers, which requires a tight integration with Android and iOS.

The system partners then develop a wide range of offerings based on the constant flow of data. Even today, drivers' assistance systems perform functions such as keeping the car in lane or braking automatically in an emergency. Tomorrow, the driver may be able to take a backseat while the vehicle drives itself autonomously. The system could also highlight free parking spaces nearby, locate the car in the event of theft, offer concierge services, reserve tables in restaurants, or book hotel rooms. Sensors monitor the internal mechanics and notify the driver when parts are worn and servicing is required. Insurers, too, have not wasted this opportunity to develop a tailored risk profile of the driver based on the driving data—from mileage and average speeds to number of interventions of the assistance systems and braking patterns. This data is then used as a basis for pricing the insurance policy.

In the future, drivers will no longer access the digital services via touch screens, but simply via voice commands. And the digital assistant in the car will also be linked to the digital assistant at home. For example, if someone taking a morning bath asks Siri or Alexa—the digital assistants of Apple and Amazon, respectively—to order a table in a favorite Italian restaurant that afternoon, the person will be driven there automatically by the car, because it already knows where to go. Much of this is technically feasible today, but a few things such as handling areas with no Internet connection or addressing data storage issues still need to be addressed.

Truck manufacturers have made the most progress when it comes to connectivity. Many commercial vehicles are already connected to their environment to such an extent that their position and speed can be monitored in real time. A current study predicts that in the future, connectivity will become a crucial starting point for developing new business models. For truck manufacturers, for example, this may take the form of capacity as a service, or the flexible provisioning of transportation capacities and direct management of fleets. Even today, 49 percent of industry decision makers say that this business may become even more attractive than vehicle sales.

Still some obstacles: onboard technologies

 Internal vehicle sensors
- How can occupant safety be improved through the use of sensors?
- How can sensor data formats be standardized?

 Software platform
- How can software updates be delivered to vehicles safely and with ease?
- How do we create a willingness to pay for functional software updates?

 Environmental sensors
- How can the driver maintain required visibility of surroundings and occupants? What limits should be applied?

 Connectivity
- How do we ensure continued functioning despite Wi-Fi gaps?
- Which data will be sent to the cloud, and which will remain in the car?

 High-performance computers
- How can safety and reliability of the high-performance computers be ascertained?
- Which tasks would be better performed on board rather than in the cloud?
- How do we ensure security of onboard computers?

 On-board data storage
- What data are continuously saved, and how can data losses and hacking be prevented?
- Who has access to the data in the car (police, insurers, etc.)?

 Redesigned human-machine interface (HMI)
- How can the HMI be reinvented?
- How will Siri, Alexa, and augmented reality influence vehicle control?
- Will there be new standards?

 Localization/navigation
- How many data points do we need to ensure dynamic traffic management?

One aspect of connected driving has particularly piqued the interest of the industry: autonomous vehicles. Over the coming years, autonomous vehicles are expected to contribute up to $1.3 trillion in annual savings to the U.S. economy alone, according to a Morgan Stanley report, including $645 billion from productivity gains, $488 billion in accident avoidance, and $169 billion from fuel savings. Once again, trucks are leading the way. A McKinsey study predicts that by as early as 2025, one in three commercial vehicles sold in Europe will be able to drive fully autonomously in certain situations, especially on freeways. This pushes down costs: currently, the driver accounts for 30 to 40 percent of the operating costs of a heavy goods vehicle. Self-driving functions can halve these costs, while at the same time ensure lower downtime and greater utilization.

Uber is also experimenting with self-driving vehicles. Again, it's primarily about costs. If Uber succeeds in deploying its cars without a driver, costs will fall by 30 percent. At the moment, the company is still a job creator: in 2015, Uber welcomed around 1.2 million new drivers into its network.

Autonomous vehicles are certainly expected to have a tremendous impact on the labor market. In the U.S. Midwest alone, several million jobs that deal with transportation, logistics, and distribution will be at risk in the coming years. Thoughtful collaboration with public policy makers is required to ensure that the benefits of automation are achieved while also retraining people who are affected by this trend.

The development of systems that enable safe, autonomous driving is the automotive industry's most ambitious project. Above all, these systems must be based on precise navigation and mapping services. So as not to lose ground to new rivals like Google in this respect, the German automakers Daimler, BMW, and Audi have jointly acquired the mapping service Here from Nokia for €2.8 billion. With autonomous driving, the data and coordinates that the car measures when on the move are constantly reconciled with the map data, which requires maximum precision down to the centimeter. A typical reading, for example, monitors the distance of the car from the curbside. This means the maps need to be of "automotive grade." Google does not achieve this classification. When owned by Nokia, Here supplied 80 percent of the global market with its maps, generating revenues of around €3 billion. The new owners, too, will supply the entire industry.

The Here mapping service is a good example of how the old linearity is dissolving in the relationship between customer and supplier. Here supplies the auto industry, and the manufacturers in turn generate huge data volumes every time their cars are used, and then sell this data to Here, which uses it to improve its product.

Daimler Swarming to Digital
If car models of the future are differentiated by their digital abilities in the same way they are differentiated by engine performance or comfort

today, automotive companies may benefit from learning a few things from Silicon Valley.

Daimler, for example, has implemented a swarm organization. On particular projects, employees come together in cross-departmental swarms and work autonomously, connected, and without hierarchies. CEO Dieter Zetsche wants around 20 percent of all employees—more than 50,000 people—to work on projects in such swarms. Everything centers around the future of mobility, for which Daimler has coined the acronym CASE: connected, autonomous, shared, and electric.

Toyota recently announced its plans to move from being a carmaker to a platform for mobility services, and to this end founded the Connected Company. Its first product, the Getaround service, enables peer-to-peer car sharing and has been undergoing tests in San Francisco since early 2017. A Smart Key Box and the right software turn Toyotas—including older models—into connected rental cars, which can be booked via a smartphone and started with a digital key. The medium-term goal is more ambitious: Toyota wants to establish its own digital operating system that controls the entire mobility ecosystem, thus enabling the automaker to gain the lion's share of the value added.

However, a do-it-yourself solution isn't the only possible strategy: Automakers such as Fiat are taking the opposite course. Since they have tight development budgets, they are working with software giants like Google on the megatrends of connectivity and autonomous driving. Classic auto suppliers, most of which now no longer supply individual parts, just complete systems, are now extending their offerings to entire software control modules. Continental, for example, no longer simply supplies tires, but complete chassis and drive components. Continental also develops products centered around the connected car, such as eHorizon, which offers predictive control of vehicle systems. The system uses positional data captured by the vehicle's sensors, and sends this to the cloud. Using this data, the onboard computer anticipates the topography of the road ahead, and optimally adjusts the engine and transmission just before a sharp incline, for example.

Another example is ZF Friedrichshafen, which has moved on from being just a supplier of transmission systems that is threatened by the advent of electric cars. The traditional firm now sells complete chassis and powertrain components, driver assistance systems, and braking and steering systems. It is also working on electric powertrains and a solution for autonomous driving.

Suppliers, then, are relieving automakers of much of the development work. A new band of manufacturers may emerge that essentially assemble the components, and see their core competencies as being connecting with end customers.

Times are changing in the mobility industry. Digitization is overturning the old balance of power. However, automakers still have a strong starting base. They have the brands, they have the customers, and they have the marketing and service infrastructure. If they inject a shot of entrepreneurial spirit from Silicon Valley into their businesses and organize intelligent collaborations, they have every chance of surviving the ensuing battle.

4.2 DIGITAL COMMERCE: ONE CHANNEL IS NO LONGER ENOUGH—TODAY'S MOBILE CUSTOMER BLITHELY SWITCHES BETWEEN THE REAL AND VIRTUAL WORLDS
Kelly Ungerman on the future of retail.

All business is local, and the managers of the drugstore chain Walgreens are keenly aware of this. Since 2010, Walgreens has gone digital: the retailer now offers customers several apps that are much more than simply a means for collecting loyalty points. With more than 8,000 stores, one may consider the massive brick-and-mortar footprint to be intimidating in an increasingly digital world where transactions are occurring online. Walgreens, however, set a clear digital value proposition of channel integration by driving synergies among web, mobile, and physical store locations.

With this focus on omnichannel integration, Walgreens today enjoys 14 million visits per week across its various digital channels. An astounding 48 percent of digital visitors claim that their next action after the digital visit is to go into a Walgreens store. In addition, Walgreens sees a 3.5-fold increase in spend between store-only customers and customers who shop both online and in-store. Mobile is seen as a store enhancer rather than replacement, with 50 percent of the company's mobile app usage happening in-store. The strategy is also allowing Walgreens to find revenue where none existed before. One of the apps allows customers to print images from social networks, and either pick up those prints in store or have them delivered.

With the massive data sets Walgreens is now able to collect across its digital and physical channels, the company can dynamically localize its offerings. Existing performance of a planogram is analyzed using data to answer key questions about why a category is behaving in a certain way. Planogram data is shared with all parts of the organization, including the e-commerce, pricing, markdown, and operations teams. They are also able to forecast their labor needs based on store-specific footage, fixtures, and inventory.[1]

There's no question: traditional retail faces radical change. "In ten years, only 10 percent of all retail revenues will still be generated by offline sales," predicts Oliver Samwer, cofounder of Rocket Internet, to which companies like Delivery Hero and Home24 belong. New online competitors are infiltrating across a broad front. They no longer concentrate just on books, consumer electronics, fashion, or furniture, but are even preparing to take on that last bastion of offline retail: groceries.

At the same time, brick-and-mortar retailers are faced with the increased expectations of their customers, who want service offerings and convenience in customer care, at checkout, and at delivery, just like they experience at the best online stores. Because customers now have greater choice and a better overview of available offers than ever before, they conduct more research before buying. As a result, they often switch channels during the buying process. They might use the local store simply as a showroom and prefer to order online instead. Before visiting a store, they might check whether the item they want is in stock; before making an offline purchase, they might use their smartphones to check recommendations, warnings, and criticisms about an item. For most consumers, the route toward making a purchase has long involved several channels, as the example from the world of fashion demonstrates.

[1] https://www.forbes.com/sites/benkepes/2014/10/09/digital-transformation-doesnt-have-to-disrupt-walgreens-shows-how/#1cc7aafa6d38; www.chainstoreage.com/article/walgreens-supports-local-assortments-jda

Even today, several channels influence our buying decisions

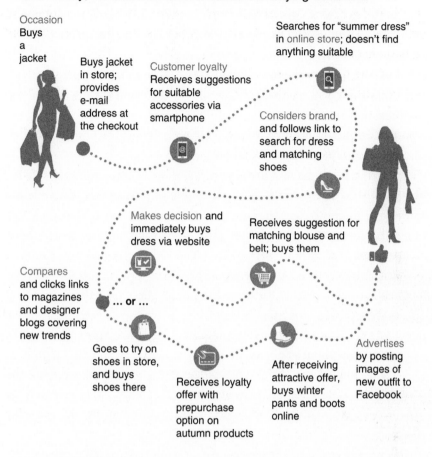

Occasion
Buys
a
jacket

Buys jacket
in store;
provides
e-mail
address at
the checkout

Customer loyalty
Receives suggestions
for suitable
accessories via
smartphone

Searches for "summer dress"
in online store; doesn't find
anything suitable

Considers brand,
and follows link to
search for dress
and matching
shoes

Makes decision and
immediately buys
dress via website

Receives suggestion for
matching blouse and
belt; buys them

Compares
and clicks links
to magazines
and designer
blogs covering
new trends

... or ...

Goes to try on
shoes in store,
and buys
shoes there

Receives loyalty
offer with
prepurchase
option on
autumn products

After receiving
attractive offer,
buys winter
pants and boots
online

Advertises
by posting
images of
new outfit to
Facebook

In 2014, a McKinsey survey showed that 94 percent of consumers actively research products and prices before making a purchase. Seventy percent read comments and ratings, and 87 percent stated they wouldn't buy a product that was consistently rated as poor. Two of the most important trends affecting retail are revealed here: "the empowered consumer," or consumers who have acquired information sovereignty; and "always-on" consumers who are constantly online with smartphones.

Advanced Analytics to Personalize the Offering

The third megatrend is personalization of offerings, and Amazon sets the standards for excelling in this using advanced analytics to automatically analyze large data volumes. The retail giant greets first-time visitors neutrally with its best sellers of the week; once it recognizes a customer, it offers suggestions based on previous purchases and search history. While searching for a book or item, a customer receives suggestions that are relevant to the search. Once the customer has placed an item in the shopping cart, Amazon recommends related products: the paper for the printer, for example, or a fitness band to go with a workout machine. Amazon generates more than a third of its revenue through such recommendations, leading many other retailers to follow suit.

In their assault on brick-and-mortar retailers, Amazon and similar players rely on a range of advantages. These businesses are generally far more agile than the cumbersome established retail firms. They have flat hierarchies and well-trained staff, and don't have to deal with "we've always done it like that" mind-sets when change is needed. Another advantage they have is in the technology. Their IT was built for the very purpose of online retail. Traditional retailers, in contrast, have to slug it out on data processing systems that have grown over decades, and that quickly become overburdened in the face of new challenges. The biggest edge that online retailers have, however, is their focus on the customer: Each contact point along the customer journey, from first contact to final purchase, is planned to make life easier for the visitor and to provide excellent support. The customer experience is at the heart of the process.

Traditional retailers still have the upper hand in some areas, though. In the best cases, they hold the all-important trump cards of a strong brand, trusting customers, and a physical presence in the form of their stores. They already have the ideal platform for a multichannel offering.

Traditional Retail Strikes Back

The smartest retailers are hitting back at their Internet rivals with their own weapons and using technology that transfers the benefits of the online shopping experience to the physical store. Fashion house Burberry has equipped its store assistants with iPads, which the sales consultants then use to customize items such as its iconic trench coat for the customer, or to order an item directly if the store doesn't have the right size or color in stock. The customer can choose whether to collect the ordered item from the store the following day or have it delivered. The mirrors in the stores have sensors that read information from radio-frequency identification (RFID) chips attached to the clothes. When a customer holds a Burberry trench coat or another item in front of the mirror, the glass displays various information about the material, cut, and collection.

British luxury department store House of Fraser is experimenting with smaller online-only stores in which customers order items from the House of Fraser online shop on special terminals, and can then choose to collect in-store if preferred. U.S. chain store Hointer also displays its fashion collection in its stores, but if customers want to try something on, they place an order for their particular size via their smartphone and the item is then delivered to the fitting room by a robot that has retrieved it from the warehouse. Robots are also being piloted in a service role in Orchard Supply Hardware stores in California. They can understand human language, and make their way to the shelves to collect items requested by customers. Adidas is also experimenting with digital technology in some of its flagship stores.

The cell phone has also become a weapon in the battle for customers. Some retailers use apps to send customers navigation aids to help them find an item they may have seen in the latest commercial. Clothing chain American Eagle Outfitters uses an app to guide customers to offers chosen by algorithms, based on previous purchases and search history. Some retailers, such as Meat Pack shoe store in Guatemala, use their apps to locate potential customers who are passing nearby or even browsing in a rival store, and then send them special offers or discount coupons that are valid for only a few minutes.

Companies are therefore targeting this deep connection between consumers and their smartphones. In a worldwide survey conducted by Motorola, 60 percent of respondents stated that they take their smartphone into bed with them, and 54 percent indicated they would rescue their smartphone before their cat in the event of a fire. Smartphones are playing a key role in the research and decision-making process of customers, and customers are assiduously using their phones even in the store, comparing prices and searching for product information. In 2015, experts estimated that 70 percent of sales made in brick-and-mortar stores were influenced by digital. This has interesting consequences: According to a study by credit card issuer MasterCard, although the number of customers visiting physical stores has dropped by more than half since 2010, sales in these stores have increased by 17 percent. Customers no longer visit to browse; they come to make a specific purchase.

Customers Want Seamless Switching between Channels

Retailers that don't want to lose their customers on this journey through the sales channels must offer a seamless shopping experience that encompasses all channels. Targeted investment in multichannel customers is worth it: U.S. department store chain Macy's, for example, has invested a lot of money in recent years in expanding cross-channel services. The retailer has observed that customers who shop at Macy's across all channels spend significantly more money than customers who use just one channel, as observed in the case of Walgreens. British retailer John Lewis tells a similar success story: A good 60 percent of customers buying items from John Lewis online use the click-and-collect service to order online and collect the items from the nearest John Lewis branch. More than half of these customers then use their visit to the store to buy additional items. As a result, despite all the competition, John Lewis has for years succeeded in increasing both its online and its in-store sales, negating the worries expressed by so many retailers of a cannibalization of offline sales by online.

Meanwhile, the e-commerce retailers have recognized the importance of physical stores. U.S. online apparel company Bonobos, for example, launched a number of showroom stores where customers can try on items to ensure the size is right. However, the order is still placed online—purchases can't actually be made in these stores. Even Amazon has recently opened its first physical locations in the United States, selling books, ironically. The customer is king, and because customers are embracing multichannel experiences, retailers that operate only one sales channel will lose ground.

Technologies and customer behavior are changing rapidly

Most important digital and multichannel consumer trends

🛍	All channels the right way	Omnichannel shopping is no longer new; it's the norm
↟↟$	The overinformed customer	Prices, options, and ratings are available at any time
🖐	The whole world a fingertip away	Smartphones are highly personal devices and the backbone of our daily lives
📱	Online and in-store purchases merging	Smarter devices and tailored, location-specific services
🗨	Polarizing shopping experience in store	To convenience formats or flagship stores
👤	Always available	Customers expect 24/7 service, information, and interaction

Intermediaries Vie with Retail for Customer Contact

How will digital dynamics change retail in the coming years? Several signs indicate that competition will grow in intensity. And as with Uber in the taxi industry or Airbnb in the hotel industry, new intermediaries are also appearing in retail. They compare the prices and offers of retailers, and provide recommendations to shoppers. By offering customers this convenient bundling of offers, comparison portals like Shop.com and Zulily are vying with traditional retailers for the important direct contact with customers, while at the same time siphoning off some of the added value. One provider, Wish, even goes one step further: its smartphone app connects consumers directly with manufacturers and wholesalers in the fashion and accessories industry in China, thus replacing the retailer completely. Although customers have to wait several weeks before delivery, they are rewarded with prices that are up to 80 percent lower. The app already has more than 150 million users, a worrying sign for classic retail.

However, whether online or offline, retailers must offer their customers added value if they are to remain in business. Only those that continuously develop as customer needs change, that decisively leverage the possibilities of multichannel retail, that expand their data and analytical skills to become more efficient across the entire value chain, and that provide tailored offerings to the customer will survive in the long term in the highly competitive retail environment. How retailers can operate in the complex world of sales channels to deliver profit, the prerequisites they need to set, and the skills they need to build are outlined in Chapter 5.1: Omnichannel: A Presence across All Channels.

4.3 WHO STILL NEEDS BANKS? FINTECHS THREATEN THE ESTABLISHED BUSINESS MODEL

Somesh Khanna, Vik Sohoni, and Michael Bender on the digital future of the finance industry.

"We're sorry to inform you that your business loan application has been rejected." For business owners who hear these words from Santander, all is not lost. Santander refers rejected customers to its cooperation partner Funding Circle, a financial technology (fintech) company. Funding Circle describes itself as a loan marketplace for small businesses. Fifty-six thousand private investors and institutions have risked some $2.4 billion in this marketplace since 2010, lending to 19,000 companies in five countries. They lend to those that no longer receive credit from the mainstream risk-averse banks bound by strict guidelines.

Funding Circle promises its lenders an attractive risk-return profile and professional credit checks of applicants. The website shows a list of loans recently granted: For a $110,000 loan to a manufacturing company with a term of two years, investors receive interest of approximately 6.5 percent per annum. A $50,000 loan to buy stock returns 10.8 percent interest each year over three years, and a $30,000 loan returns a mammoth 16.6 percent in a year. Attractive returns in times of zero interest rates, these are demonstrating Funding Circle's ambitious mission statement: "We want to revolutionize the outdated banking system."

It's a philosophy shared by most of the 12,000 fintechs worldwide. Investors particularly like financial start-ups: in 2015 alone they lent them around $21 billion in capital. Some, such as Funding Circle, SoFi (student loans, mortgages), and Lending Club, are now valued at more than a billion dollars.

Much Is at Stake

The traditional financial institutions have clear weaknesses compared to the new players. The banks have long neglected digitizing their value chain; overworked and bloated IT systems, old habits, and new regulatory requirements slow their efforts. On top of this, most institutions have still not recovered from the financial crisis of 2007–2009, and the low interest rates put pressure on margins. Cost reduction programs are the order of the day across the board.

Even retail banking offers little to smile about. Deposits have almost become a loss business, while at the same time customers are reluctant to pay fees for checking accounts and online banking. Banking services are regarded by many as a commodity where the main focus is affordability.

It's against this backdrop that these fintechs are muscling in on the banks. They work more quickly and cheaply, and boast greater innovation. They have young workforces and unburdened IT systems, and they are free of regulatory pressures. They understand what customers want, and deliver simple apps with streamlined digital processes. Opening an account with N26, for example, a fintech with a banking license that specializes in account management via smartphone, takes less than 10 minutes. Users simply enter their personal details, complete verification with a video call, and in no time at all they have access to a fully functioning account with a credit card number. At a brick-and-mortar savings bank, opening an account can take a whole day.

Fintechs are also offering products that never existed before. Lending Club, for example, offers a platform where private individuals can lend money to other private individuals. Another example, Kiva, is a nonprofit whose mission is to connect people through lending to alleviate poverty. Donations of as little as $25 can be made to help an entrepreneur start a business in a developing country, or a child go to school, or a household get access to energy.[2]

However, these new players will not, and don't intend to, replace the traditional financial institutions. They always focus on individual elements of the value chain. Primarily, it's in retail banking where the fintechs are attacking the established banks. They play on people's changing habits and the new technological possibilities. For example, the majority of consumers now own a smartphone, a key element in mobile transactions. This frees clients from the local bank, with proximity no longer a priority. The fintech start-up Raisin, for example, is a marketplace for investments throughout

[2] https://www.kiva.org/about

Europe. The company provides customers the ability to deposit money in countries across Europe so that they can access better fixed deposit rates.[3]

Financing for business customers, as offered by Funding Circle, is not yet so common. Although the fintechs are cheap, convenient, and user-friendly, and that counts for a lot in this segment, a specific understanding of the needs and restrictions of this target group is also needed—customer advice is essential. Yet the effort is worth it for fintechs: small and midsize enterprises (SMEs) are particularly open to online support in financial matters, according to surveys.

The established banks—also on the lookout for a new business model in these times of low interest rates—are being truly challenged by the fintechs. A McKinsey study extrapolated that if banks don't respond, up to 35 percent of their profits will be threatened in the next few years. However, the flip side of the digital threat also reveals an opportunity. If the banks succeed in learning from the fintechs and are able to apply this knowledge to their own processes while at the same time entering into joint ventures with the new start-ups, not only can they stave off their decline, but they could even increase their profits well beyond 40 percent.

Potential impact of digitization over two to three years
Proportion of profit as %

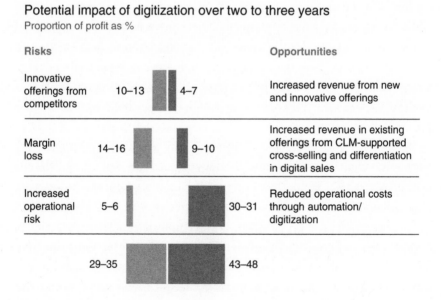

Risks			Opportunities
Innovative offerings from competitors	10–13	4–7	Increased revenue from new and innovative offerings
Margin loss	14–16	9–10	Increased revenue in existing offerings from CLM-supported cross-selling and differentiation in digital sales
Increased operational risk	5–6	30–31	Reduced operational costs through automation/digitization
	29–35	43–48	

[3] https://www.raisin.com/

The Bank of the Future

If banks want to seize their opportunity, they first need to focus on their strengths. Unlike fintechs, banks already have a large customer base and broad product portfolios, and they have built trust in their brands over decades. Even the expensive local branches could be turned into a strength as part of an omnichannel concept where customers freely switch between checking their statements on their smartphones, buying shares on their laptops, and visiting the branch for personal advice.

Above all, the banks have a still unleveraged treasure trove of data concerning a range of areas such as customer transactions and loan default rates, right through to how investors respond to interest rate changes. Conventional data processing lacked the power to analyze these enormous volumes of data due to the sheer size, complexity, and poor structure of the data. However, advanced analytics—powerful computers, efficient logarithms, and intelligent programs—allow these data volumes to be analyzed to predict future developments.

These advanced analytics enable banks to better understand the needs of their customers, and to address specific customer groups more directly with tailored investment products. Big data analyses also help to estimate credit risks, and can form the basis for completely new products and services. Facebook and Google show how this can work. For example, banks can develop software that analyzes existing transaction data, as well as some external sources such as payment behavior with PayPal, to enable an immediate decision on a loan application. Banks that intelligently analyze their wealth of big data have every chance of asserting their dominance as data companies in the heart of a data-based ecosystem. Naturally, the industry will still be about financial transactions in the future, but banks can spread their competencies across a much broader area than they do today and develop into service providers for customers' day-to-day needs.

The bank of the future will build an ecosystem of its own services and partner offerings around a digital platform. For example, if a customer researches mortgage conditions on the bank's website, the bank's insurance partner can offer home insurance products at the same time. Partners may also include, for example, a manufacturer of bathroom fittings, which could offer stylish faucets for the new home.

Other bank customers may be pinpointed via their smartphone data while out shopping, and be sent special vouchers to entice them into a nearby store.

The bank of the future would like to be the digital hub and fulcrum of customers' daily lives

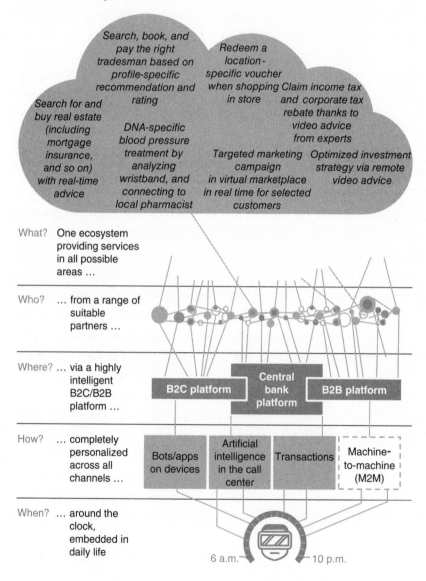

Granted, traditional banks still have a long way to go before they become a digital platform offering customers lifestyle choices and making commissions from partner companies rather than just being purely financial institutions. However, at least when it comes to the technical foundations, the banks don't have to work alone. Collaboration with fintechs is possible, with varying levels of intensity.

The loosest example is an alliance with a fintech: The London-based Metro Bank, for example, has a deal with the fintech Zopa, which benefits both parties. In the era of low interest rates, Metro has a difficult time investing its customer deposits profitably. On the other hand, Zopa, a peer-to-peer lending platform, has more loan applications than private investors, so Metro provides cash and earns higher interest. It's a win-win situation.

A closer collaboration is a participation: In 2015, for example, Credit Suisse bought a $165 million stake in Prosper, in return for 10 percent of its shares. The peer-to-peer lending platform was valued at $1.9 billion in the financing round. Banco Bilbao has been even more radical in its efforts to buy into the digital future. The 150-year-old Spanish bank has taken over a number of fintechs: In 2016, it took over the Californian fintech Holvi, an online lender focusing on SMEs. In 2015, Banco Bilbao acquired a 30 percent stake in Atom, the United Kingdom's first online bank, whose customer contact strategy is optimized for mobile devices. Prior to this, Banco Bilbao had already acquired the U.S. online bank Simple, the Spanish big data start-up Madiva Soluciones, and Spring Studio, a Californian design studio.

This highlights another strength of the established banks: despite the much-lamented lack of capital, they clearly have the money to acquire interesting ideas and talent. However, despite fintech acquisitions, their path to a successful digital future still remains uncertain. To ensure success, the financial institutions and all of their employees must shift their mind-sets to adopt a philosophy that all fintechs have in common: to think of each transaction in terms of the customer need and customer experience.

4.4 DIGITAL HEALTH: THE FIRST INNOVATION IN HEALTH CARE THAT CAN REDUCE COSTS IN THE LONG TERM

Sri Velamoor and Basel Kayyali on the rocky road to the digitization of health care.

The smartphone counts steps, the Fitbit fitness band records calories burned, heart rates, and training progress, the mySugr app uses movement data and food diaries to predict blood-sugar curves for diabetics, and the app Tinnitracks plays music to sufferers of tinnitus that filters out specific frequencies, thus neutralizing the hearing disorder. Digital solutions for both the ill and the healthy have been around for a long time, and are eagerly downloaded. According to a leading e-health publisher, more than 50 percent of American mobile phone users have downloaded a health-related mobile app.[4]

Health care institutions have been slower to embrace the possibilities of digitization than the patients themselves. And yet they could benefit considerably. Committed digitization of the value chain in Sweden, for example, has meant substantial savings for the health care system. In 10 years, a gross saving of up to 25 percent is possible. Although not enough to reduce expenditures entirely, it would significantly lessen the expected cost increases.

Digitization of the Swedish health care system using the latest e-health technologies could save 25 percent gross by 2025

Health care expenditure in Sweden, in SEK billions

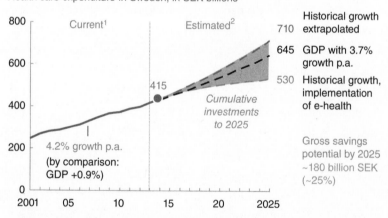

1 Historical data 2001–2010 updated based on broadened definition of health care expenditure as of 2011
2 Estimate based on 2005–2013 data on total health care expenditure and number of visits/days admitted to primary care and hospitals

Source: IHS Global Insights; Statistics Sweden

[4] https://www.ncbi.nlm.nih.gov/pmc/articles/PMC4704953/

Digitization offers particularly high potentials for the health care sector. Ever-present sensors combined with apps and systems that emphasize human-centered design and smart algorithms (advanced analytics) to analyze the accrued data volumes could collectively revolutionize medicine and wellness, if the system wasn't beset with its inherent braking mechanisms.

Just consider MyTherapy, for example, an app that helps patients to take their prescription medications—which medication, how much, when, and how often. Older patients with multiple diseases in particular have to take a number of medications at the same time. Numerous studies have shown that very few patients are capable of this. According to a World Health Organization estimate, medication compliance in industrialized countries is only 50 percent in the case of long-term treatment. In the United States, nonadherence accounts for almost $300 billion a year in additional health care spending.[5]

In the digital world, there are mobile solutions that tackle this very problem. With the app MyTherapy, patients can simply scan the bar codes on the packaging using their smartphones, and after entering the prescribed intervals for taking the medicine, they receive alerts at the corresponding times. Game elements in the app help the user to stay on track. Not only does the patient benefit from better compliance, but the health care system also benefits from not having to treat follow-up problems caused by noncompliance.

Lack of a Suitable Business Model

While such an app is an excellent idea, there's no suitable business model for it. In many countries citizens get access to basic health care for free, and they are willing to pay 99 cents at most to download the app. The health insurance companies demand clinical studies on efficacy before they consider paying for things. The pharmaceuticals industry invests millions in such studies, but this is impossible for a start-up. Physicians have little motivation to recommend such apps to their patients. This may have to do with the fact that they are unfamiliar with the various apps

[5] https://www.theatlantic.com/health/archive/2012/09/the-289-billion-cost-of-medication-noncompliance-and-what-to-do-about-it/262222/

or have little faith in the clinical relevance or quality of the app. Matters concerning reliability or data protection almost always play a subordinate role. Furthermore, a physician who recommends such an app does not immediately gain from it financially and may have to spend time explaining it. This leads to a difficult predicament: although there is proven added value for digital health at a system level, no one wants to pay for it. The patient has already paid for health care through his or her contributions, the health insurance company is willing to pay only for proven individual added value, and the physician doesn't want to be the person who puts time into it without being compensated.

As such, the fundamental mechanics of the health care market in many countries stand in the way of the nationwide adoption of digital. Remuneration is based on fee-for-service models in which invoices are billed for individual services. The quality of treatment and the success of the outcome are not included as components of the remuneration. The United States, which is not exactly a model when it comes to health care costs, now proposes a different way: the government health insurers Medicaid and Medicare are leading the way by including a quality component for hospitals in their remuneration models. Medicare issues financial penalties to hospitals whose readmittance rates are too high, for example. Such outcome-driven models create a financial incentive for service providers to focus even more on the quality of treatment.

Some U.S. states are implementing even farther-reaching changes to medical remuneration. For example, they measure the outcome of a treatment based on several quality parameters. Above-average service providers then receive a financial bonus. Assessments of childbirth deliveries, for example, include the rate of complications, the frequency of readmission of mother and child, and the proportion of expensive C-sections. The hospital receives the full fee only if it meets or surpasses the average. If not, deductions are applied.

It's a revolutionary step because it shifts the risk from the insurance companies to hospitals and medical staff. It sets an incentive for higher-quality and more effective services—including the use of digital health care apps that the physician can recommend to achieve overall better treatment outcomes. Take the example of how online consultations are reimbursed in Delaware: Aetna pays for an online physician if the family practice is closed, if a normal physician's appointment cannot be arranged at short notice, or if the policyholder is out and about.

However, not all the prerequisites for digital health care are in place. If collaboration between health care players is to be optimized, not only is a seamless exchange of data necessary, but also a viable business model for digital innovation (such as that offered by performance-related remuneration for health care services) and an informed and accountable citizenry willing and able to shift health choices and behaviors.

The basic philosophy is this: Digital health care providers offer their services for free to patients with insurance. Compensation is paid by the health insurance company only if the data of the respective patient shows that use of the app led to lower costs. This is possible with complex mathematical models if there are sufficient user figures and detailed data. In most cases, data already exists in this form in the health care system, but is not yet available for such purposes.

At the same time, the entry barriers blocking digital health care innovators must be lowered. Developers that offer useful services must not fear the possibility of lawsuits because data privacy laws were breached or because of an unintentional failure to comply with regulatory conditions. An amendment to the data protection law is needed: if patients expressly wish their health data to be used by a third party, legislation should not prevent this. Patients should have the right to allow their data to be used by third parties; the job of the health care system is to ensure safe and simple access to the existing data.

Who Will Establish a Central and Open Innovation Platform?

To enable digital health, an open innovation platform is required that has access to the highly standardized billing data of the health insurance companies, and also makes this available to the digital development partners. These certified third-party providers in theory then deliver innovations to the health care system. They boost the innovation engine, as demonstrated by the launch of multiple open data initiatives by the Centers for Medicare & Medicaid Services (CMS) in the United States. To receive access to the health data of patients, the third-party providers must in turn make their own data available on the platform—not only to avoid user lock-in, but to measure whether use of the individual digital solutions has led to measurable outcome improvements. And since this is sensitive data, a trustworthy governing body such as the Department of Health and Human Services must ensure that unauthorized access is prevented by using a powerful identity, access, and data release management system.

The British National Health Services (NHS) was an early adopter of digital medicine. After a few stumbles, it has now made £4.7 billion available for a digitization agenda with the aim of saving 8 to 11 percent of overall health costs. The British are targeting improvements in productivity by aiding the optimization of hospitals' and general practitioners' practices with services such as online appointment booking, patient reminder services, and online consultations, as well as by addressing the demand side. The NHS promotes digital aids such as step counters and fitness apps that help people remain healthy, apps that help to reduce health risks and to quit smoking, and apps such as mySugr, which helps manage diabetes.

The British have realized that if the health care system does not build a central platform itself, others will. However, this can be done only by companies with very long staying power and plenty of money, which once again leads back to deep-pocketed tech companies such as Apple and Google.

Apple is taking a twin-track approach with its ResearchKit and CareKit platforms. ResearchKit is an open-source software platform that invites physicians and researchers to build apps. Volunteers will download these research apps—which, if permitted, can also access other health apps on the smartphone—to their iPhone, allowing data to be collected for medical research. Apple hopes that, by doing this, its iPhone will become a tool for medical research. ResearchKit enables medical researchers to investigate various conditions like asthma, breast cancer, and Parkinson's disease. Top U.S. universities and research institutes are on board with this project.

CareKit is aimed at the patients themselves. The platform is designed to help patients manage their conditions better, while also allowing their vital signs to be shared with their treating physician. In early 2016, Apple launched four self-developed modules: Care Card, which reminds users when it's time to take their medicine or exercise; Insight Dashboard, which records symptoms and relates them to the measures from the Care Card module; an app that keeps track of mental health; and Connect, which sends the data to the physician or a family member. Apple itself is not able to access the individual data, and has committed to respecting and protecting privacy. CareKit is also an open-source platform—partners are invited to develop apps on this platform to extend the range of services. Combined with the acquisition of Gliimpse, a personalized health data collection/dissemination platform in 2016, Apple is well positioned to become a key enabler for patients to more directly influence and redirect health decisions.

Naturally, the established players in health care technology are also attempting to develop a platform and secure a central position in a new medical ecosystem. Philips is bundling its business as Philips Healthcare with a product range from toothbrushes to magnetic resonance imaging (MRI) scanners, and, in addition to the hardware, has also developed software for managing entire hospitals. General Electric operates its Health Cloud, which not only sells server capacity, but also rents software for the health care system (software as a service). IBM acquired Truven, Explorys, and Phytel, companies that have collected vast amounts of health data over the years, and uses this wealth of data as the basis for solutions in population health management. Microsoft has launched its own health cloud boosted by Cortana, its proprietary artificial intelligence (AI) capability, to become the preferred platform for developing digital health solutions. Siemens Healthineers has a clear digitization strategy with Teamplay, a cloud-based platform for digital solutions, which is used in many hospitals.

Predictive Maintenance for People

Although the players in the digital health care industry may still be finding their place, there is no lack of vision. In the United States, pioneers are working on population health management. The idea mirrors what machinery manufacturers have already achieved with digitization: predictive maintenance, where a part is repaired in time before it fails. To transfer this concept to people, volunteers send the health data collected via their health and fitness apps to a central body, which then evaluates it. If worrying deviations from the norm are detected—for example, if the user is increasingly overweight with rising blood pressure—the program responds and recommends targeted exercise regimes and a nutrition plan—all via an app that also records the impact and reminds the user if a unit has been skipped. The tailored program even includes a voice assistant with artificial intelligence that acts as a personal health coach and can answer questions. With this predictive maintenance, the user's health is improved before he or she actually becomes ill.

The question isn't so much whether we will use digital health services in the future, but rather when, and who will provide and regulate these services. Existing health care organizations like the large health insurance companies in the United States and the British NHS still have an invaluable lead over Google and Apple with their access to highly standardized and granular patient data. This lead can be defended only by health care systems that are open to innovation and willing to shape it. The window in which this must be done is already open, and waiting is not an option. Otherwise, there is a risk that—just as in other industries—the digital champions won't be the incumbents.

4.5 CONNECTED BUILDINGS
Hugo Sarrazin, Kabir Ahuja, and Mark Patel on the buildings and smart homes of tomorrow.

A brave new world at home: tomorrow, when the alarm buzzes, the freshly brewed coffee is already prepared. The coffee machine knows when it's time to start. The hot water tank has also been heated up in time thanks to the self-learning system, which knows that the family starts taking showers at 7:15 a.m. on weekdays. Once everyone has left the house, the robot vacuum cleaner starts its work, having received the signal that everyone has gone and the noise won't disturb anyone. The washing machine also turns on: electricity costs are currently low and no further hot water consumption is expected, so the cycle starts. From her workplace, a mother performs a quick security check on her PC, and notices that the alarm system is armed but a bathroom window is open. Using a smartphone app, she accesses the home's command center, which activates the window's electric motor and closes it.

Connected home: a wide range of digital possibilities

Health and well-being
Activity tracker, vital signs upload, alarm button, activity monitor for children/the elderly, medications, health

Energy efficiency
Meters, climate controls, lighting, domestic appliances, sockets

Safe living
Smoke detectors, temperature sensors, CO sensors

Housework
Cleaning and vacuuming, appliances and stocks

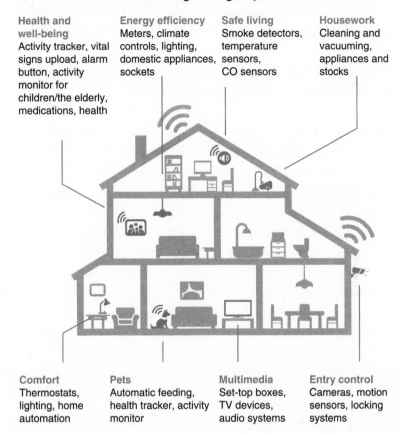

Comfort
Thermostats, lighting, home automation

Pets
Automatic feeding, health tracker, activity monitor

Multimedia
Set-top boxes, TV devices, audio systems

Entry control
Cameras, motion sensors, locking systems

A pipe dream? Not entirely: astonishing technical solutions like those in the house of the future just described are already possible. All kinds of buildings are becoming smart: residential homes and garages, offices, shopping centers, train stations, factories, universities, schools, and hospitals. Connected buildings offer greater convenience, increased security, reduced energy consumption, and completely new usage models. In the near future all critical systems will be fitted with sensors and connected to the Internet or cloud—the Internet of Things (IoT)—from heating and air-conditioning systems to locks and video monitoring. It will extend even further as all devices learn to communicate with each other, from the media center around the TV screen to the smart oven to the refrigerator to the robot vacuum cleaner and iron. Just as broad is the range of value propositions and business opportunities this opens. The building of the future is smart.

This new ecosystem of the connected building can be described across four dimensions.

The first dimension concerns customers, who are in turn divided into four groups:

1. Consumers in the smart home
2. The public sector with smart buildings such as universities and administrative buildings
3. Industry with smart factories and production halls, or infrastructure-related buildings like train stations and airports
4. The entire commercial sector with smart shops, shopping centers, and warehouses

The second dimension relates to providers that serve these customers. They develop products and services that leverage the Internet of Things to provide infrastructure that transforms "dumb" buildings into smart buildings. Many already have a history of delivering individual products, such as heating systems, and now, with sensors and software, they can deliver complete climate control solutions, for example, that can be controlled via a smartphone or tablet.

The third dimension outlines which customer needs are addressed by these offerings, such as security. There are a number of core value propositions at play: security (including access control, monitoring, and notification), home automation, energy management, and so on.

The fourth dimension describes the technologies on which the offerings are based. New demands are placed on all components, including sensors, hardware, data platforms, IT security, and much more.

Commercial: Shopping and Working in Smart Buildings

The typical office building is also changing drastically. It identifies employees based on a small RFID sensor, and automatically opens the right doors

The smart building offering is broken down into four areas

		Description	Examples
1	Customers	User groups that use IoT technology in buildings or municipal infrastructures	• Consumers • Retail • Industry • General public
2	Key industries	Branches of industry that provide packaged offers aside from pure IoT technology for buildings or municipal infrastructure	• Construction • Utilities and communication • Facility management
3	Use case groups	Description of how a user uses the technology regardless of the key industries	• Protection and security • Supply management • Interaction with people • Smart devices • Information and entertainment
4	Technology stack	The technology stack that covers the full spectrum of IoT technology—from hardware and software platforms to applications	• Business applications • Enablement platform • Data infrastructure • Connectivity • Hardware • IT security

for them. It calculates the route that visitors must take to their meetings, and highlights the way with dynamically illuminated signs. It controls elevators based on the meetings marked in the online calendar.

Naturally, the building also regulates the climate control systems based on weather forecasts, and is even connected to neighboring buildings to which it can feed excess heat generated either in its own power plant or via solar panels on the roof. Soon, there will even be entire facades of office buildings that generate electricity via solar energy. Models are even being discussed where construction companies sell or rent out their facades or solar roofs to an energy company.

In the building of the future, all technical equipment from the elevator to the climate control system constantly transmits data, which is analyzed for the purposes of predictive maintenance. The technician intervenes before a critical component fails, rather than after the elevator is broken.

In Amsterdam, a 14-story office building called The Edge boasts not only the kinds of solutions relating to security, climate control, and efficiency just described, but also intelligent software solutions to cater to occupants such as:

- Sensors that detect motion, and inform the cleaning personnel which areas have seen particularly high use.
- A system that dynamically allocates workplaces. This manages the workforce in such a way that entire floors remain closed on days when relatively few people are in the office, which saves on heating and operating costs.
- Automatic lighting and temperature control to ensure the perfect lighting for each desk currently in use and a comfortable working environment.
- Robot vacuum cleaners with industrial-grade performance keep spaces clean.

Although The Edge has been in operation for some time now, further digital use cases are still being implemented. For example, the number of smartphone apps for tenants is constantly being expanded. The most recent addition was an app with information about the traffic situation in each area of the building, with provisional forecasts on the best times to journey to and from the office. A virtual facility manager also integrates perfectly into The Edge. Previously, a human facility manager had to oversee the heating, elevators, and other facility technology, and check whether inspections were due or problems had occurred. Now, sensors in all the critical technology functions transmit their data to a control center. The virtual facility manager in the form of a program monitors deviations from the norm and times of use. It identifies when unplanned maintenance is required if a part is close to failure, and orders regular inspections.

Cameras, sensors, and control software are also making their way into supermarkets, department stores, and shopping centers. Cameras and sensors track our movements through aisles, intelligently controlling lighting to steer our gaze to attractively lit offers, note the locations where we appear interested in something, what we touch, and which shelves need to be restocked. These systems can also be used to monitor store staff and to identify any security concerns within the stores. In shopping centers, the systems can identify visitor flows and guide them accordingly. For example, if the ground floor becomes too crowded, visitors are notified about a special offer via a Bluetooth beacon: "Huge discount on the third floor!" All of these developments are still at early stages of maturity and adoption.

Consumers: Comfortable and Safe Living

The first components of the smart home have long been on trial in residential homes. For example, since as early as 2010, ADT has offered a remote-controlled security package under the brand Pulse. The package is used to control alarm systems, lighting, climate control, and appliances. Contact sensors on windows and doors report intruders and are directly connected to a monitored security service.

Now products with machine learning capabilities are embedded in homes—for example, in the kitchen. Whirlpool offers the smart French door refrigerator, which automatically switches to party mode if its doors are opened frequently, and increases its refrigeration power and ice cube production. The company also has a smart washing machine that allows for remote start/pause, gives details of how much time is left in the cycle, and sends alerts when done.[6] Samsung manufactures a refrigerator with a built-in camera that allows owners to view the contents of their fridge via smartphone when the door is closed. We even see innovations like the Juno oven, which automatically cook a number of different recipes, react to the food inside, and allow video monitoring of your meal.

Neatmo has launched a security camera that can distinguish whether an animal or a human is moving in the bushes, and sounds the alarm only if the situation is deemed to be threatening. The system is so smart that it recognizes people and pets that belong to the household. Other companies, like August Home with its smart locks, have taken the smart home one step further and integrated with digital service providers to offer features like opening your home for package delivery or managed access control for Airbnb guests.

The technical prerequisites are already in place, in part because prices for sensors have fallen dramatically. The market is beginning to show real signs of strength and is growing fast, with penetration at about 30 percent for at least one smart device per home and a compound annual growth

---

[6] https://www.cnet.com/news/spring-cleaning-at-cnets-smart-home-starts-with-a-new-washer-and-dryer/

rate of 30 percent. A good quarter of new spend will be on security, around 20 percent on energy systems, 16 percent on smart domestic appliances, and around 14 percent each for lighting and home entertainment.

Perhaps most importantly, with technological advances in voice control and artificial intelligence, the intelligent assistant is now a viable control center for the connected home. This new trend has changed the control point for the home and shifted focus from the devices to the experience of interacting with a home. Tech giants and start-up attackers have developed solutions delivered through both existing devices (e.g., smartphones) and new stand-alone products (e.g., Amazon Echo, Google Home).

Industrial: Robots as Workmates

Just as with homes, offices, and shops, in the next few years industrial and logistics buildings, train stations, and even entire public spaces will become increasingly smart.

Robots will take care of more of the work in large warehouses when goods are marked with sensors that free electronic assistants of the need for a storage system or to remember a specific position. Instead, packages can be stacked wherever it is most logical. The robots can always find them easily through the sensor. Amazon is already using such technology in its warehouses with Kiva robots. Factories will see the same transformation. In the age of Industry 4.0, smart machines can communicate and interact with each other, not only optimizing production, but also enabling fully automatic processing of orders and goods.

Airports and train stations will become mobility hubs and intelligently combine various mobility concepts simultaneously, ensuring that ordered goods currently in transport are delivered to the correct location.

Public: schools, universities, and public administration

The public sector is the country's largest property owner, with transit hubs, schools, government buildings, and so on. Smart facility management of these buildings is similar to that of residential homes and office buildings. Again, it's primarily about climate control, energy consumption, and security. Many public buildings stand empty for certain periods, such as school holidays and weekends, while others are not fully occupied.

Intensive research is currently looking at ways to reduce the enormous heating and operating costs. For example, the Massachusetts Institute of

Technology (MIT) together with the Fraunhofer Institute and various large companies like Ericsson, Philips, and Volkswagen are working on the "SenseableCity Laboratory" initiative. One of the studies concerns the idea of personalized climate control. Referred to by the researchers as "local warming," the idea of the concept is to ensure that only those areas in which people are situated are heated or cooled. The system uses measurements to track the movements of people through the building, and fast-acting infrared heaters are activated wherever someone currently stands. Everyone gets their own tailored climate control, with the thermal cloud following individuals to different rooms—greater comfort with greatly reduced heating costs.

Smart digital solutions have also been developed for roads. In Los Angeles, Philips has implemented its CityTouch connected lighting system, which intelligently monitors and manages street lights. This has helped reduce the city's energy usage for street lighting by more than 60 percent, while also incorporating environmental noise-monitoring systems on light poles that help detect violations and respond in a timely manner.[7] Smart street lamps have even greater potential: the masts could be used to build a public Wi-Fi network, and even serve as charging points for electric cars. Thus, a fluid transition from the concept of connected buildings to a smart city is possible.

Whose Standard Will Prevail?

There are many players in the market that offer individual solutions for smart buildings. The key questions, however, are these: who will become the system integrator, who will develop a platform, and who will establish a standard that connects and combines isolated solutions in a user-friendly way? For all companies that are targeting only one specific area of this booming market, another question arises: in which of the emerging ecosystems will the other players also flourish? Essentially, there are four options:

1. Look for partners with whom joint standards can be established to ensure the systems are compatible with each other and able to communicate.
2. Connect with an open-source ecosystem that offers interfaces for integrating self-developed apps that control the respective system.

[7] http://images.philips.com/is/content/PhilipsConsumer/PDFDownloads/Global/ODLI20161110_001-UPD-en_AA-Evolving-applications-with-Philips-Lighting-in-Los-Angeles.pdf

3. Create a self-contained system in a segment that itself promises high revenues, and dispense entirely with the idea of connecting to an ecosystem.
4. Ambitious players can develop their own platform for an ecosystem.

Several competitors are competing to gain the cherished position at the heart of the emerging ecosystems. For example, Telefonica has incubated an entirely new business called Geeny, a consumer IoT platform. It allows consumers to create one hub for all their smart things while controlling for security and privacy. Example use cases include monitoring whether the stove has been left on and turning it off, tracking your dog's location, activity and sleeping habits, and identifying when an elderly person is in need of help. All of this can be done from one software interface. Geeny also enables companies to create smart IoT products. Its partner network of hardware vendors, developers, design experts, connectivity providers, and system experts allows it to help organizations create an IoT product in 100 days.[8]

In the United States, Comcast has invested in buying the iControl platform that powers its Xfinity home solution and is building a network of compatible connected devices. Vivint has taken a similar approach, but with even more selectivity on integration and more proprietary hardware.

Apple has also launched its own HomeKit with the same aim. This system creates a framework for device manufacturers to plug into, despite the need for proprietary hardware. After they join, their products can be controlled from any Apple device, including Siri, who could be asked to perform commands such as "Turn off the corridor light." When it comes to Apple's business model, HomeKit is less about tapping new revenue sources, but rather about reinforcing the value proposition of Apple devices.

Search engine giant Google is also working on a platform. In 2014, Google acquired the start-up Nest, a specialist in remote-controlled home heating and climate control systems, for $3.2 billion. In 2016, Google Home launched—with only moderate success. The centerpiece of the system is a large loudspeaker that also listens and can respond to commands to control domestic electronics. Unlike its competitors, Google has only started

---

[8] McKinsey; https://geeny.io/

integrating with other providers at scale; first it wants the technology to establish itself and prove the value of Google Assistant. In the Google business model, the smart home is very much seen as a key part of the information ecosystem.

Amazon has also developed a platform for smart buildings, and it too uses a voice assistant, Alexa. Alexa acts an interface, not just for Amazon itself but also for a number of third-party devices and services—with a goal of strengthening Amazon's core business by being the primary conduit for information in the home. Other tech companies are also pursuing this market. Samsung, for example, acquired and is expanding the platform SmartThings to play a central role in smart homes, and has recently launched Bixby to compete with Amazon and Google.

There have also been some initial forays into B2B. Mozaiq, for example, a consortium of companies such as ABB, Cisco, and Bosch, is working on a standard platform for smart buildings. This is an open software platform intended to ensure that all smart devices in the home of the future are able to communicate with each other in a simple and user-friendly way.

However, none of the competitors has yet penetrated the market at scale, and no standard has yet been developed, which is creating hesitation among construction companies that integrate connected home products. The smart security, heating, and lighting systems in homes cannot communicate with each other, leaving customers with isolated solutions. The scarce availability of qualified tradespeople is also slowing down success. Today's typical electrician or heating installer may not yet have the capability to install a smart system. Another factor slowing down progress is smart customers: as long as the cost savings delivered by smart energy management in connected buildings continues to be offset by the energy consumption of the many sensors and adjustment motors, smart buildings will not be economical. However, the vast number of start-ups clamoring to make their mark in this area shows that there is potential. Companies like Sensibo, Netatmo, LIFX, Ecobee, and others are helping to develop the market.

The smart building market is wide open. We are seeing a young industry in which sectors that previously had no contact with each other are growing together. They are forming new ecosystems that promise significant growth, and are establishing a new normal in-home and outside-the-home living. The growth is chaotic, but it is building from modest beginnings, with real opportunities for accelerators like interoperability and intelligent agents to truly make all buildings smart.

4.6 THE DIGITAL REVOLUTION HAS REACHED ELECTRICITY UTILITIES

Adrian Booth and Mark Patel on the strategy of the German utilities in response to the digital intruders in their core markets.

For 150 years, it was relatively straightforward to run an electric utility. Customers were unable to choose any company other than the regional monopoly, demand was predictable and growing, and electricity was produced in a small number of large power plants that for a long time ran on coal, and later oil, gas, hydro, or nuclear power. Prices were calculated to allow for profits after costs. In fact, the energy utilities were similar to the public sector—with one small difference: some of them generated profits for shareholders in a predictable, low-risk, and sometimes significant manner.

Those times have gone. Many energy utilities are fighting for their lives. As if the pressures created by the nuclear energy phaseout and the challenges of renewable energy weren't enough, they are also experiencing a revolution in their customer relationships and the overall technology of the industry.

Since the liberalization of the energy market and the end of regional monopolies, a lively group of energy providers has emerged. These companies—such as Yello—don't have their own power plants, and instead concentrate fully on the trading of purchased electricity volumes. Online portals like Choose Energy and Verivox show price comparisons of all providers, and can even register customers with their preferred provider and cancel their old service. The big digital providers of Google, Amazon, and Apple are also muscling in between the established energy firms and their customers by further expanding their established or emerging ecosystems. When customers are already controlling their heating and alarm systems with their smartphones, it's a logical step to control energy consumption via the Apple platform too, putting energy utilities at risk of losing their dominance over the vital interface with the customer and becoming mere commodity suppliers.

Digital Means Increased Competition

The digital wave, which has now penetrated the entire value chain of the energy companies, does not make life any easier. End customers, for example, are gradually being upgraded to smart meters. In one way, this is good news for utility companies. They no longer need to send a person to read meters, because the smart devices are fitted with sensors connected to the Internet, constantly transmitting all the consumption data, though not always to the energy suppliers. Instead, the data may be sent to a cloud and the servers of external data centers.

In the United Kingdom, for example, every household is to be fitted with a smart meter by 2020. However, the customer data will no longer be sent to the individual utility companies, but to a cloud, to enable competition. This is bad news for the traditional energy companies, which will lose their exclusivity over the sensitive data. In areas that have competitive retail providers, competitors will be able to analyze the consumption habits of individual customers and provide them with tailored offers, possibly more cheaply than before.

Things have also changed at the other end of the utilities' value chain—with the way electric power gets generated. Instead of a small number of large power plants, today thousands of decentralized producers feed their electricity into the grid. It's complex to predict feed times and volumes for solar and wind power, but smart grids can address this by measuring the received energy volumes at thousands of feed-in nodes, and transmit the data digitally to a central computer. In New York, there is an initiative called Reforming the Energy Vision (REV), which has a bold vision of not just physically enabling thousands of distributed generation points but also creating an economic marketplace that accommodates all different types of micro services, including distributed generation.

This can potentially create enormous complexity for grid operators, which are now separate from the retail and generation companies in many cases. Their central custodian role, whereby they pay money to the electricity generators and sell the energy either via the electricity markets or directly, is under threat. Since all the information about the feed-in volumes is digitally available, blockchain technology could enable direct business between energy producers and energy consumers. This could completely disrupt the trading part of the value chain that has traditionally connected energy producers with energy consumers.

So how does a blockchain work? Purchases are no longer processed via a central platform, but within a union of computers that make up the system. The computers act as a connected, decentralized register that can't be manipulated. They store transactions in continuously updated digital blocks, which are forwarded to all participating computers after each transaction. Once a block has reached a certain size, a new one is created. Together, they form a chain—the blockchain. Since the system is self-organized, there are practically no costs.

Under one scenario, the grid operators are tasked solely with ensuring that there is a marginal and reliable source of energy provided into the transmission grid. And even that may no longer be secure in the long term. As batteries and other energy storage technologies become ever more powerful, the opportunity for private and commercial consumers to uncouple themselves from the grid completely with their own solar arrays and wind turbines increases.

Energy Companies Want to Digitize Their Entire Value Chain

So many energy companies now recognize the importance of digital. Many utilities are starting to look at the opportunity to digitize processes.

Digitizing utility processes can free up extensive resources. If it encompasses the entire value chain, the operating profit of an energy utility can be increased by almost a quarter. If sensors can transmit performance data to the servers from all critical points, programs can accurately calculate times for predictive maintenance before a given point fails—which saves on personnel costs and minimizes downtimes. Of course, this also means the digital networking of all field employees and elimination of paperwork that is common today in utility field work.

The greatest potential, however, is in the interface to customers, which is often an area with significant room for improvement. Digitizing all customer contact points doesn't just save money, but also increases customer satisfaction. Most customers would now prefer to enter their details into a smartphone or laptop themselves rather than wait on hold with a call center. While this in no way means that customers now want to communicate with their energy provider only via digital channels, they do expect the same level of service across all channels. This is why employees in the call centers and in the physical offices of the utility companies must have all the relevant data and customer profiles available. Equally, the utility employee must be able to send information or offers to the customer's smartphone or home PC immediately.

As a further digitization measure, call centers are already being staffed by digital assistants: speech programs known as chatbots are now so far advanced that they are able to understand customer queries, search through data, and provide information verbally. These programs are based on AI/machine learning systems and are even able to detect the emotions of callers and respond to annoyed customers with particularly calming words.

Customer Loyalty via Digital Contact

The more advanced energy companies foster their customer relationships by using apps to provide their customers with information about energy consumption and costs, and inform them where they can save money. Others keep in contact with regular blogs or online forums, or send text alerts to let customers know when an engineer is about to arrive. Some are working on their product proposition by offering customers the choice of buying "green energy" from renewable sources, or equipping customers with solar panels and batteries to make them almost self-sufficient. Again, digital channels play a key role in customer communication.

Data is collected with each customer interaction, which will become a critical differentiator in the competition for the energy customer of tomorrow. If utilities are able to retain critical data from smart meters and smart grids, they will have the framework for tailored offerings. For example, energy companies could take over the management of climate control systems in buildings, offering significant discounts. The concept can even be scaled up: energy companies could form alliances with property developers and systems manufacturers, and take over energy management for entire residential areas, industrial facilities, or office buildings.

They could even find new sources of revenue in smart, connected buildings if they are able to provide the remote-control systems for the electric appliances in addition to the electricity itself. E.ON has already made inroads into this market, and acquired a 20 percent stake in the start-up Thermondo, a European manufacturer of low-carbon heating systems. Thermondo promises energy efficiency, and offers its customers complete packages for retrofitting homes with condensing boilers, solar power, or fuel cells. Communication is online, and Thermondo takes care of planning with clever algorithms, submits the necessary applications to local authorities, and procures public funding. Following installation, the firm coordinates with the energy supplier, as well as the chimney sweep and service teams. It's an excellent central position in the home heating ecosystem. E.ON and its competitors would love to have a similar offering in the energy market.

Challenges across Three Dimensions

Energy companies, then, see themselves faced with a three-dimensional challenge: (1) Digitization is destroying the old order. (2) New economic ecosystems are emerging in which they must find their place. (3) Smart grids and meters have created new business models and rivals, while connected buildings open up new markets.

To survive, the energy giants must develop their business architecture. They need to digitize their processes, communicate with their customers across new channels with new messages, and extend their product offerings. This will be possible only if they first reinforce their foundations with strategies ranging from a two-speed IT architecture to new big data analytical capabilities.

The digital transformation of energy utilities is undoubtedly a major project, and the question as to who will be the supplier of the future is a long way from being answered. However, energy producers still have much to gain: greater productivity, greater revenue, more reliable grids, new business fields, and more satisfied customers. They also have a rare opportunity: After 150 years, they can completely reinvent their strategy, structure, and processes. Those that do nothing will most likely be squeezed out by the new competitors. Those that revolutionize their business and go digital will seize the opportunities offered by the markets of the future.

Overview of the most important action areas in the digital transformation of energy suppliers

New ecosystems	**New fields**	• Smart grids • Smart living • Connected buildings • Distributed energy production	• Energy services • Preventive maintenance • Digital billing • Digital energy trading
Business architecture	**Customer experience**	• Digital front-end processes • Multichannel trading • Digital marketing and social media	• Seamless customer journey across all customer interfaces • Customer life-cycle management • Customer journey management
	Product and value proposition	• Open development environment • Digital innovation	• Smart products and components
	Value added	• Automated back-end processes • Analytics and intelligence	• End-to-end digitization • Employee productivity
Foundation	**Technology**	• System and data architecture • Interactive mobile devices	• Connectivity • Big data and advanced analytics • Data security
	Organization and culture	• Project culture • Cross-functional cooperation • Flat hierarchies	• Digital talent management • Agility

4.7 TELECOM GIANTS UNDER PRESSURE: WHO WILL BE AT THE HEART OF THE EMERGING COMMUNICATIONS ECOSYSTEMS?

Brendan Gaffey on the distribution battle between hardware manufacturers, content providers, and telecom companies.

The trigger for the revolution is tiny: a surface area measuring just 6 by 5 millimeters, and 1 millimeter thick. These are the dimensions of the eSIM. Just like its larger predecessors, this new storage card ultimately connects mobile devices to the Internet and cellular network. However, it's not so much its minuscule dimensions that make it revolutionary, but rather that the "e" stands for "embedded."

Currently, subscriber identity module (SIM) cards are sent out by a wireless provider and inserted manually, usually by the customer. The programmable eSIM is installed by the manufacturer in smartphones, tablets, fitness trackers, smart watches, game consoles, smart glasses, cameras, or home medical equipment—anything that's always online. The eSIM will also allow users to make calls from their wearable technology. The Samsung Gear S2 classic 3G smart watch, for example, incorporates an eSIM that lets users choose their carrier, and can make phone calls and access the Internet independently of a phone tether.[9]

The prospect excites customers, but worries telecom companies, which played a dominant role in the early days of cell phones back when transmission capacities were low and within their control. Telecom companies sent their customers the SIM cards, and were in a central position with high added value. If future SIM cards can be reassigned to any provider, wireless operators stand to lose their most important customer loyalty lever—the cost of switching. This will lead to profits and revenues being redistributed in the interrelationships among telecom groups, hardware manufacturers, Internet providers, and content providers.

Who Will Win in the Battle for the Center of the New Ecosystems?

New ecosystems are emerging, and all market players want to be at the center where the value added is greatest, rather than at the periphery and feeding off scraps. Will the hardware manufacturers like Apple and Samsung be victorious? With eSIM, in the future these companies will be able to predetermine the wireless providers for their smartphones, and allow customers to change provider with a simple click. It is also a logical step to suggest hardware manufacturers could purchase transmission capacities and infrastructure on the market themselves and squeeze out the wireless providers. Or will "content is king" prevail, a philosophy embraced by content providers like Netflix? The video streaming service relies heavily on self-produced TV series and movies, and has attracted millions of new customers in the process. As a newcomer to the market, Amazon now also produces its own content.

9 www.zdnet.com/article/samsung-gear-s2-classic-3g-first-esim-lets-you-switch-carriers-remotely/

Facebook is also betting on virtual reality (VR). The social media company bought Oculus, the virtual reality headset company, for $2 billion. The Oculus Rift offers all manner of digital experiences, from virtual car chases to complete virtual tours of property for sale. The device is able to trick the brain into believing that the body is experiencing what we see.

A number of players have already moved into this market, the most successful of which is Sony, with its PlayStation. Together with the related area of augmented reality, an attractive growth market has opened up. The new industry—which already generates between $3 billion and $5 billion a year in revenue—is predicted to grow to between $80 billion and $100 billion in revenue by 2025, according to a study by Goldman Sachs. Although almost all revenues are currently generated in gaming, business customers are expected to account for approximately half of the revenues by 2025. VR headsets can help designers by displaying virtual information, help surgeons by showing virtual lines along which to move their scalpels, and even help soldiers aim their rifles.

The telecom giants have much to lose. Their once-lucrative call, messaging, and video services have long been offered for free by aggressive competitors, and they are also on the defensive when it comes to content and platforms. Since 2013, overall revenues of telecom companies in the United States and Europe have been falling by around 0.5 percent a year. And this decline is now threatening to escalate. Various worst-case forecasts predict a fall in industry revenues by as much as 30 percent by 2020.

To halt this trend, some firms are using their still-healthy cash resources to buy into companies that produce content and programs that can be distributed via the telecom infrastructure. In late 2016, U.S. telecom giant AT&T tabled an $85 billion bid for Time Warner, whose portfolio includes film studios and the broadcaster CNN. Prior to this, AT&T had just closed its acquisition of DirecTV for $49 billion. A few years earlier, cable provider Comcast acquired the NBC Universal media group. And in 2015, wireless provider Verizon acquired Internet pioneer America Online (AOL), and later Yahoo! in 2016.

However, takeovers alone will not be enough to save the profitability of the industry. To ensure that telecom groups don't end up as poorly paid

Digital players systematically capturing business from telecom industry

		Services	Examples
Communication		Messaging	WhatsApp TALK
		Voice	skype WhatsApp
		Video calls	skype Tango ooVoo
Content		TV/video	NETFLIX You Tube hulu tv
		Other	iTunes hungrygowhere gameloft
Other		Retail	amazon.com ebay
		Advertising	Google
		Device platforms	Microsoft

commodity suppliers of a base infrastructure, they need to improve in three areas: first, they need to streamline a core business that has become slow and ponderous through the years; second, they need to identify growth markets and develop strategies for capturing them; finally, they need to manage regulations since industry structure and consolidation will be key drivers.

Streamline Core Business

In slimming down costs, digitization—the very phenomenon that necessitated this need for more streamlined processes—can help. From customer acquisition, registration, payment processes, billing, and customer support through to contract termination, every step of the customer journey now comes under the microscope. Each step of the journey offers the possibility of replacing expensive human labor with digital assistants with the aim of end-to-end digitization of the customer contact process, with greater service levels and lower costs than before. Of course, administration and technology also need to be streamlined. Surprisingly, these new digital processes not only are more cost-effective, but generally also lead to greater customer satisfaction if implemented correctly. Instead of having to wait on hold with a call center, many customers are happy to resolve their queries themselves digitally.

Opportunities in New Service Sectors

Once their processes have been trimmed down, the telecom groups can attack future growth markets. For six important growth markets, the wireless providers are in a very good starting position in the sense that their networks are ready for the data streams. Those markets are:

1. *Wearables:* Who will connect the fitness bands, VR headsets, smart watches, and running shoes to the Internet? How will revenue be generated from this, and what will the business model be?

2. *Smart houses:* Which Internet connection will be used to control the heating and climate control systems, roller shutters, elevators, and all the other features of the smart homes of tomorrow?

3. *Connected cars:* Autonomous driving, lane departure warning systems, emergency braking systems, service data—who will process the enormous stream of data that the vehicles of tomorrow will produce?

4. *Internet of Things:* All machines fitted with sensors that constantly transmit performance and usage data—who will enable transmission of this vast data pool?

5. *Digital health:* The connected patient will soon transmit a steady stream of data—will it be via the networks of the telecom companies?

6. *Cloud computing:* Who will operate the data clouds—the data and software centers where all of the data are transmitted and processed?

The key questions are: What role will the telecom groups play in these growth areas? Will they, as in the past, only supply the transmission technology, which in the future will be a cheap and interchangeable commodity? Or will they succeed in assuming a central role in the emerging ecosystems? Will they be able to get their SIM cards into the devices, or will they be squeezed out by the manufacturers, who will then have control over the choice of wireless provider? Will they simply transmit the data to the data centers of other cloud operators, or will they be able to provide the necessary data centers and software services? And will they be able to build expertise in data analysis and offer their external partners services in areas ranging from customer support to billing and payments? The formula is simple: the more service, the greater the value added, and thus the less interchangeable the provider.

AT&T, for example, is keenly tapping new service sectors, and has established itself as the hub of a new ecosystem in the process. The company is leveraging its huge customer base and the trust that it has established over 100 years to offer security and convenience packages centered around the home. For subscriptions of between $30 and $65 a month, residents' windows and doors are monitored if they are away, and a local security company is notified and checks the premises if a window or door is opened. An alarm also sounds in the event of smoke, fire, or flooding. In terms of convenience, the packages also include remote control of heating and lighting, as well as monitoring of pets and babysitters via camera. Customers can view the camera on their smartphones or tablets when they're away, and also control functions of the various systems.

To make all of this possible, sensors, cameras, and adjustment motors must be installed in the home by contract suppliers of AT&T. Together with the subscription fee, this delivers the company one-off payments of $30 to $150, while emphasizing to the customer that the equipment is worth much more. AT&T manages its network of equipment partners, local installers, and local security firms, and—as the provider of the offering and controller of the customer relationship—is able to reclaim the lion's share of the value added. And in times of minimal fixed-line telephone income, predictable annual revenues of $400 to $800 per customer are estimated. This is why the idea is already being copied: Swiss telecom group Swisscom has a very similar offering called Smartlife.

The other players in the emerging ecosystem are also doing the math. Google and Apple are already fitting their mobile devices with an eSIM, and promising customers a seamless transition from one wireless provider to another. They are also pushing into new business sectors. Google sought a slice of the smart home pie in 2014 when it bought Nest, a connected homes company that had already established itself in the market with its smart thermostats and smoke alarms. The traditional suppliers in this market, manufacturers of heating systems and thermostats all the way through to lawn mowers, also want to get a foothold in these new ecosystems and connect their devices.

Battle of the Business Models

Perhaps even more interesting than the battle of the providers is the battle of the business models. Telecom firms rely on the monetization of communications, with most companies also selling hardware. The manufacturers of home equipment rely on add-on services related to their hardware, whereas the media giants from Silicon Valley rely on data. Nest wants to earn revenues not only from its smart thermostats, but also from the consumption data of customers. This aggregated data is valuable for all industries centered around the home. Even outsiders are entering the market: Amazon, for example, now produces TV series for online streaming. Not only does this generate revenue in the area of online media, but it also opens up entirely new opportunities in the area of personalized and targeted advertising. Why not buy the dress of your favorite actress's brand in one click during the stream? Access to consumer data is driving some of the mergers and acquisitions (M&A) decisions as well, including Verizon's acquisition of AOL. With changes in privacy rules in the United States, this is an even more lucrative play.

The battle lines have been drawn, and the distribution war has begun.

4.8 DIGITAL LOGISTICS: THE DRONE ALWAYS RINGS TWICE
David Frank on driverless trucks, fully connected containers, and small drones that deliver packages to our homes.

No more children's tears on Christmas Day—this was Amazon's reasoning for leasing a fleet of 40 Boeing 767s in 2016. In 2013, parcel delivery firms in the United States were unable to cope with the demand of Amazon orders in the run-up to Christmas, causing hundreds of thousands of presents to go undelivered in time. Even after the holiday period, Amazon managers continued to complain about their delivery partners' lack of transport capacity at peak times. It was reason enough to seek to become more independent on long-haul deliveries. In the United States, Amazon now operates several thousand trucks, and has a license for chartering cargo ships; and, for the last mile, the company has for a long time been experimenting with drones and driverless vehicles, as has Alibaba, which founded its own logistics company, called Cainiao.

These developments are doubly painful for the logistics industry. It's bad enough that their biggest customers are performing some of their deliveries themselves, but what if their customers discover that they could organize their logistics on their own? What if they compete directly against freight carriers, parcel delivery firms, and cargo airlines?

Megatrends pave the way for new players and business models

Next-generation commercial transportation and logistics

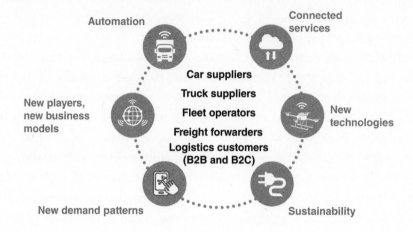

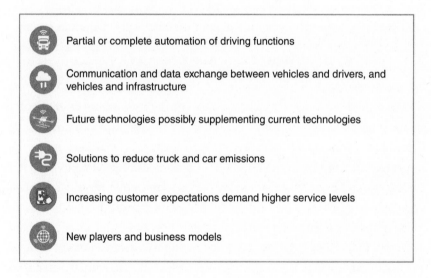

Even without their customers becoming competitors, the cards are already being reshuffled in the logistics industry. The development of digital technology and changing consumer trends are allowing, and in some instances forcing, new business models to develop. Everyone is affected, from truck manufacturers to bicycle couriers: the dividing line runs between long-haul distributors and those specializing in the last mile, or delivery to the customer.

Will Traditional Haulers Become Redundant?
Other far more disruptive changes are also possible. One of these is the imminent mass production of driverless trucks. Ironically, the very technology that haulers currently purport to welcome—enabling a 30 to 40 percent reduction in operating costs for trucks—is a stepping-stone on the road to their own demise.

A traditional hauler's core business currently consists of acquiring freight for its trucks, something that is much easier to organize via an independent online platform. As these orders are increasingly received digitally, and data about routes, cold chains, diesel consumption, and servicing needs are transmitted by sensors and are trackable online, and if drivers are no longer needed, then the traditional entry barriers into the hauling industry disappear. That will be a particularly enticing scenario for truck manufacturers.

Why shouldn't Mercedes and the other manufacturers offer the services for which they build their trucks? In the passenger car sector, the automakers are already experimenting with this model with Car2go and DriveNow. In a McKinsey survey of the truck industry's decision makers, almost one in two respondents said that capacity as a service—providing and managing flexible transport capacities—could be a more attractive option for manufacturers than truck sales. What may have sounded at first like a pipe dream is now not so far away. By as early as 2025, one in three commercial vehicles is expected to be capable of fully autonomous driving in certain environments such as freeway driving.

Even today, the logistics industry is experiencing dramatic change through the Internet of Things. For example, UPS has fitted its trucks, delivery vans, warehouses, and cargo with sensors that constantly transmit data to UPS servers. Using advanced analytics, computers are then able to optimize routes and minimize waiting times. Each year, UPS vehicles now travel approximately 90 million fewer miles on the road and consume almost 8 million fewer gallons of fuel, and driver waiting times have been reduced by around 100 million minutes.

Online connectivity has helped the logistics industry save money in all areas. The shipping industry and ports, for example, can save around $18 billion by digitizing their operations in this way.

Internet of Things helps eliminate inefficiencies in logistics

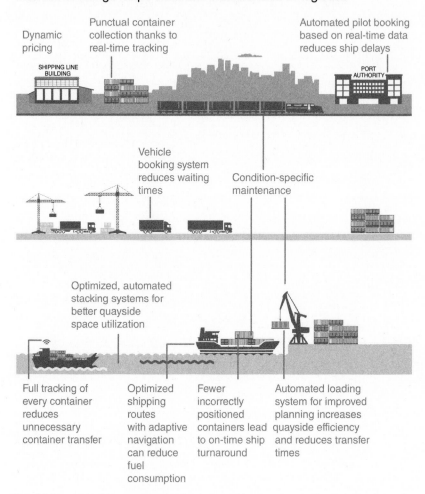

Dynamic pricing

Punctual container collection thanks to real-time tracking

Automated pilot booking based on real-time data reduces ship delays

SHIPPING LINE BUILDING

PORT AUTHORITY

Vehicle booking system reduces waiting times

Condition-specific maintenance

Optimized, automated stacking systems for better quayside space utilization

Full tracking of every container reduces unnecessary container transfer

Optimized shipping routes with adaptive navigation can reduce fuel consumption

Fewer incorrectly positioned containers lead to on-time ship turnaround

Automated loading system for improved planning increases quayside efficiency and reduces transfer times

Revolution on the Last Mile

For logistics companies, most of the changes will occur on the last mile, where the parcel is delivered to the customer. Worldwide, parcel delivery firms generated over $75 million in revenues in 2015, with growth rates between 7 percent and 10 percent in developed markets such as the United States and Germany. If the firms were able to save on driver costs for the delivery vans, costs would fall even more than for trucks. Drivers account for 60 percent of overall costs. The industry is now looking at ways to reduce this cost. It's not so easy, because under the current system, delivery vans can't be dispatched without a driver. Otherwise customers would have to find their parcels themselves in the loading area.

But that, too, is changing. Most likely, we will soon see a small, electric version of the classic delivery van on our roads—known in the trade as an autonomous ground vehicle (AGV). This is the smart version of the delivery van, with lockers on the sides that correspond to parcel sizes. Once the AGV reaches the customer's address, it sends a text message to the customer, who goes to the AGV and enters a code to retrieve the package from the locker. AGVs will need supervision. Supervisors will be employed in the offices of the parcel firm to watch for emergency signals and error messages, and to monitor the images sent back from the cameras built into the AGVs. However, that supervision is scalable—just one controller can monitor eight to 10 of these vehicles.

Moving further along this continuum, small, electrically powered trolleys or "droids" may well soon be trundling along our sidewalks en route to the customer, at a leisurely pace of 2 to 6 mph. They will carry only one parcel, and park immediately outside the house door; the notification and unlocking process will be the same as with AGVs. Because the droids are small and slow, their operation poses minimal risk, and a supervisor can monitor 50 to 100 of these types of units.

In less accessible areas outside of cities, or for urgent deliveries such as medications, it will soon be feasible to use flying drones. These can carry parcels weighing up to 30 pounds, and can reach their destinations very quickly in a straight line. These, too, will need to be monitored, and one controller should be able to supervise eight drones.

Another real disruption in the form of a completely new business model looms on the horizon, and it relies on crowdsourcing. In this disruption model, the delivery company operates the online platform on which the orders are placed, as well as the distribution hubs. Private drivers or even taxi drivers then register and use an app to check whether there is an opportunity for them to perform a delivery on a journey that is already planned. This creates a flexible network that doesn't require high investment from the parcel delivery firm, and generates costs only when revenues are generated.

This concept is already a reality in an analogous space, The start-up Postmates, which started as a delivery service for restaurants that don't have their own delivery service, operates a similar business model. Postmates provides an app that connects restaurants and freelance drivers, taking a commission in return. Now others have also latched onto the idea: UberRush works just like Postmates. When they're not transporting customers, Uber drivers deliver parcels, again receiving their orders via an app.

And alongside all these new and emerging technologies, one technology from the nineteenth century still holds its own in certain areas: bicycle couriers are hard to beat for city courier work. In terms of volumes, however, they are of very little (and diminishing) significance. In 10 years, the cyclists will hold just barely 2 percent of the overall delivery market, whereas the competition from autonomous vehicles and drones will account for around 80 percent. The rest will continue to be delivered by conventional delivery vans, predominantly for business customers with high parcel volumes.

The autonomous driving systems will appear soonest in countries with the highest wage levels. Logistics companies in Europe and the United States must therefore start developing their strategies now in view of the amount of time required to build the necessary resources in personnel and IT. Moreover, substantial investment will also need to be earmarked and deployed to win in this changing landscape.

Notably, substantial investment is not something that Amazon has ever shied away from. The online retailer and best customer of the parcel delivery industry has for a long time been experimenting with its own service for the last mile, running pilot programs in a number of cities across the globe. In its AmazonFresh groceries business, for example, Amazon uses its own delivery services. In the face of this, the German parcel delivery firm DHL has deftly broken free of its industry boundaries, and now operates AllyouneedFresh, an online supermarket that already had more than 300,000 users by the end of 2016.

While this type of spirited innovation is a good beginning for traditional players, if Amazon really does take control of its entire delivery

chain—container shipping, truck transportation to the distribution centers, and final delivery to the customer—the established players in the
industry will lose out on significant revenue, limiting their ability to
spend and innovate further. This begets the classic death spiral of companies struggling to maintain pace in a changing landscape. No wonder,
then, that the parcel firms are looking for new ideas. UPS, for example,
is now equipping hundreds of its UPS stores in the United States with
3D printers. Instead of sports shoes being delivered via a container ship
from China, the customer can now have them produced according to
Nike or Adidas specifications from the print shop around the corner.
These could even be personalized with a monogram or pink soles and
delivered by express courier. Ships and trucks are no longer needed in
this case.

In summary, the landscape is changing rapidly and radically, and the
time is now for traditional players in the logistics space to examine their
positions within the value chain. They must identify areas for strategic
investment in innovation, and create enduring relationships with customers through enhanced value propositions and journeys.

4.9 E-GOVERNMENT: PUBLIC ADMINISTRATION GOES ONLINE
*Martin Lundqvist on the digitization of public administration, and what citizens
can expect.*

It was a revolution in the public sector: "No more printed forms or letters." That was the directive of the Danish government to public authorities
during the recent financial crisis. Today, almost all contact that citizens in
Denmark have with their local authorities is via the online portal at www
.borger.dk. All registrations and deregistrations, and applications for benefits or permits are entered here. Every citizen and every company receives
a secure user ID, which they use to register for online public administration services. The electronic forms are digitally signed, and officials no
longer print out the forms in the council offices to process them. Instead
the process is all digital, and decisions are made automatically. It's often
astonishingly fast. Danish entrepreneurs generally receive confirmation
that their start-up has been registered as a business immediately after they
send in the application. There is no waiting at counters, and no frustration
over forgotten documentation. Instead of visiting the council offices, it's a
simple online application.

An analysis by McKinsey suggests that capturing the full potential of government digitization could free up to $1 trillion annually in economic value worldwide through improved cost and operational performance. Shared services, greater collaboration and integration, improved fraud management, and productivity enhancements enable systemwide efficiencies. At a time of increasing budgetary pressures, governments at national, regional, and local levels cannot afford to miss out on those savings.

Governments around the world are doing their best to meet citizen demand and capture benefits. More than 130 countries have online services. Estonia's 1.3 million residents can use electronic identification cards to vote, pay taxes, and access more than 160 services online, from unemployment benefits to property registration. The United Kingdom's gov.uk site serves as a one-stop information hub for all government departments. Such online services also provide greater access for rural populations, improve quality of life for those with physical infirmities, and offer options for those whose work and lifestyle demands don't conform to typical daytime office hours. However, despite all the progress made, most governments are far from capturing the full benefits of digitization. To do so, they need to take their digital transformations deeper, beyond the provision of online services through e-government portals into the broader business of government itself. That means looking for opportunities for improving productivity, collaboration, scale, process efficiency, and innovation.

While digital transformation in the public sector is particularly challenging, a number of successful government initiatives show that by translating private-sector best practices into the public context it is possible to achieve broader and deeper public sector digitization. Six levers are described next, each illustrated by success stories.

Win Government-Wide and Agency-Deep Commitment to Specific Digital Targets

The launch of gov.uk in 2012 marked the creation of one of the most accessible digital government services in the world. Its success in providing citizens, businesses, and government users with accurate, streamlined, and comprehensive services is due to strong central leadership and implementation provided by the United Kingdom's Government Digital Service. This unit of the government's Cabinet Office was charged with overseeing the country's digital strategy and implementing the transformation of its service provisioning to what it described as "digital by default."[10] By including seasoned digital leaders from different public departments, the Government Digital Service gained the needed experience and expertise, as well as the buy-in of those departments. A clear mandate helped steer the implementation and build awareness.

The unit worked to sustain momentum for the sometimes challenging change efforts by being as transparent as possible. It published its strategy, scheduled targets for each department, and reported performance against those targets frequently. According to government estimates, gov.uk saved £42 million in government spending within a year of its launch. In October 2013, it had, for the first time, two million visits in one day.[11]

Establish Government-Wide Coordination of Digital Investments

To better coordinate large-scale digital projects across the government and generate cost efficiencies, Denmark established IT Projektraad, a digitization council reporting to the Ministry of Finance, to function as its central IT steering group. The agency's goal is to ensure that the benefits and gains targeted in a project's business case are realized. This has allowed it to apply a test-and-learn approach, using pilot projects to ensure that investments are effective and then bringing lessons learned to other agencies. To that end, the digitization agency requires government institutions to adhere to specific methodologies and guidelines when planning their IT investments. It also develops and shares best practices, conducts risk evaluations for projects over a certain cost threshold, participates in project reviews, and helps oversee the government's IT project pipeline. Such central oversight has helped the Danish government reduce unnecessary investments, enforce common standards, and build greater project synergies.

Redesign Processes with the End User in Mind

In 2011 the Netherlands released i-NUP, its government-wide implementation agenda for e-government services, to prioritize citizen- or user-centered design by boosting convenience and trimming red tape. One of

[10] Government Digital Strategy: December 2013, UK Cabinet Office, 2013, https://www.gov.uk.
[11] "£10bn Saved in 2012/13: Efficiency and Reform 2012/13 Summary Report," UK Cabinet Office, 2013, gov.uk.

the implementation rules, for instance, states, "We do not pose superfluous questions. Data included in one of the basic registrations will not be asked for again."[12] Under the plan, municipalities would serve as "citizens' desks" and be the first line of contact to field or refer questions, supported by a website, customer contact center, and central phone number. As of 2014, most municipalities are connected to a single access number.

The plan called for a similar overhaul of the country's government-to-business services. To make that happen, the Dutch launched a comprehensive digital infrastructure project led by the national digital governance agency, Logius. The project steering group included central and local governments and public IT agencies. Together, using world-class standards, they defined the technical specifications for the 13 central databases involved and their interconnections. They also created a government-wide dashboard to highlight project status and risks, and used conferences and social media to disseminate and refine key lessons with public-sector IT managers around the country. As a result of these initiatives, physical visits to municipalities and government offices have decreased significantly. For example, the number of visits to Rotterdam municipality offices decreased by around 50 percent from 2010 to 2013.

Hire and Nurture the Right Talent

Digital transformations call for specialized skills that are in high demand and therefore increasingly hard to come by. Government organizations often struggle to compete for such talent since the private sector frequently can offer higher wages, a more entrepreneurial culture, and more clearly defined career paths.

However, a few governments have found ways to attract or nurture talent for their digital projects. In South Korea, for instance, a significant portion of government IT infrastructure is centralized in a few data centers providing numerous e-government services to citizens. The size and breadth of these centers makes it possible to offer IT staff engaging career paths with the chance, for example, to improve a variety of online services while tackling the challenges of managing a large-scale data center. In the United Kingdom, the government actively seeks to attract talented

---

[12] "One Digital Government: Better Service, Greater Convenience," Netherlands Ministry of the Interior and Kingdom Relations, 2011, www.e-overheid.nl.

individuals from the private sector by offering fast-track career opportunities for high performers. For example, the government CIO and the head of digital services spent most of their careers in the private sector. In addition, high-performing graduates are offered fast promotion opportunities in various government service areas, including IT.

Use Big Data and Analytics to Improve Decision Making
The U.S. government has been one of the most active in leveraging data to support government decision making. In 2009, it created a legal and privacy framework that led to the creation of Data.gov, a repository of government tools, resources, and information on anything from energy and science to global development and health. In all, more than 85,000 data sets are available to help businesses and private citizens conduct research, develop web and mobile apps, and create design visualizations. To populate their data troves, government departments were required to identify and share their most valuable data. Competitions, such as Apps for America and Apps for Democracy, have been organized to attract talented developers to build applications that use government data.

Protect Critical Infrastructure and Confidential Data
Data security has become a top national security issue. In 2013, the World Economic Forum identified cyber attacks and critical systems failure as two of the most dangerous global risks. Beyond financial losses, cyber attacks may pose serious reputation risks for companies and governments. Governments can protect critical infrastructures and confidential data through several initiatives. For example, most major developed economies have created a national cyber security strategy in the past five years. They are also developing information-sharing mechanisms to detect and respond to cyber threats more quickly. One example is the UK Fusion Cell, which brings experts from government and the private sector together in an information-sharing and threat-analysis hub.

Regardless of where a public-sector organization is in its digitization journey, these six lessons can help as it starts, scales, or evaluates its program. The stakes are high. When digital public-sector transformations succeed, citizens and businesses will benefit from better access, and governments can operate more nimbly and achieve substantial savings.

CONCLUSION: OPPORTUNITIES IN THE EMERGING ECOSYSTEMS

Digitization is destroying the old business models and creating space for new ones—in addition to the nine emerging ecosystems described here, there are many more. Smart cities, precision farming, digital fleet management, and solutions for field engineering teams are areas where digital thinking means new business opportunities.

As industry boundaries dissolve, markets are redistributed; and as agile start-ups snatch customers away from the established leaders in every field, it's time for critical stocktaking: Is our business under threat? Are we using the new technologies correctly? Have we identified new revenue potentials? Companies that want to succeed in the new markets need to work on their business architecture, which we will look at in the next chapter.

□-□-5-□-□

WHAT? DEVELOPING BUSINESS ARCHITECTURE

THE DIGITAL AGE *demands new skills: companies that want to be successful in their industries and the emerging ecosystems must get their functions and processes in shape for the new era.*

What do successful digital companies have in common? They all base their products and processes strictly on the needs of the customer, which is why this chapter on the development of the business architecture starts with the customer experience. We describe how a shopping or service experience can be orchestrated across numerous channels, we identify the opportunities of automated pricing, and we dive into the world of social media, which has revolutionized marketing.

We then move on to the product and its value proposition. In keeping with the new digital philosophy, products are no longer launched in perfect condition, but come to market in their basic configuration, and are then rigorously further developed. Real-time customer reactions are incorporated into the ongoing development, and the products and services approach perfection in iterative loops.

The value chain also faces sweeping changes as the Internet of Things, robots, and artificial intelligence revolutionize production, the supply chain, and administration. To link robots, machines in production, and the supply chain, connectivity is needed as well as technical platforms that interact with sensors and actuators.

5.1 OMNICHANNEL: A PRESENCE ACROSS ALL CHANNELS
Lareina Yee and Martin Harrysson describe how companies leverage all sales and communication channels to the maximum.

Iron and steel are very traditional industries. Yet in the digital age, even heavy industries are now treading new paths in sales and distribution. The Chinese iron and steel group Baosteel offers its entire product range, from sheet steel to specialist aluminum products, via its online platform Ouyeel. Customers are able to find all the information they need on the user-friendly site in a single click. The steel manufacturer has digitized its entire ordering and delivery process, while also offering other services on the platform such as financing.

Baosteel demonstrates the concept of omnichannel, where customer sales and customer contact occur across all channels. It is no longer limited to classic retail and its end consumers. It has now spread to all industries, from banking, insurance, and energy utilities right through to purely B2B industries. In all cases, it's clear that digitization is fundamentally changing not only how customers find information and make purchases, but also how companies and their existing and potential customers communicate and interact.

Omnichannel Is Both a Challenge and Opportunity for All Industries
Until just a few years ago, some transactions in banking and insurance were conducted via one channel only for regulatory reasons. People who wanted to open a bank account or take out an insurance policy had to complete at least the final step offline, and legally verify their identity in the bank branch, at the insurance agency, or at the post office. With digital verification methods, even these final steps can now be performed across multiple channels. Start-ups like Socure, WebID, and The ID Co. now offer identity verification processes via video or smartphone, thus digitizing the final step to opening an account or taking out a policy even in this complex regulatory environment.

Travel and hospitality service providers not only are working intensively on digitizing their customer contact processes, but also face immense competition from digital intermediaries and platforms like Priceline and Expedia, which are investing huge sums in marketing, in an effort to gain direct customer access.

And as our opening example shows, the digitization of customer contact has even become commonplace in B2B sectors like heavy industry. While Baosteel operates its own platform, its rivals sell their steel by the ton on Alibaba. Chemicals group BASF also sells its chemicals to Chinese small and midsize enterprises (SMEs) via Alibaba.

The multichannel approach not only is used to inform customers and sell products, but also offers a direct link to the company. Insurers, for example, have opened up the digital channel to enable car drivers to submit damage reports with a photo from their smartphones. Health insurance customers can scan their medical receipts with an app and submit claims for reimbursement. It's no coincidence that one of the top priorities of Allianz is the radical digitization of all relevant customer contact points.

In Five Years, the Millennials Will Be the Strongest Consumer Group

The pioneers of development are the retailers and service providers that have contact with the end customers. They are now preparing for a generation of customers who grew up in the digital age. In five years, people born after 1990 will be the strongest consumer group. According to a survey, 77 percent of this generation spends three or more hours online each day; for 56 percent, their smartphones are their most important shopping tool, and even though they have a lower income on average than the general population, they are above-average spenders online.

Brick-and-mortar retail has responded to the needs of young people with an omnichannel strategy, providing offers across all sales channels. This is also known as a multichannel strategy or 360-degree commerce. In implementing such a strategy, the company must decide in which sales channels, on which platforms, and at which contact points it wants to be visible to its customers, and how to interact with them. Customers today want to be free to decide which channels they use to find information, to make purchases, and to receive their goods or services. They want to be able to move seamlessly between these channels and contact points.

In the early years, the online activities of main-street retailers were predominantly defensive—to ward off their online competitors. Today, the established retailers display their full strengths. They use their stores as a customer contact weapon where customers can physically experience the goods, receive advice, and even collect or exchange goods that they ordered online. They've done it so successfully that online-only retailers are starting to think multichannel. Amazon is now opening physical stores and collection points where ordered goods can be collected. This shows that even the new digital retailers mustn't underestimate the old brick-and-mortar model. At the beginning of 2016, a good 90 percent of all retail revenues were still generated offline.

Strategy and Implementation: Structure Is Everything

In many industries that deal with the end customer, digital measures have only led to a set of further sales and marketing channels—online, mobile devices, social media, and chat forums. In many cases, this has simply exacerbated the classic channel conflicts, with the managers of the respective sales channels competing more against their colleagues rather than against the competition. To ensure this doesn't happen, it's worth bearing in mind some fundamental rules.

Six characteristics of pioneers in multichannel business

What the pioneers do

🏆	Multichannel strategy	• Define an **ambitious multichannel vision**, closely linked to the corporate strategy • Undertake **targeted steps** and investments in areas in which they want to achieve excellence
🧍	Customer journey	• Focus **fully on the customer**, regardless of channel • Ensure **seamless customer experiences** that focus on customer needs
📊	Findings, not data	• Focus on findings for improved **decisions** and increased **sense of responsibility** • Experiment with iterative and comprehensive **test-and-learn approach**
🚚	Flexible supply chain	• Offer **flexibility and choice** when it comes to fulfillment options for customers • Optimal use of **infrastructure**—particularly stores—and optimum basic processes
🗄	Dynamic technological ecosystem	• Invest in scalable back-end infrastructure with APIs to link old and new systems • Establish **12–18 month rolling plan** • Use **MVP approach** (minimum viable product), particularly for customer-facing processes • Enable customers and employees
🗂	Organization and operational model	• Establish a culture where **digitization predominates** • Increase the digital quotient of all employees • Centralize resources; introduce cross-functional teams and methods • Promote the digital organization (C-suite) • Combine new and existing talent: 1 + 1 = 3

Set the Right Targets

The aim is simple: companies need to offer their customers a consistent experience across all channels and across all contact points. But what does this actually mean? In retail, for example, it includes services and offers, such as customers being able to check on a smartphone whether an item they saw in a commercial is available in the nearest store. Or perhaps targeting customers who are browsing in a store with vouchers or discount coupons sent to their smartphone. For electricity and gas customers, it means addressing them by name when they visit the website and log in. Banks have integrated their services in such a way that customers can start filling out a loan application on their smartphone before going to bed at night, and then complete it in their branch the next day on their lunch break and sign the contract.

For companies, work starts with the strategic issue of which channel mix is best for the target customers. What roles do the individual channels and platforms play, and how can they be integrated into a true multichannel offering? The question as to which channels a company doesn't want to include in its strategy is also implicit: does an energy utility need to be present on price-comparison sites, thus starting a price war?

These questions can be answered only if managers precisely understand the needs of their target customers. To do so, they need to understand the customer decision journey from initial contact with an offer in a shop window or on the website, through the research phase and the consideration phase, to the actual order and potential after-sales services. This journey differs vastly from customer to customer, which makes it even more important to ensure customers are able to switch seamlessly between channels. "The art of selling is the same across all channels," according to Andy Street, head of marketing at successful British multichannel retailer John Lewis, "which is why we need to ensure that customers don't have to worry about which channel they're currently using because they get the same offer presented in the same way on whichever channel they choose."

Keys to Success: Data

To fully understand the customer journey through the various channels, companies rely on data. Modern market researchers, or customer insight specialists, leverage customer satisfaction data at all contact points. Data scientists then study where potential customers exit the journey, and use this data to identify where friction and dissatisfaction exist. The results are then presented to management, which looks at ways to bridge these short-comings. And since today's customer needs and habits change dynamically, data analysis is not a one-off process, but must be a constant cycle of measuring, analyzing, and optimizing.

Keys to Success: Organization and Culture

Optimizing the customer experience at the various touch points can succeed only if the optimizer consistently thinks from the customer perspective, which requires the committed abolition of company silos and departmental thinking. However, this can happen only if the sales channels are not managed individually in separate organizational units. And yet this is still the reality in many companies, which have grown with the new channels, setting the ideal prerequisites for serious channel conflicts. The only remedy is to think like the customers, and trace their journey through the contact points with a cross-departmental and cross-functional mind-set.

Customer-centric thinking is a key marker of digital organizations for most companies. However, it requires cultural change and the willingness to test and learn. Whenever new channels or contact points emerge, companies should use them to approach customers. If the response is positive, the channel can be expanded; if it's negative, the company can make a quick exit. Nevertheless, companies must be constantly willing to innovate, and be prepared to accept failure.

U.S. fashion chain Nordstrom, for example, established its own cross-functional teams in an "innovation lab" to conduct these quick tests. British retailer John Lewis constantly trials new technologies in its stores. Most recently it tested smart mirrors; a customer clicked on an item of clothing, which the integrated computers then portrayed as a virtual and 3D image superimposed onto the customer. If customers liked what they saw, they could scan the QR code and place the item in a digital shopping basket. John Lewis then sent the customer the mirror image by e-mail as a service. "Great fun and an excellent idea" was how the project team summed up the trial—and then promptly terminated it. Although the idea was a popular gimmick among customers at first, it failed to produce any new findings on customer behavior or increased sales.

Keys to Success: Technology

To be successful across all channels, companies need to rethink their technology. It should no longer be seen as just a support function, but must instead be developed into a core competency.

To support customers through all touch points, data must be collected at each point and aggregated in the background. Not only does this require extremely powerful databases, which are increasingly based in the cloud, but also integrated IT systems. Once in place, software is needed to analyze the aggregated data. Only once a company has identified whether customers leave its online store after just a few minutes of browsing without buying anything, or leave after viewing products and possibly placing a product in the shopping cart, will it know whether it needs to improve the offering, the loading times of the pages, or the buying process.

Only companies that employ analytics software that can show where an ordered product is in the supply chain at any given time—in the warehouse, in the sorting center, or already in the delivery van—can offer their customers services like "track and trace." The website, especially the version for mobile versions, must be continuously optimized with new features. A home page that crashes due to overloading means lost revenue.

However, upgrading the technology means investment. U.S. home improvement chain Home Depot, for example, announced plans to invest around 40 percent of its overall investment budget in technology and IT over the next three years.

Amazon, too, the pioneer of online retailing, has long operated across numerous channels, and is continuously testing new ideas—such as the supermarket of tomorrow, which it launched as Amazon Go. Its grocery store customers check in on a smartphone, are greeted personally, and then are directed to products that may be of interest, either because they have bought them before or because they're reduced in price. The smartphone points the way to the relevant shelf, the customer scans the codes of his or her purchases, and drives home—no lines, no checkout. Payment is made with the credit card associated with the app, just like online shopping, and the receipt is e-mailed to the customer.

5.2 DYNAMIC PRICING: UP-TO-THE-MINUTE PRICES

Ramji Sundararajan on dynamic pricing, and why two people can pay vastly differing sums for the same product, from the same provider.

A typical online fashion retailer has a range of seven million items, while the major multicategory providers like Amazon have much more. In addition, the most successful online retailers change their prices for the individual items every 15 minutes. How is this possible? If you're now trying to calculate how many employees are required to work tirelessly in their offices analyzing price elasticity trends and how these affect individual prices, you're on the wrong track. Dynamic pricing is fully automatic, with computers taking over the work of calculating and processing huge volumes of data about competitors' prices, sales promotion figures, potential customers' search trends, product ratings on Internet forums, and even comments on Twitter and Facebook. Depending on the company's strategic aims, whether it's maximizing market share or profit, an algorithm calculates the optimal price when necessary, sometimes refreshing every minute.

Dynamic pricing, which was introduced in 2005 by Amazon and others, saves the margins of online retailers because online shoppers have become shrewd bargain hunters. Price-comparison websites and ratings communities have enabled the sort of transparency that never existed before, and aggressive new retailers often explode existing price structures with cheap introductory offers. Dynamic pricing plays a crucial role in boosting both consumer price perception and retailer profitability. Typically, dynamic pricing can unlock a 3 to 8 percent return on sales rapidly and is a huge competitive advantage.

Retailers retaliate with two different versions of dynamic pricing: One version optimizes prices for an entire range, which apply to all customers across the board. This is ideal for products that are easy to compare, such as brand items. The second version calculates a tailored price for each customer individually. This works better when direct comparisons are more difficult such as with insurance products or travel.

Algorithms Find the Best Prices

Luckily for retailers, the best price is not always cheaper than competitors' prices. As experiences in local retail have also shown, customers form an opinion on whether a store offers good value for money or is expensive

Digitization disrupts the conventional ground rules of pricing in retail

		Challenges for pricing
1	Consumers have access to unlimited information	Never before have customers had so many ways to research products and compare prices in real time
2	Information in real time	Real-time information on competitors and consumer behavior enable multiple price changes in one day
3	Customer expectations are changing	Experiences with new providers have changed customer expectations of pricing and promotions
4	The dynamic customer	Customer decision journeys now follow multiple channels—and the customer expects that

based on relatively few prices for specific products. In supermarkets, for example, impressions are generally formed on frequently purchased items like milk, butter, and detergent, which is why retailers choose these products for their aggressive special offers.

And it's no different online. The important thing is to know the products on which customers base their opinions about value for money. Once again, the best example is Amazon: The e-commerce giant defines key value items throughout each of its categories, which it consistently offers at lower prices than its major competitors. In the case of ink cartridges for printers, for example, Amazon knows that most buyers first look at the price of a twin pack of black ink. In 2016, Amazon undercut its two strongest competitors for this product by more than 20 percent. However, when it came to the single pack of black ink, which is also a frequent buy, Amazon was only just under its competitors. Yet these low prices are more than compensated by the prices for colored ink: yellow, blue, and red are between 33 percent and 57 percent more expensive than at Amazon's competitors.

The great thing about digital pricing is that the company is constantly learning. Computer programs track the responses of customers and competitors to a new price in real time: Are sales moving as planned? How many people showing an interest fail to make a purchase? Where do the new customers come from—price-comparison sites, websites of competitors—or did they come to our website specifically? All the findings are immediately entered into the pricing model, which constantly updates and adjusts.

Companies that optimize their prices based on this formula even do away with the old 80/20 rule according to which 20 percent of products actually account for 80 percent of revenue and profit. Take the example of Amazon with cell phones: Around 80 percent of its revenue is made from selling devices that account for around 20 percent of its business in this category. The remaining 80 percent of items comprise accessories like chargers, connection cables, headphones, and smartphone cases. Although they account for only 20 percent of revenue, they still deliver 50 percent of profit. These are typical long-tail products. They remain in the assortment for years, long after the corresponding cell phone has been surpassed by newer models but is still used. In main-street stores, it isn't cost-effective to continue stocking such a vast array of accessories, because the retail space is just too expensive. However, online retailers with their enormous and cheap warehouses can healthily boost their margins with these very items.

All the major online retailers have now established dynamic pricing systems, and the idea is also coming to brick-and-mortar retail. The U.S. retail chains Sears and Home Depot, for example, are now able to vary their in-store prices at the push of a button after installing electronic price labels in some sections within their stores. Once electronic price labeling has been established across the board, this opens up dynamic pricing opportunities even for multichannel retailers who started off in the physical space. Ultimately, today's customers expect a consistent offering across all channels, even when it comes to prices.

Individually Tailored Prices

Tailored pricing goes one step further. In this case, the retailer attempts to classify the individual customer—for example, by analyzing which device was used to reach the website. If an expensive iPad was used, the system immediately shows a higher price than is displayed to a different customer using a cheaper product running the Android operating system. A cheaper offer is also shown to customers who have been redirected to the provider's website from a price-comparison site. For a long time, systems have noted whether someone has previously visited the website and shown an interest in an offer. If the customer views the same item again on the website, the system forces a decision by promising a discount for an immediate purchase or offering free add-on services.

Once customers see through these pricing strategies, they are often less than amused, which is why many travel operators have given up differentiating customers according to the devices they use. Too many customers vented their frustration at being shown a higher price following a quick browse on their expensive iPhone than they were shown later at home on their old PC. However, price differentiation according to the route taken to the website is still very much in force among the core players in the travel industry.

The concept of tailored pricing is an area of interest for companies in many industries. Insurers are working on ways to better price individual risks, while energy companies want to incorporate individual consumption habits into their offers. And it's not just in the retail space where dynamic pricing is winning out—the enterprise space is also experimenting with the concept, for example in the chemicals and steel industries. Steel distributor Baosteel's online marketplace Ouyeel has created the kind of price transparency that never before existed in the industry. And BASF now trades on Chinese retail platform Alibaba, selling chemicals to thousands of predominantly SME clients in Asia.

Five Modules of Dynamic Pricing

Dynamic pricing plays a crucial role in boosting both consumer price perception and retailer profitability. A robust dynamic-pricing solution should consist of five modules, all working in parallel to generate price recommendations for every SKU in the assortment:

1. *The long-tail module* helps a retailer set the introductory price for new or long-tail items through intelligent product matching. The module determines which data-rich products are comparable to new items (which have no history) or long-tail items (which have limited historical data).
2. *The elasticity module* uses time-series methods and big data analytics to calculate how a product's price affects demand, accounting for a wide variety of factors, including seasonality, cannibalization, and competitive moves.

3. *The key value items (KVIs) module* estimates how much each product affects consumer price perception, using actual market data rather than consumer surveys. This enables the module to automatically detect changes as to which items consumers perceive as KVIs.

4. *The competitive-response module* recommends price adjustments based on competitor prices updated in real time.

5. *The omnichannel module* coordinates prices among the retailer's offline and online channels.

While a best-in-class solution includes all five modules, companies can often begin with only the KVI and competitive-response modules. These help companies nimbly respond to competitive moves on key items, while they add the rest of the modules over time.

Dynamic-pricing solutions should include five modules

Long-tail module helps set the introductory price through intelligent product matching	Elasticity module calculates how a product's price affects demand	KVI module estimates much each product affects consumer price perception	Competitive-response module recommends price adjustments based on competitor prices updated in real time	Omnichannel module coordinates prices among the retailer's offline and online channels

Companies looking to lay the groundwork for a functioning dynamic pricing system know it can be done—and the effort is worth it. Some e-commerce retailers have achieved margin gains of two to three percentage points—and in an industry that operates with such tight margins, that can make the difference between being an industry leader and a follower.

And with results like that, concepts soon catch on. In the next few years, dynamic pricing is likely to become a core competency in business. The next wave will affect the B2B sector, where prices in many industries still lack transparency. Such new openness could trigger shock waves. Just think of the current practices in industries like steel or chemicals. In the

B2C sector, the trend is increasingly moving toward more customized offerings, including tailored prices.

The big question is whether customers will rebel. Just because something is technically feasible doesn't mean it will be accepted, as the example from the travel industry shows, where companies had to give up price differentiation based on whether a customer was using an expensive Apple product or a cheap no-name PC. However, there are other options for setting tailored prices, and they will pose an interesting challenge for creative companies.

5.3 DIGITAL MARKETING: TAILORED MESSAGES ACROSS ALL CHANNELS

Brian Gregg on why content is king in digital marketing, and how companies can master the discipline.

On average, people look at their cell phones 200 times a day to check for messages. A 20-year-old today has already received 20 million marketing messages during his or her young life. In the 1990s, this figure would have been only a million. Adult U.S. citizens spend just under six hours online each day, and it's not much less in Europe. In the United States, Google generates more advertising revenue than all the country's daily newspapers put together.

We chat, we tweet, we text, we e-mail, we post photos to Instagram, and we watch videos on YouTube anytime, anywhere. Our use of media has changed radically. And just as radical are the upheavals in marketing. As conventional advertising reaches ever-dwindling numbers of the younger generation, so continuous measures to build brand awareness and trust online become more important.

The established marketing companies need to reinvent themselves. Instead of planning broad, individual, successively scheduled campaigns, today multiple campaigns specifically aimed at micro-target groups continuously run in parallel. Instead of mass communication, consumers want personalization; instead of slogans, they want stories. Instead of broadcasting marketing content mainly in advertising slots and commercials regardless of whether it interests the audience, today the ultimate challenge is to deliver content that is interesting enough to be shared between friends (earned advertising).

And naturally smartphones are the medium of choice for most consumers. Marketing content needs to take into account the restrictions of mobile devices, such as the small screen, which limit presence, not just for banner advertising. Search engines show only a few hits on small screens, which means it's imperative that ads appear at the top of the list. Conversely, mobile devices offer new opportunities such as geomarketing where the location of the consumer is identified via the smartphone, and local offers can then be sent to the screen to entice the potential customer to visit a nearby store.

Digital marketing is subject to different mechanisms than traditional ones, and demands a restructured marketing organization

Traditional marketing	Digital marketing
One-time	Always-on
Push	As required
Standardized	Personalized and targeted
Paid	Owned + earned + paid
Planned in advance	Agile
Create	Create, measure, optimize
Fixed budgets	Flexible budgets

Finding the Right Channel for Each Message

The various digital communication channels present marketing with different challenges. By analyzing customer and usage data, marketers can address individual target groups specifically in these channels. In this new world of performance marketing, companies no longer buy advertising space on individual websites, but instead pay to reach target groups across a range of sites. The target group filtering is based on previous surfing habits. Tracking customers who viewed a certain product on store websites, particularly if they placed the product in the shopping cart but didn't complete the purchase (retargeting), is particularly effective. They can then offer the same or a similar product again since the customer has already shown an interest.

Search engine marketing is also aimed at very specific customer segments and purchases. Search engine optimization (SEO) optimizes the content and links of a company's website to the algorithms used by Google so that the website appears right at the top of the hit list. Search engine advertising (SEA) purchases the top positions for paid advertising in the Google search results. Being positioned among the top hits is crucial to the success of both SEO and SEA. Between them, all search results that are not visible without scrolling receive less than 10 percent of all user clicks.

SEA is paid per click, and that can get expensive. For example, in the United States, Google charges $2.90 per click for the top position in results returned for the search term "buy wine." Companies that want their ad to be positioned at the top of the list for the keyword "mortgage" can expect to pay $15.30 for each click. And the search term "insurance" costs $31.10 per click for the top position. In other words, it's easy for companies to calculate how high the conversion rate must be to make such an investment worthwhile.

Marketing in social media is where it gets exciting, On Twitter, Facebook, Instagram, and the rest, it's not about advertising slogans, but more about storytelling. This means a completely new way of thinking and organization for marketing departments; they need to think more like editors and less like advertising agencies. Content marketing is a key discipline in today's digital marketing, and is explained in more detail next.

Content Is King

What story am I telling to whom? How, where, and when will I tell it? These are the questions that content marketing must answer. The last question is simple to answer: always. Essentially, there are four central success factors for digital content marketing:

1. *Continuity.* Companies need to be always on, because today's consumers expect continuous communication. This means producing more content in smaller units. For example, Burberry regularly publishes not only videos about its current collection on its YouTube channel, but also music videos with the greatest possible reach.

2. *Authenticity.* Companies need their own authentic content that is appropriate to the respective platform. The messages will achieve their aim only if the users feel the content producer is competent in that field. For example, American Express gained significant reach with customers when it launched the OPEN Forum, which provides a platform for customers to connect with experts to help them solve many of their pressing business challenges, while at the same time connecting them with American Express's brand messages. Content doesn't necessarily need to be product-related, as Red Bull shows with its long-term involvement with sports and its resulting credibility in the field. The content should also be tailored to the medium: the communication style used on Snapchat, for example, is more spontaneous than the language used on narrative blogs, while the imagery on the virtual pinboard Pinterest is different from that found on Instagram, which mainly centers around snapshots.

3. *Relevance.* Content marketing must understand precisely who the relevant customers are, which channels they use, and the kind of content they respond to. For millennials, explanatory videos are clearly important. We learned through research with McGarryBowen and Kraft Foods conducted by Google that 59 percent of 25- to 34-year-olds indicated they cook with either their smartphones or tablets handy. As a result, hardware chains like Home Depot, Lowe's, and Ace Hardware have uploaded vast numbers of instructional videos to YouTube. In its online magazine *Turn On* and on its YouTube channel, electronics retailer Saturn explains the technology of its products. Supermarkets Safeway and Whole Foods have their own online cooking shows. The investment is worth it for retailers: In a survey of young adults, one-third revealed they had bought a product after watching the corresponding instructional video. A meta-analysis conducted by Google of 56 European case studies shows that in three-quarters of the observed cases the return on investment from YouTube campaigns was higher than that of TV commercials. In other industries, on the other hand, up-to-date content is what counts. This means producing more and more content in ever-shorter cycles, particularly during major events like the soccer World Cup. Adidas

and Nike, for example, each put together their own editorial teams that virtually commentated live on matches on social media, while supplementing this with online content.

4. *Interactivity.* Virtually all companies with an active online presence have at some point engaged directly with customers, who expect a fast response to a direct question. Take the example of United Airlines: because travel issues tend to generate a particularly high volume of queries on social media, the airline now promotes its 24-hour customer service on Twitter, Facebook, and LinkedIn to set itself apart from the competition.

How to Succeed in Content Marketing

To master all of these challenges, marketing needs to reorganize itself. It needs technology, organization, oversight, and control systems.

- *Technology.* A content management system can help the marketing team manage publishing processes and make them more efficient with the use of simple user interfaces. Media asset management (MAM) or data asset management (DAM) also stores images, videos, and text centrally, thus minimizing duplicate production. Analysis tools measure the impact of content, and in the event of negative responses, improvements can be made based on the data. Finally, targeting management systems and audience management systems help companies deliver the right content to the right target groups.
- *Organization.* Not only must processes be adapted to the new challenges, but the organization also needs to change. Classic marketing functions like strategy and creation are now supplemented with roles such as editor, writer, and content manager, whose skill profiles bridge editorial work and marketing expertise.
- *Oversight.* A coordinator oversees the right mix of paid content and owned and earned content. Owned content refers to all content that the company curates itself, be it on its own website or on its Instagram account. Earned content refers to the reach achieved when a post is shared, liked, reposted, and commented on by other users. Even though this unpaid reach may at first appear to be the company's ultimate aim, it's actually the mix that's the most important. The

transitions must be seamless for customers. Thus, successful earned content campaigns often lead to monetary gains.

- *Control systems.* Content marketing also requires continuous testing, measuring, and improvement. However, the success of content should not be measured just by its reach, but also by whether it goes viral—X percent of users share it with Y percent of their contacts. Customer responses can also be analyzed using special text analysis software and divided into positive, negative, and neutral contributions. This enables companies to identify successful content early and to initiate targeted seeding to broadening the content's spread.

After Content Marketing Comes Programmatic Marketing

How will online marketing continue to develop? The trend toward precise, data-driven targeting of specific target groups will grow significantly with new advanced analytics approaches. Completely automated algorithms will increasingly be used to control the publication of digital marketing content. This is known as programmatic marketing. For example, when a user visits a website, the advertising space on that website is offered to advertising platforms in real time, and those spaces are allocated in a bidding process lasting just milliseconds—real-time bidding.

So what does this mean for the online marketing organization of a company? There must be a core team of in-house online marketing experts who understand these new technologies and their opportunities, and who ensure that the advertising budgets are deployed as efficiently as possible and continuously optimized. Too many companies currently outsource this work to external service providers. Expertise at the crossover between marketing and technology will become a new core competency for businesses that includes selecting the right marketing systems and tools. This poses a significant challenge to most of today's marketing employees.

5.4 DIGITAL PRODUCT DEVELOPMENT AND OPEN INNOVATION: RETHINKING PRODUCT DEVELOPMENT

Michael Uhl and Belkis Vasquez-McCall on how digitization is changing development processes in all industries.

The Sonos speaker comes with an app that controls the digital radio, sends different songs to speakers in different rooms, and saves personal playlists for all members of the household. Today, all devices are connected to the

Internet, transmitting data collected by their sensors. Cars have long since become four-wheeled computers. The products that brighten up our everyday lives and keep the economy going have changed. They're becoming smarter as software's share of the value added increases. For example, the car of today has more lines of programming code than was contained in Windows Vista, and it's increasing all the time.

Software requires that development departments in many industries now rely on the methods of programmers. This is digital development, a structured route to new products and services. The developers combine digital and technological innovation in an agile, cross-departmental approach that drives projects to production stage with the end consumer in mind at all times. In this process, speed is more important than perfection. Try, fail, and learn are the core components of this method.

The digital innovation process (DIP) is determined by guiding principles, starting with modular structure. Developers begin with a focused project, and then transfer the results to neighboring areas. All innovations target the customer. In turn, customer feedback is then immediately reincorporated back into development. It's agile and fast. The digital development process is efficient and never stops. The product is being constantly developed.

The definition of the digital innovation process (DIP) follows five best-practice design principles

Principle	Description
1 Modularity	• Assembly kit principle allows process to be expanded (e.g., adapt to new idea sources) • Enables flexible adjustment (e.g., Fast Tracks)
2 Customer focus	• Unconditional and early focus on the customer with early pilot for example • Continuous iterations using customer feedback
3 Agility	• Fast decisions on implementation/adjustments as well as resource deployment • Run times vary by project scope
4 Efficiency	• Permeability of promising ideas • Short decision paths and optimal support for implementing the business idea
5 Continuous further development	• Iteration of the process itself and incorporation of feedback and experiences • Update frequency lessens with maturity

The DIP should initially be defined as a minimal version, then tested and refined

Open Innovation and Open Development: Tapping into the World's Creativity

This product development philosophy was born in the digital economy and is now being adopted in the innovation processes of traditional analog products. Largely autonomous cross-departmental teams work on focused tasks and are committed to achieving specific stage targets without the interruptions of steering committees and management meetings—it's the best of the start-up scene applied to business: independence, fun, and speed.

By using a special interface or crowdsourcing platform, open innovation allows outsiders to contribute their ideas, and ideally bring them to market readiness using specially provided software tools. Open innovation doesn't necessarily have to be limited to an entirely digital innovation process; it can also supplement a traditional development process.

Surprisingly enough, the pioneer of open innovation wasn't a digital company at all. It was Lego. Starting as early as 2005, the toymaker invited both adult and young enthusiasts to become part of its design team via the Legofactory.com website. This platform offered these would-be designers free software for designing their own Lego parts, and the best ideas were selected to be included in the range. Lego received both ideas and criticism via the Legofactory.com website. Particularly eager and technically proficient users discovered several weaknesses in the program. In 2012, Lego stopped the program because the individually designed and produced kits were too expensive for customers.

Once again, the master of open innovation among the digital companies is Apple. The computer maker established application programming interfaces (APIs) for software engineers, giving them access to Xcode, a development environment in which apps can be written for the iPhone and iPad. After a testing process, the apps are then sold on Apple's App Store. The developers enjoy the revenue, while Apple enjoys the commission and the value added to its hardware that allows its customers to do even more.

Many other digital companies like Google and SAP are also using open innovation, and even telecom groups are tapping into the creativity of outsiders. Since an increasing number of products now incorporate software elements, the best example being smart TVs, this approach is interesting for a lot of industries.

Companies that want to establish an open platform should bear in mind some basic rules. It's important to define clear targets at the outset: what should the platform and its users accomplish? Then motivation needs to be considered: how will the codevelopers be rewarded? The third stage involves assessing the ideas and solutions, and the fourth stage focuses on organizing the network.

Open development environments: 10 success factors

Network design	1	Define **clear targets** for the open network
	2	Redefine **relationships** with current partners and establish new ones
	3	Leverage open network **across the entire value chain**
Partner management	4	Precisely tailor **own innovative contribution**
	5	**Support partners**
	6	Use **network** to complete the **bulk of the work**
Network assessment	7	Check **business model for robustness** early on
	8	Continuously evaluate **new ideas**
Network support	9	Manage network with **own top talent**
	10	**Monitor performance** of the network

Agile Product Development of Digital Products:
Faster and Smarter to Market

At a time when customer tastes are changing ever more quickly, the traditional method of product development has proven increasingly unsuitable. It's too slow, there's too little feedback on the latest customer preferences, and there's nowhere near enough flexibility. The product design is fixed long before the start of production, and in most cases can no longer be adapted dynamically to customer needs after market launch.

Agile product development overcomes these shortcomings as traditional companies look to the methods used by start-ups, which studiously examine trends and consumer preferences, and use their findings for product ideas. These are then tested and developed in a dynamic process, interacting with customers, even involving them in the early design phase.

Prototypes are tested on the market, and the product's final specifications remain flexible right up to product launch. Start-ups work by the philosophy that a product is never finished, but remains in constant development based on customer reactions.

One of the first to use this innovation process was Google: Even the company's Gmail product was developed by a cross-functional team that comprised marketing, sales, and IT. First, the idea had to be approved by the Google Product Council, whose members include cofounders Larry Page and Sergey Brin, as well as CEO Sundar Pichai. Once teams have passed this test, they are allocated a budget and assume responsibility for their results. To successfully negotiate the path from idea to market launch, the developers must pass through three stage gates. Each of these gates to the next phase has clearly defined criteria, and each month, the team must report to CEO Pichai. Beyond this, no further coordination is needed in the company.

Agile product development requires an organization that is independent from the company. Samsung operates its Global Innovation Center as an independent unit with reporting lines running straight to the CEO. The money for projects comes from the various divisions, which specify strict stage targets for development. In turn, the divisions must create structures that enable fast responses and quick decision making. To recruit the best talent, the Global Innovation Center is based wherever there is a particularly high density of digital natives. Development centers are operated in New York, Silicon Valley, Tel Aviv, and Seoul.

To leverage external expertise and ideas, Samsung's Global Innovation Center also participates in start-ups. A Samsung developer always switches to the freshly acquired company for up to one year to support the firm through to the proof of concept. However, the Global Innovation Center doesn't work just with start-ups; it also works with other large businesses in the spirit of progress. For example, the South Koreans partnered with Intel to start the country's National Internet of Things Strategy Dialogue.

A complete rethink of product development is needed. In the past, patents and internal expertise formed the primary source of innovation. This has now given way to the realization that markets are always more innovative than individual companies can ever be because market stimuli have become more important. Acting fast and trialing products in the right networks have become core competencies. Nonetheless, patents and intellectual property rights (IPR) will continue to be important in the future—they are the platform for innovation.

5.5 PRODUCT DESIGN: LEARNING FROM SOFTWARE DEVELOPMENT

Florian Weig on how the philosophy of software development is infecting every industry, and what engineers can learn from big data.

Why does the iPhone 7 Plus have two cameras? In 2016, buyers searched in vain for the reason. The hardware to take 3D photos was in place, but the software was missing. It's typical Apple: the firm launches products that offer all the essential functions, but still leave their options open for additional functionality. Once the software for 3D images is ready, there'll be an update, and the iPhone won't just be able to shoot stunning 3D photos, but will also be ready for augmented reality or the overlay of additional computer-generated information or virtual objects. Exciting new features like these keep the device interesting for consumers even after long periods. The model is upgraded without changing the hardware.

Digitization fundamentally changes product development

Product Design thinking	• Understand **customer needs and their causes** • **Real-time feedback** determines the design • **Feature-based design**
Process and tools Acceleration and virtualization	• **Agile software development** making inroads into product development. **Feature road maps** instead of product road maps • Virtualization and simulation (the digital twin and digital factory) • Integrated PLM/PDM[1] systems allow **easier development, greater anticipation of risks, and better forecasting of quality defects**
Advanced analytics Transparency through data	• Data transparency in development enables significantly improved **development efficiency (e.g., 5D BIM)** • **Machine learning delivers real-time transparency of project progress and product profitability**

1 PLM: product life-cycle management; PDM: product data management

Apple is entirely on trend with its understanding of new products and their development. Companies no longer bring finished, unchanging products to market; instead most regard product development as a dynamic process that continues throughout the product's life cycle. This type of development centers around the internal software, and is becoming increasingly important in products of all industries. It's called feature-based design. Digitization is fundamentally changing product development, from the product concept and development processes right through to data-driven decisions.

Rapid Improvements Rather Than Long Product Life Cycles

Design thinking is revolutionizing the way products are being developed, with a much stronger focus on customer needs, real-time incorporation of customer feedback in follow-up products, and products launched in ever shorter cycles.

The Customer Is King—and Codeveloper

By analyzing comments made on social media and online forums, and by analyzing sales data and information from sensors built into their products, engineers today have a much better idea of which product features and capabilities are really used and valued by customers. Our cars, for example, record how drivers use the electronic assistants, and send the information to the manufacturers as standard. This gives automakers a clearer idea of which features their customers value, which can then be used in later product development. Manufacturers of medical equipment also track every image produced by their devices and how each device is used.

Incorporating Data in Real Time

Never before has so much information about customer preferences and usage habits been available. The job of development teams is to reconcile this data continuously with the usage profiles of their products. Wherever there are shortfalls, including where they are caused by changing preferences or habits, adjustments are made.

Classic design consultancies like Veryday and Lunar have established a strong position in the development of digital products. As the ancestors of all modern designers put it during the Bauhaus era, "form follows function," which is why Veryday and Lunar have added digital talent to their designer teams. It's known as user experience (UX) design. The result is products that combine elegant and functional hardware with intuitive user interfaces and menu control. Since this competence has become so important, McKinsey recently acquired both firms.

Feature-Based Design: Gradual Improvement

Feature-based design was initially used by software companies and later adopted by related industries like telecommunications and the semiconductor industry. Now even domestic appliance manufacturers and automakers develop products based on individual features: Products start out with basic features, and are gradually improved. For example, most of today's automakers use a specification called Autosar, which is used to add new features to their models by installing new software modules.

Feature-based design offers benefits for both manufacturers and buyers:

- *Customers* increasingly expect products to remain fresh and new in a world that's developing faster all the time.
- *Companies* secure additional revenues with consistently high margins.
- *Society and the environment* benefit because the product platforms on which new features are added have longer life cycles, thus integrating better into the circular economy of tomorrow.

The new product development philosophy is also changing the customer relationships of sellers, who remain in constant contact with their buyers, and can earn additional revenues throughout the lifetime of their equipment. Electric carmaker Tesla is a shining example of this. Its cars come equipped with all the hardware necessary for semiautonomous driving, including sensors and control units. In 2014, the firm offered its customers the opportunity to upgrade their vehicles with an autopilot system. The software was sent to them for $3,000—a lucrative add-on with a very high margin.

Process Digitization—Acceleration and Virtualization

Tools are constantly being redeveloped to accelerate and virtualize processes. Core elements of agile development include feature road maps, virtualization and simulation, and smart systems for product life-cycle management (PLM) and product data management (PDM).

In the past, there was a development plan or road map leading to the finished product. Today, the product is only an indication of its current position on the development line. Engineers and programmers work according to a feature road map, developing individual modules that are then combined into a single product. However, each individual module is renewed in its own innovation cycle, and this can go very quickly in the case of software. In addition to the classic engineer who is responsible for one or more components, there is also a "feature lead," who is responsible for a specific module such as a camera in a smartphone or a navigation system in a car. The feature lead plans several product generations in advance, and drives forward development.

And even moving away from software features, digitization has changed product design and development processes in other areas. Everything is becoming digital; processes are running faster, and becoming more transparent with big data analytics. Take machinery construction for example. ASML, the world leader in photolithography machines, uses lasers to map circuits onto wafers (the substrates for chips) and is able to upgrade its customers' machines via software updates. These machines have built-in sensors, which continuously transmit data to ASML. After analyzing the data, the ASML engineers first develop ideas and then write programs to deliver improvements—for example, to ensure greater precision when aligning circuits with each other. These programs are then downloaded to the running machines via an app, increasing the performance of the machines without a panel being unscrewed.

And since everything today needs to be faster, developers use digital tools—such as in the design of new chips, where advanced simulations have now replaced hardware prototypes. Just four weeks after the start of a development project, engineers today have a virtual semiconductor on which they can fully test the functionality of the new chip, to which they can make changes without running into delays. This halves development time compared to the previous testing of prototypes. And once the chip emerges from the virtual space and is baked in silicon, it almost always works immediately, because virtual development enables more and better tests, and delivers considerably higher quality. In the past, developers seldom managed without building a second prototype, which could take another three to six months.

Honda offers another example of how digital tools are used. The Japanese carmaker is borrowing technology from Hollywood to learn more about crash behavior in the form of highly advanced graphics processors that the film studios use for their special effects. Honda combines its crash simulation software with 3D visualization programs to understand what happens to the vehicle structure in a crash. The system visualizes the energy wave that runs through the car after a collision. The warp patterns spread out like ripples on the water. The special effects software perfectly visualizes the destructive waves, enabling engineers to track the flow of forces and identify weak points in their design.

Virtual Training Is Faster and Cheaper

Today, it's often much cheaper and faster to simulate a real machine as a virtual image to carry out tests or provide training.

For example, developers of the Lockheed F35 stealth fighter saved $100 million just by training their service personnel using a virtual jet rather than a real one: with 3D real-time visualization, or immersive engineering, the digital twin was almost exactly the same as its physical counterpart. Computer simulations are replacing many test flights. Physical air combat training in particular is extremely expensive and difficult, which is where augmented reality in the simulator comes into its own. The technology has helped Lockheed Martin to achieve more streamlined development processes, more efficient tests, and even better integration of production processes in its factory.

Simpler Development with PLM and PDM

Product life-cycle management (PLM) systems are based on product data management (PDM), and are used to integrate all the information generated during a product's life, ideally across the entire value chain.

During the design phase, PLM prevents duplicate developments: Its database contains all the previous development work of engineers in a modular and parameterized system. An engineer about to start modeling a transmission system can access the preceding model, and if the dimensions are wrong, they can be extrapolated, which is just one of the benefits of the parameterized storage system.

Transparency Drives Efficiency

Advanced analytics and machine learning are playing an ever-greater role in development departments, generating a level of data transparency never seen before. As a result, processes can now achieve unprecedented quality and efficiency.

All the data concerning the development process is stored in a single database—from designs, schedules, e-mails, documentation, customer correspondence, and supplier information right through to personnel deployment planning. Today, this mass of big data can be analyzed for correlations with advanced analytics, and examined for potential success levers.

The pioneer of these applications is the British firm QuantumBlack, which has its roots in Formula One auto racing. Working with a Formula One team, the firm used its Nerve racing algorithm to analyze all the unstructured data accumulated over the course of a racing season. The aim was to increase the hit rate in the thousands of development projects conducted throughout the racing season to make the cars faster and more reliable. QuantumBlack linked project results and data with data about the structure of the development teams, identified correlations and causalities, and defined success levers based on the findings. Almost immediately, the ratio of new parts that led to actual improvements doubled, laying the foundations for the world title.

However, advanced analytics can also uncover elements that hold the productivity of developers back by shedding light on surprising relationships hidden in the sea of data. For example, McKinsey analyses for a client revealed that putting a development project on hold for just one week leads to an 8 percent loss in productivity. Also, the size of the team affects results. More than seven engineers on one team is too many, with each extra team member bringing a 7 percent productivity loss for the company in question. Another practice popular among global companies, where employees who are spread around the world work on the same task, also hinders progress: each additional time zone costs the firm on average around 5 percent in productivity. On the other hand, simply knowing the other people in the team has a positive effect. Teams that have worked together before are around 7 percent more productive than the average.

Artificial Intelligence Even Calculates Profitability in Advance

Using cost data, market data, and the assumed inverse demand functions, which are continuously compared against the current situation, machine learning systems with artificial intelligence can today forecast the likely profitability for each planned product variant, both per unit and across the entire life cycle. These data-driven predictions replace the previous extrapolation forecasts, and have thus led to a significantly higher hit rate.

Further Disruption to Be Expected

New technologies and new opportunities are appearing all the time, and developers in companies need to brace themselves for further disruption that will rock their job profiles. For example, will today's 3D printers that produce prototypes in industries like machinery construction be used in full production? It would mean a completely new relationship between development and manufacture. And equally exciting is the question as to whether the trend toward customized production will lead to a co-creation model between customers and developers. We could see an entirely new product design process. Although still very limited, such a model is already being trialed with Nike iD where customers are able to customize their athletic shoes online from a selection of features.

The concept of co-creation has fired the imaginations of industry visionaries, who are already asking: Does a company even need to produce products anymore? Or will a viable business model emerge where the company simply offers a platform that provides co-creators with a basic design and the necessary customization tools? Once designed, the customer can then print out the product in the nearest 3D print shop. It may sound farfetched, but it's already happening. For example, in a number of online games, the players create and design their own characters—the company simply provides the platform and gamer network. Developers are barely needed—the customers do it.

5.6 FASTER, MORE FLEXIBLE, MORE EFFICIENT: SUPPLY CHAIN 4.0

Enno de Boer and Sumit Dutta on how digitization is changing every point in the supply chain.

Consignment warehouses have long since moved on from pickers running around racks with printed lists putting together shipments. Robots now bring entire racks to the workers or even put customers' shopping baskets together themselves. Computers show workers equipped with smart glasses and headsets the correct routes through the warehouse. The workers then assemble their deliveries in the aisles, and scan the products with their smart glasses to avoid errors. Routes are calculated with sophisticated algorithms to optimize journey times. Everything is wonderfully digital and efficient, unless a new algorithm is needed because the old one had weaknesses. In the conventional model, that can take a long time. The requirement has to be specified; a budget has to be applied for; an order is sent to a trusted software company, which takes away development work from employees who can't program; a prototype is tested; and sooner or later, maybe six months or so down the line, the new algorithm is installed.

With digitization, it's not just the logistics chain that runs faster than before; offices are also setting a new pace. When a leading European e-commerce company decided to make its picking processes more efficient, the team worked a whole day to determine whether the algorithm could be improved. After some quick research, they found a routing algorithm for making pickers' routes through warehouses more efficient. The team then optimized this algorithm to the company's needs, and the chief information officer personally implemented it throughout the system. This was possible because they had programmed the warehouse management system, which is ultimately the heart of warehouse operations itself, rather than installing an inflexible standard product. Comparison tests on the performance of the new algorithm revealed that pickers' routes were reduced by 10 to 15 percent. After just six working days, the solution was so advanced it could be installed in all of the other warehouses.

This example is a perfect illustration of the management approach needed for the digital age. Speed and customer-centric thinking count. Fast, data-driven decisions are made; development work factors in fast failure; there is an eagerness to experiment, as well as transparency and team spirit.

There's plenty of opportunity for failure right now because logistics currently faces massive upheaval. Big data and advanced analytics, the ability to search huge unstructured data volumes for correlations and causalities, together with robot technology and the Internet of Things, are revolutionizing the management of the supply chain. Sensors are everywhere, and everything is connected. Each step is automated, every aspect is analyzed, and logistics companies and their customers are the winners.

Success potential: using Supply Chain 4.0 levers, huge potential can be tapped in all categories

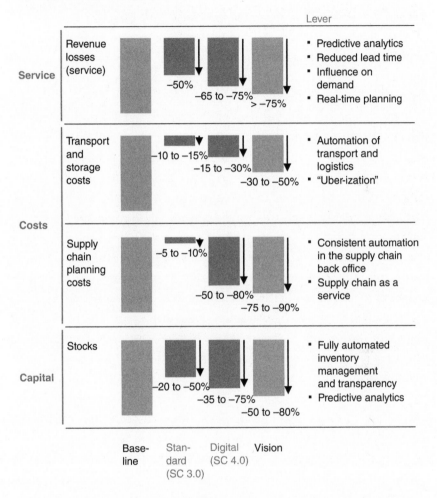

	Lever
Service — Revenue losses (service)	• Predictive analytics • Reduced lead time • Influence on demand • Real-time planning
Costs — Transport and storage costs	• Automation of transport and logistics • "Uber-ization"
Costs — Supply chain planning costs	• Consistent automation in the supply chain back office • Supply chain as a service
Capital — Stocks	• Fully automated inventory management and transparency • Predictive analytics

–50%
–65 to –75%
> –75%

–10 to –15%
–15 to –30%
–30 to –50%

–5 to –10%
–50 to –80%
–75 to –90%

–20 to –50%
–35 to –75%
–50 to –80%

Base-line
Stan-dard (SC 3.0)
Digital (SC 4.0)
Vision

Following on from Industry 4.0, Supply Chain 4.0, as it has become known, saves a lot of money. According to a McKinsey study conducted in 2016, Supply Chain 4.0 reduces transportation and warehousing costs by 15 to 30 percent, and revenue losses resulting from nondelivery by as much as

65 to 75 percent. With better scheduling, retailers can reduce stock on hand by 35 to 75 percent, depending on the industry, and planning and order processing costs by 50 to 80 percent. Customers in turn benefit from more accurate delivery times and more flexible logistics companies, which can tailor the place and time of deliveries to suit consumer preferences.

Seven Innovations That Revolutionize the Supply Chain

In 2016, the Supply Chain 4.0 Innovations Survey examined which currently foreseeable innovations would change the supply chain in the coming years. Of the 53 innovations identified, seven have the potential to disrupt the current business model.

Better planning with big data and advanced analytics supported by machine learning systems that have artificial intelligence will optimize every step in the supply chain. In addition to internal data, planners of delivery routes, warehouse stocks, and requirements also use external information ranging from traffic reports to current consumer demand. Predictive analytics can model demand trends, and already some companies are using such a cloud-based analysis model from the provider Blue Yonder. UPS, for example, used on-truck telematics and advanced algorithms to optimize routes and reduce engine idle time, saving the company over 39 million gallons of fuel and avoiding 364 million miles of unnecessary driving.[1]

Semiautonomous and fully autonomous trucks are one of the most important innovations. In a recent study, McKinsey found autonomous trucks result in approximately 10 to 15 percent lowered fuel consumption by optimized driving, and 15 percent reduction in carbon footprint due to optimized driving. Mining group Rio Tinto already uses driverless haul trucks in its mining operations. Experts, however, don't expect driverless trucks to appear on public roads within the next five years.

With 3D printers, the rules will also soon change when it comes to warehousing and product availability, particularly for slow-moving items and spare parts. In 2015, Amazon experimented with installing 3D printers in its delivery vans, and even patented the idea. Orders are printed on demand in the delivery van itself, with extensive customization possibilities and unprecedented delivery times. Bosch has invested a lot of money to test 3D printing of metals and ceramics, which it hopes in the medium

[1] https://www.linkedin.com/pulse/20-examples-roi-results-big-data-adam-ab-bloom

Seven innovations will fire the change
Evaluation of average change potential on the Effect-Disruption Matrix

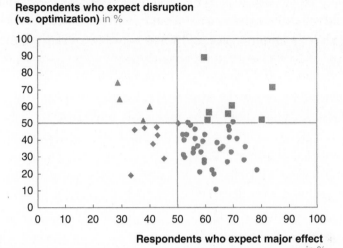

Respondents who expect disruption (vs. optimization) in %

Respondents who expect major effect in %

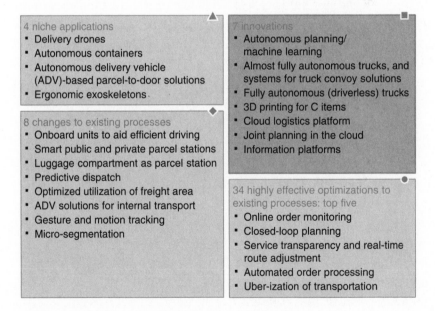

4 niche applications
* Delivery drones
* Autonomous containers
* Autonomous delivery vehicle (ADV)-based parcel-to-door solutions
* Ergonomic exoskeletons

8 changes to existing processes
* Onboard units to aid efficient driving
* Smart public and private parcel stations
* Luggage compartment as parcel station
* Predictive dispatch
* Optimized utilization of freight area
* ADV solutions for internal transport
* Gesture and motion tracking
* Micro-segmentation

7 innovations
* Autonomous planning/ machine learning
* Almost fully autonomous trucks, and systems for truck convoy solutions
* Fully autonomous (driverless) trucks
* 3D printing for C items
* Cloud logistics platform
* Joint planning in the cloud
* Information platforms

34 highly effective optimizations to existing processes: top five
* Online order monitoring
* Closed-loop planning
* Service transparency and real-time route adjustment
* Automated order processing
* Uber-ization of transportation

Source: SC 4 Innovation Survey—responses of 76 experts from various sectors

term will allow it to print spare parts for machines on-site. Airbus and General Electric are also already using 3D printers to produce individual aircraft and turbine parts. Yet despite the highly promising applications, a

McKinsey study estimates that it will still be another 10 to 15 years before 3D printing becomes the norm.

Logistics Platforms and Shared Planning

Cloud logistics platforms offer significant benefits such as dramatically increasing truck fleet utilization. Cloud-based logistics platforms connect shippers and transport service providers, optimizing utilization and mileage driven. An unlimited number of companies, both customers and freight forwarders, can register via a simple app and connect.

Shared planning in the cloud between manufacturers and their suppliers also means more efficient collaboration. Cloud-based logistics also reduces the bullwhip effect where supplier purchase orders always fluctuate more strongly than consumer demand, leading to excess overstock, overcapacity, and higher costs. With cross-company shared planning, changes in demand are reported in real time, which means companies can respond accordingly and prevent overstock and overreactions. Companies in the field of consumer electronics are already very closely integrated with their suppliers, and use planning solutions such as E2open to deliver seamless planning.

Information platforms on which companies share nonconfidential and nonanonymized data provide the fuel for advanced analytics, which enables more precise predictions of demand and optimized logistics routes. Information shared on these platforms includes details about disruptions in supply chains, hacking attacks on systems, traffic updates, and much more. The challenge is to expand such information systems and then establish a reliable connection to the IT infrastructures of customers. Experts believe that these information platforms will become widespread in just a few years.

First Steps toward Supply Chain 4.0

The journey toward the supply chain of the future must start with some critical stocktaking. Management must review the entire supply chain to assess its suitability for the switch to digitization. Data flows, analysis capabilities, hardware and software, talent, and processes must all be analyzed at every point in the supply chain, and assessed on a 1 to 5 scale where 1 denotes predominantly paper data and 5 denotes digital excellence. The findings will then form the foundations for the digitization process. Initially, very specific, isolated projects are recommended—for example, projects focusing on achieving greater efficiency in pick processes or improved forecasting. This type of approach will help yield the agility and pace of start-ups.

The efforts to digitize the supply chain are worth it, but will not deliver cost reductions on their own, but rather a range of solid improvements.

- *Faster pace:* Delivery times for fast-moving items will be reduced to a few hours thanks to more precise estimates and planning based on the analysis of large data volumes. Soon, logistics companies will switch to predictive shipping, where products are sent for dispatch even before the order has been received from the customer. Amazon has already patented such a method that calculates freight and routes. Once an order is received, the system searches for the product on a delivery van in the region, and the driver is promptly directed to the delivery address.
- *More flexibility:* Planning cycles and periods in which the company is unable to respond are minimized by real-time planning methods. Instead, planning becomes a revolving process in which dynamic adjustments are possible. For example, if a product is already on its way to a customer, the customer can still have it redirected to a destination that's more convenient. Similar to developments such as software as a service, we will see supply chain as a service where service providers assume responsibility for the company's entire supply chain. Companies pay the service provider according to the services used, which means they don't have to invest in their own resources or capabilities. Another trend that will deliver greater flexibility is the "Uber-ization" of transportation. Crowdsourcing enables people with free capacity, such as Uber drivers who currently have no customers, to deliver packages. All of these solutions make delivery networks far more agile.
- *Greater depth of field:* Customers want increasingly customized products, and mass production of tailored products is now expected. This requires micro-segmentation of customer groups, with companies having to readjust to much smaller target groups while offering a broader palette. In terms of the supply chain, customers will expect

to be able to choose from a wide offering of logistics solutions and select the one that precisely fits their needs.

- *More precision:* The next generation of key performance indicator (KPI) systems will deliver real-time transparency across the entire supply chain. These will range from management KPIs such as the service levels to operational data such as the precise position of the delivery vans at the current time. We will see machine learning systems that automatically identify risks and immediately modify parameters—for example, calculating new truck routes. An automatic control center will independently react to a wide range of problems and deviations without any human interventions with continuous system learning.

- *Greater efficiency:* The efficiency of supply chains is increasing sharply because both physical tasks and the entire planning process are going digital. In the warehouse, robots are taking over all the work; autonomous trucks and delivery vans will assume driving responsibilities on longer routes, while delivery bots and drones take over the last mile. To deliver greater utilization, supply chain organizations will pool capacities and form a network whose organization must in turn meet the needs of all its members.

5.7 DIGITAL LEAN: THE DIGITIZATION OF PRODUCTION
Varun Marya and Gianluca Camplone on the five fundamentals of digital production.

Let's look ahead to the factory of tomorrow and beyond: Drones with 360-degree cameras fly through the warehouse area capturing images that are translated into 3D drawings to optimize material flow and work flows. Autonomous transport vehicles trundle across the factory floor and through the production halls while, alongside human workers at the assembly lines, robots assume the arduous tasks. All the machines are in working order; with predictive maintenance, there is almost no downtime, as data are automatically captured and sent to the cloud. The 3D printers produce prototypes and spare parts, and apply customizations to the finished products at the end of assembly lines. There's no refuse or scrap—the factory of tomorrow doesn't produce waste. Data are exchanged throughout the value chain from the raw material right through to the product in use. This is digital lean, the evolution of lean manufacturing, whose principles have conquered the world of manufacturing since its Japanese beginnings in the 1980s.

Digital Lean: The Same Aims as Lean Production

Digitization is giving new impetus to the concept of the continuous improvement process, one of the cornerstones of lean production. This is because digital technology is strengthening the competitiveness of companies in the three core areas: it helps to control costs, eliminate waste, and optimize production. Huge productivity increases are possible.

Today, productivity and quality studies can be simulated on computers, which dramatically reduces development times. Stock inventory warehouses are redundant because demand forecasting is so precise that companies are virtually able to manufacture to order. With predictive maintenance, machine availability will approach 100 percent rather the current 40 to 80 percent. Optimized processes and smart energy consumption will enable energy savings of up to 20 percent compared to today. The automated transport systems in the factory will work far more cost-effectively and efficiently because they are no longer restricted by rail systems. Robots in Factory 4.0 are cheaper to program, and constantly learn with artificial intelligence. Employees will be more skilled, with continuous training and development. Considerable savings beckon in the entire production value chain of tomorrow.

The philosophy of digital lean doesn't end at the factory gates. With the Internet, companies can now largely integrate their own processes with those of suppliers and customers. For example, automakers can analyze information about the activities of their suppliers together with up-to-date consumption data of customers from social media analyses to predict future demand patterns. As a result, the auto industry is able to make extremely accurate predictions regarding the extent to which extra features will be ordered with sales of new cars, enabling more precise production planning. Other companies use the Internet to manage their branched production sites. A large energy utility, for example, monitors all of its drilling rigs in the Gulf of Mexico from a central control room.

A by-product of digital lean even allows a restructuring of the global distribution of labor. Because manufacturing is far more flexible and automated than before, hardly any individual work steps will be out-sourced in future, and even the offshoring of full production to low-wage economies will be virtually eliminated. "Local for local" is the new philoso-phy: factories manufacture locally for local demand. This will be a blow to developing countries because the labor cost advantage will no longer be as relevant. However, one of the benefits for industrial nations is that some of the workplaces lost as a result of advances in productivity will be transferred to the new manufacturing.

The productivity gain in digital production is brought by the widespread use of data analyses, sensors, robots, and other new technologies such as 3D printing, all driven by the large-scale use of computer capacities and servers. And yet the aims are the same as lean production in the past. It's about increasing productivity and reducing waste, from machine down-times to nonproductive worker activities. And just as before, the transfor-mation primarily centers around three central dimensions: the technical system (processes and tools), the management system (organization and performance management), and the human resources (HR) system (skills and attitudes of employees). Digitization also brings a fourth pillar into play: data, IT, and networking as value drivers.

Five Central Themes for the Transformation

Five central themes have emerged from previous experiences of digital transformation processes.

1. *Digital lean significantly increases productivity.* With persistent cost pressures, most companies try to increase productivity by two to four percentage points each year. As numerous studies have shown, digitization has the potential to make production 15 to 20 percent more efficient. This requires several individual solutions work-ing together across the entire value chain. For example, predic-tive maintenance and remote monitoring of machines can reduce downtimes by 30 to 50 percent, significantly increasing equipment utilization. Optimizing labor efficiency also has great potential. Digital performance management and large-scale use of ever more powerful robots that can replace human labor not just in produc-tion, but also in logistics, can increase working productivity by 40

to 50 percent. Advanced analytics of extensive volumes of machine data in real time can identify inefficient processes and quality problems. Because the entire process of sales forecasting is becoming much more accurate with big data, companies can dramatically reduce warehouse stocks while also improving delivery capacity.

2. *Digital lean isn't about IT, but about business.* Although the IT department provides the tools for digital production, it isn't responsible for how it's deployed. On no account must the digital transformation process begin with the question of how the new technology can be integrated into the old IT system. Digital lean starts at a much more fundamental level. It's about how the business should look in the future, and what that means for the value chain and business model. For example, a manufacturer of sports apparel wants to make sports shoe production much more customized. This changes the value chain dramatically. To leverage the cost benefits of production in low-wage economies, companies today accept long shipping times for container shipments to Europe and the United States, as well as the equally low flexibility. Soon, the wholesale use of production robots not only will make high-wage economies competitive, but it will also reduce the time to market from product design to start of sales, it will reduce freight costs, and, thanks to the greater flexibility of automated production, it will even be able to deliver cost-effective product personalization.

3. *Digital lean is a job for top management and cannot be delegated.* To date, only a few companies have a structured plan for addressing the topic of Industry 4.0. According to a recent study by McKinsey, only 15 percent have formulated an actual strategy. Around 20 percent have defined responsibilities in their organization, typically as a staff function without the authority to make direct decisions. Where line functions do have responsibility, these are usually too low in the hierarchy, and therefore also lacking the strength to combat inertia. Once again, the methods used to introduce lean production at the end of the last century can help; if the transformation is to deliver value quickly, the company management must take control.

4. *Digital lean requires a holistic transformation approach.* Just like the transformation to lean production, the digitization of the factory at scale tackles all components of the value chain and prepares them for digital. Many of these individual initiatives are coordinated centrally and must include a program for equipping employees with the necessary skills, and a plan focusing on how to establish digitization throughout the company. This is Digital@Scale. Isolated projects that are not linked to other projects or anchored in the foundations of the transformation are of little help, and often fail in their early phases.

5. *Despite digitization, analog humans are still needed in digital lean.* Although the technical infrastructure for Industry 4.0 is quickly installed, human expertise is still needed, with new roles in the production process that will require new skills for most. The worker at the assembly line now turns into a troubleshooter who intervenes if something goes wrong with a robot. He or she needs to understand the production machines and be able to control them. Maintenance engineers no longer unscrew machine panels, but instead use a computer to view the calculations for predictive maintenance. Quality controllers no longer inspect manufactured parts, but continuously check live production. Production planners no longer draft linear processes, but rather design flexible and self-learning manufacturing. Foremen and team leads no longer physically show the team occurrences of scrap or waste, but instead show them the actual data on the computer. New job profiles will emerge throughout the factory. Data analysts will search the mass of production data for correlations and causalities, reconcile their results with those of colleagues in other factories to find best practice models, and put together recommendations for production staff. IT integrators will ensure that the factory's IT infrastructure is seamlessly integrated into the IT landscape of the entire company and will manage the interfaces.

The McKinsey Digital Capability Center (DCC) provides an opportunity to practice the production of tomorrow today. The five centers in Chicago, Singapore, Aachen, Beijing, and Venice demonstrate how the latest technology is used throughout the operational value chain from development through to production and service. McKinsey operates the Chicago DCC in partnership with the Digital Manufacturing and Design Innovation Institute (DMDII), and collaborates with other technology providers and research institutes. The hands-on workshops at the DCC help companies approach Industry 4.0 systematically and purposefully.

The end-to-end digitization of production poses a significant challenge to management, but the good news is that this is evolutionary development, not revolutionary. In other words, following a thorough analysis of requirements and holistic planning of the transformation, digitization must not be implemented across the board at the same time. Instead, companies would do well to start quickly with the digitization of production, and learn from the experience. The next project will then run much more smoothly, with employees developing the necessary skills and experience, and leaders learning what develops best by itself, what is better achieved in partnerships, and what needs to be bought in. It is vital to emphasize to all employees that digitization is an opportunity, not a threat.

Indicative quantification of value drivers

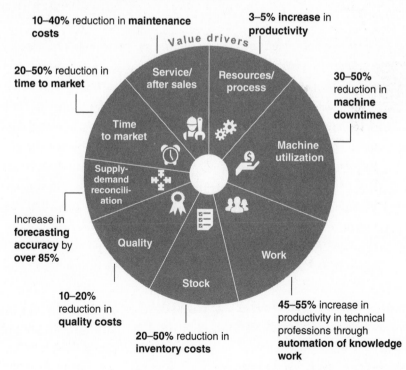

10–40% reduction in **maintenance costs**

3–5% **increase** in **productivity**

20–50% reduction in **time to market**

30–50% reduction in **machine downtimes**

Increase in **forecasting accuracy** by **over 85%**

10–20% reduction in **quality costs**

20–50% reduction in **inventory costs**

45–55% increase in productivity in technical professions through **automation of knowledge work**

Value drivers:
Service/after sales · Resources/process · Time to market · Machine utilization · Supply-demand reconciliation · Quality · Work · Stock

5.8 DIGITIZATION IN THE OFFICE: BOTS TAKE THE REINS
Alexander Edlich on the automation of administration.

Will the next book about digitization be written by a skilled robot? Quill, a software program from U.S. start-up Narrative Science, analyzes data and transforms it into natural language using artificial intelligence. In just a few seconds, reports and essays are produced that read as though written by a real person. Other tools are making the work of young attorneys superfluous by deeply analyzing vast quantities of documents in the shortest time, and searching for any points of relevance to the current case faster than any human could manage.

The astonishing capabilities of Quill shed light on a side of digitization that is often forgotten: automation and robots are not just revolutionizing work in factories and warehouses, but also in offices. Forty-five percent of all tasks for which people are paid could already be executed by machines in 2015, according to a study by the McKinsey Global Institute. A further 13 percent of the tasks could be automated by technologies that are currently being developed, such as those focused on software that enables robots to understand human language. According to the study, in around 60 percent of all occupations, 30 percent or more of all tasks could be performed by machines. Even 20 percent of management tasks could be performed by robot workmates.

Smart Process Automation Is Revolutionizing Office Work

The conventional robot is emulating how its human models interact with computer software programs in the workplace. It can learn Word and Excel, and even knows how to use enterprise resource planning (ERP) systems. In general, it works according to rules, and only processes structured data rather than learning. Experts call it robotic process automation (RPA). RPA allows many tasks that still currently require human labor to be handed over to the bot, which can perform them considerably faster, without growing tired.

Robots with the necessary software can prepare the monthly or quarterly reports for businesses where previously data often had to be mined manually from several different sources. The reports created by the software are even formatted well and perfectly readable. This saves costs, and frees up resources for the more critical work of interpreting the data. Very

Sixty percent of professions in the United States could be automated by 30 percent or more

Potential of technology-based automation of employee activities in the United States[1] (cumulative)
Automation potential in % (100% = 129 million)

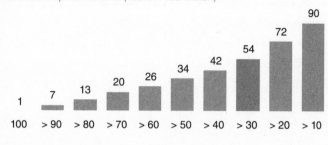

100	> 90	> 80	> 70	> 60	> 50	> 40	> 30	> 20	> 10
1	7	13	20	26	34	42	54	72	90

Potential of automation of professions in the United States (cumulative)
Automation potential in % (100% = 775 professions)

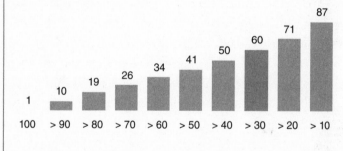

100	> 90	> 80	> 70	> 60	> 50	> 40	> 30	> 20	> 10
1	10	19	26	34	41	50	60	71	87

Job examples	• Seamstress • Logging equipment operator	• Shelf stacker • Travel agent • Dental technician	• Bus driver • Nursing assistant • Web developer	• Fashion designer • Manager • Statistician

1 We define automation potential as being the work activities that could be automated by adapting current technology

Source: BLS 2014; O*Net; McKinsey analysis

soon, fully automated processes in finance could allow the annual accounts to be created at the push of a button. New employees in the company would have all the necessary information and tools they need for working productively right from the first minute. In this brave new world of work, many employees could have a virtual assistant ready to take on rule-based activities on call.

However, cognitive computing, also known as artificial intelligence, is where things get really interesting. Here, the machine emulates cognitive functions; it learns, solves problems, and presents the results of data analysis in natural language. One famous example is Siri, Apple's virtual assistant, which can respond to spoken queries asked by iPhone users, and search the Internet for answers. Siri translates simple voice commands into text and gives simple responses. More powerful assistants understand language and are able to analyze text and tone in the respective context, fully mirroring human interaction. The software Amelia from the firm IPSoft, for example, runs on IT help desks, and can perform tasks such as issuing employees with a new password if they've forgotten their old one.

Machines like Watson from IBM and Google's DeepMind take a different direction, and are able to learn from data and use their enormous computing capacity to think through problems that humans would find impossible. The various approaches and tools can be combined to produce the cognitive engine that works based on the model of the human brain, just with greater capacity. The cognitive engine is designed to fully understand humans; the only thing missing is feelings, but those may yet come.

How Will Companies Change When Office Work Is Automated?

If robots and software programs replace human work, this costs on average around 13 percent of the wages paid for work in a developed country like the United States. At a stroke, moving this work to low-wage economies becomes less attractive because offshoring costs on average almost 40 percent of the wages in developed countries.

A British insurance broker today automatically processes 3,000 claims a day—all managed by a grand total of four employees. And the subsidiary of a major European energy utility has automated several important processes in administration, including billing, collection of consumption data, and consumption management. What was previously handled by 250 employees is now managed by 110 robots, overseen by 11 human supervisors. One of the biggest wireless providers has automated 15 complex administrative processes, which is equivalent to 35 percent of its work volume. Now 160 robots process around 500,000 transactions a month. And it doesn't just reduce costs. Since the results are more reliable than those produced by human employees, sales staff on the frontlines have more capacity because they don't have to keep checking back with the head office to query an incorrect entry.

Machines, then, are superior in terms of both cost and quality, with robots and computers producing more accurate results. They rigidly follow their programming, so errors are not a factor. And even if production is ramped up, the same quality is achieved with large volumes as with smaller volumes. Robots don't need breaks. They can work around the clock if necessary. And something else that's particularly important in times of increased compliance regulations is that machines record their activities in seamless logs, and any activity can be verified later.

However, since it will be possible to fully automate only a handful of jobs in the near future, work content and processes will need to be redefined. For example, if banks use machines to review loan applications, employees have more time to advise customers, thus producing more applications a day. Financial advisers no longer need to analyze the financial data themselves, and can therefore work more on creative investment strategies. Robots can even help develop investment strategies, meaning recommendations that were previously given to only the best customers because they tied up so much adviser capacity can now be granted to every customer as robo-advice.

Automation Is Relevant Even for Complex Jobs

The opinion still persists that automation is suitable only for the work of poorly qualified and low-paid workers. However, the study by the McKinsey Global Institute comes to a different conclusion: even around 20 percent of management tasks can be handled by machines. They can analyze reports and presentations for operational decisions, check status reports for compliance with targets, and even prepare HR decisions. In turn, managers have more time for thinking, for communicating, and for managing, and that time needs to be used wisely. The more intensive the use of data, the more managers can benefit from automation—for example, in investment management where data volumes can be leveraged and turned into recommendations far more systematically using artificial intelligence and machine learning systems than is possible by a human.

Occupations where creativity and the ability to understand and respond to emotions are needed are safe from automation for now. Just 4 percent of all professions in the United States center around creativity, although the ability to empathize with others is still needed in 29 percent of all work activities. However, even these jobs aren't safe from automation in the long term. Even now, software exists that can interpret human feelings.

Automation Is More Than a Technological Decision

Technology is, of course, a key element on the road to intelligent process automation; however, this is primarily a strategic decision that must be made by top management. The management must assess the extent to which the company is affected by the changes, and decide whether to develop a specific strength in the area and be at the forefront of change, or to hold back as a follower and avoid the mistakes of the pioneers. Ultimately, managers must decide how to adjust the operational business model of their company, from the organization and culture to the development of talent and skills. Past experience shows that companies that selectively automate their processes and reduce costs quickly with robotic process automation have to redefine all of their processes on the road to intelligent process automation. The lessons of business process reengineering of the 1990s are still relevant. The key objective isn't simply far-reaching automation of all processes, but to improve the overarching business system.

It is still uncertain how soon automation will become widely adopted in offices. On one hand, it depends on the pace of technological developments, and on the other, on how quickly the technological possibilities will be accepted and implemented in companies. Industries with a strong reliance on pure software solutions lead the way. They quickly achieve significant savings with manageable investment. The finance industry, where processes can be automated at relatively little cost, is a good example. The more hardware that is required, or the more security provisions and legal regulations that have to be met, the longer the switch to automation takes.

Management must have a good overview of how their own industry's parameters are developing, while at the same time gaining a feeling for the economics of automation. This specific IQ of company leadership could become the difference between success and failure in the business world of tomorrow.

CONCLUSION: DIGITIZATION IS CHANGING EVERY FUNCTION IN THE COMPANY

Successful digital companies base their products and processes strictly on the needs of the customer. We have seen how the business architecture is being redeveloped starting with the customer experience. Products and value propositions are brought to market in keeping with the digital philosophy. The value chain also faces sweeping changes—the Internet of Things, robots, and artificial intelligence will shape the future.

In this chapter, it has only been possible to describe the most important changes, but there are far more—including the next generation of customer life-cycle management and the introduction of new commercial models.

Rolls-Royce, for example, fundamentally revised the commercial model for engines by having customers pay for operating hours rather than the equipment. The strategy is possible only with sensor technology and predictive maintenance. Procurement is also fundamentally changing as a result of digitization, virtually forcing the introduction of omnichannel capabilities even in the B2B sector. Ultimately, it is clear that every function in the company will benefit from digitization.

□-□-⑥-□-□

WHAT? STRENGTHENING THE FOUNDATION

HOW WILL IT *get in shape to meet the challenges of digitization? What help will be available to analyze the enormous data volumes? And what type of organization does a company need to succeed in the digital world? This chapter explores the foundations for this success.*

Speed is the hallmark of the digital world. Fast development times, short cycles, and rapid change are factors that overwhelm most traditional organizations. The first section of this chapter describes how companies can build a two-speed IT architecture. This involves a robust IT system deployed for stable functions with minimal need for intervention, and an agile, fast IT system for everything aimed at the rapid pace of digitization. We then move on to data, the new gold. Big data and advanced analytics—vast accumulations of unstructured data and its intelligent analysis—are critical success factors today. And since data theft can jeopardize success, we also describe ways to protect it. With the advent of the Internet of Things, software is making its way into everyday objects, and is also covered in this section on IT and technology.

However, digitization is also changing the culture and organization of companies, especially with the emergence of the chief digital officer (CDO), and we explain what this role does. Companies in the digital age need agile, cross-functional, flat hierarchies, and we explain how to go about it. Everyone wants digital talent, and we describe how to find it and retain it. Also in the new ecosystems, most companies work with a network of partners, whose interaction needs to be managed, and the final section of this chapter describes how.

6.1 TWO-SPEED IT: ACCELERATING THE PACE FOR THE DIGITAL AGE

Naufal Khan on the new challenges for IT, and how companies from the analog age can meet them.

Fintechs are making life difficult for banks. Accounts can be opened online in five minutes, small loans can be approved just as quickly, and money can be invested with a single click. The new digital companies are leaving the traditional credit industry behind. What's the answer? The IT departments and systems of banks aren't cut out for this fast pace. When it comes to such sensitive data, security is always the top priority. The fact that the large financial institutions (at least some of them) are still able to keep up is due to their two-speed IT architectures.

Digitization has increased the pace of innovation throughout the business world, and customers' expectations have risen. As a result, companies in many industries have been forced to dramatically increase the performance of their IT. However, restructuring the entire IT architecture of a company is always fraught with incalculable risk, big investments, and high costs. Change on that scale can put a company's ordering, billing, or accounting systems at risk of failure during the reorganization. On top of this, they are expensive and protracted processes. Instead, smart IT managers came up with the idea of running two systems in parallel: an agile, fast, often cloud-based system that can work with apps for all processes targeting the customer (front-end system), and a stable, solid, cost-effective system with its own data center or rented capacity in the cloud for all non-customer-related operations (back-end system). An integration platform, or middleware, connects these two IT worlds.

In the agile section of the IT architecture, engineers work in tight units in integrated teams with common goals. Programmers build apps in fast sprints and feed the underlying computers with the necessary data. Customers access these apps from their smartphones or computers—for example, checking the prices of wireless providers, quickly and easily switching between prices and products, choosing services, or changing their payment options. Existing customers can check the status of their accounts or ask questions. Companies use apps to communicate with potential and current customers, and to generate business. This new style of business development doesn't work just with private customers, but also increasingly with enterprise customers. Customer feedback is immediately incorporated into the further development of the digital offering.

The time and costs required for these tailored solutions are worth it because innovative apps and a fast response to customer needs can set a company apart from the competition. Indonesian wireless provider Telkomsel, for example, developed a self-service mobile app for its 150 million customers. Key functions include new contracts, as well as contract extensions and amendments. In just six months, the team developed functions that would normally have taken two years to implement on a stable IT system.

In the back-end IT system, on the other hand, one thing counts above everything else: no outages. The loss of inventory, billing, or customer data, or the failure of supply chains can lead to terminal business damage. Cost efficiency achieved through harmonization and standardization is also highly important. The back-end system runs the major programs that keep the company alive: the enterprise resource planning (ERP) system, customer relationship management (CRM), the standard cost model (SCM), and everything to do with logistics and administration.

Three Routes to a Two-Speed IT

Essentially, companies have three options for establishing their agile IT system: They can build on something that already exists in their organization, they can start from scratch, or they can acquire a company with the necessary skills.

Travel group Thomas Cook took the first route. It isolated the customer-facing areas of its IT organization, separated them from routine tasks, and, in so doing, gradually established a two-speed IT architecture. For this solution to work, there must already be processes within the IT organization that are worth transforming. Additionally, it requires significant investment in middleware systems to decouple customer-facing processes from the back end.

Starbucks decided to start from scratch. The firm was unable to identify a suitable starting point in its existing IT system, and therefore established a completely new IT organization separate from the old one, to take on the agile role in a two-speed IT architecture.

Reference architecture for two-speed IT

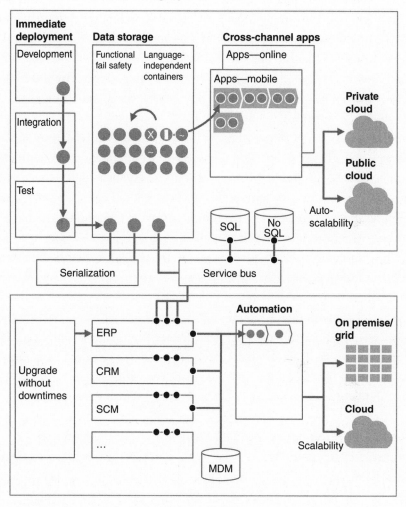

U.S. insurer Allstate was in a rush, so it acquired a company with an agile, fast-paced, and innovative IT team. The advantage of this approach is that Allstate lost no time with a long-drawn-out transformation process, or with establishing an agile IT structure over an even longer time. Instead, it could immediately start work on developing attractive digital offerings for customers. Companies that choose this route are convinced that the costs of integrating the new organization into the existing one are lower than the additional profit leveraged from fast market entry.

Companies that build an agile IT can reckon with a lead time of around 18 months before the new system delivers valuable contributions. This type of restructuring revolves around a strong crossover of business and IT. All processes in which fast changes count or that enable the company to set itself apart from the competition will in future be the responsibility of the agile IT team. As such, these IT systems need to be modernized and adjusted accordingly, and strict governance is required to manage this change. As a first step, a close interface must be established between business and IT. Cross-functional teams of marketers and programmers must be formed, products and services must be organized into teams, and a product owner must be appointed for each product and each service to coordinate developments and communicate with the organization. The product owner acts as a coordinator and moderator, but not a manager.

The more independently the teams are able to deploy their talents, and the more independently the agile IT is able to act in the organization as a whole, the faster the company will be able to deliver attractive customer offerings. Discussions with suppliers and consultants who plug holes in the skills of the organization and offer even greater flexibility also run in parallel to this process. The team has shared goals that are achieved in iterative sprints. These teams develop apps for customers, while other teams ensure the stability of the underlying IT architecture on which the apps are built.

The Agile IT Often Accelerates All Elements of the Organization

The fast IT organization typically concentrates on processes in which there is direct interaction with customers and where rapid adjustments are often necessary to remain competitive and meet customer requirements. In many cases, the agile IT element even spurs on the IT engineers who work on the more stable IT, resulting in a self-intensifying system that in turn can accelerate the entire IT transformation.

A major bank, for example, successfully implemented a two-speed IT structure. It soon became apparent, however, that the apps used by customers to move money or view account information also necessitated changes to the back-end systems that provided and modified the customer data. As a result, not only were the customer-facing systems made faster, but the systems in the processing department also became part of the fast architecture. This also required changes to the delivery model to support the fast cycle times while managing the interdependencies.

This could prove the beginning of a move toward a completely agile IT organization. The advantage is that employees who don't feel up to the challenges of agile IT can remain in the steadier but no less reliable departments with the gentle transition process over a prolonged period. The aim is to achieve an IT architecture that mirrors the architectures of digital giants like Amazon, Facebook, and Google, where technology is fully integrated with business targets and they work in unison to identify, establish, and meet business goals.

This is where digital product management comes in. Managers who lead a development team are not responsible just for an app and its use, but possibly for the entire purchase and payment process through to order confirmation and notification of delivery dates. This kind of end-to-end responsibility leads not only to shorter lead times, but also to increased quality of the end product or service. Managers' job profiles now include numerous tests and experiments in which market strategies are trialed with different objectives. Customer data and feedback are collected and analyzed, and the results are immediately incorporated into further developments. Other tasks include developing a set of key performance indicators (KPIs) used to measure the success of the team.

The combination of an agile, fast-response IT structure, a digital product manager, small teams of entrepreneurial talent, and cutting-edge scalable architecture has formed the backbone of the astonishing success of the likes of Amazon and Google. Today, companies from the analog world can also benefit from the strategy.

6.2 BIG DATA AND ADVANCED ANALYTICS
Holger Hürtgen on the path to better, data-driven decisions.

How can Amazon recommend a novel that actually interests me after just a few book purchases? How does Spotify know which hit song will appeal to me next after just a few downloads? And how is it that online fashion retailers are able to recommend clothes that I like even though I've only viewed a few of their pages? We are no longer surprised by this. We just expect it. But very few of us know how it works.

Online stores and apps like Spotify collect accessible data about their customers: what we buy, what we look at, which website we came from, which device we are using, what time of day it is, how often we visit, and what else we look at. Advanced analytics software then sifts through this vast sea of data searching for patterns, which the company can then use to make predictions about our behavior. Online retailers, for example, love lookalike modeling, which is the search for statistical twins, on the assumption that someone who leaves behind the same data trail as we do will have similar needs to ours. Once one twin likes a song, video, or pair of pants, the other immediately gets a recommendation for the same item.

Big data and advanced analytics aren't just useful for retailers. They also help manufacturers and service providers make better, fact-driven decisions. Despite this, many managers and employees still base their decisions solely on personal experience or statistical planning. In the past three years alone, more data has been generated in the world than in the rest of human history. Companies that are able to leverage these data volumes can gain an immediate competitive advantage. Big data and advanced analytics deliver the tools for better, faster decisions, and although technology plays an important role, it is by no means everything. Added value is generated where the technological possibilities and corporate goals intertwine. Because the very core of the company is affected, from the corporate strategy and the business model right through to its growth prospects, once again the executive management must be on board. A big data strategy needs to be driven from the top.

The Three Success Factors of Big Data and Advanced Analytics

For companies that want to drive their businesses forward with big data and advanced analytics, three levers are needed: the company must formulate a vision outlining its objectives; data analyses should be tested in defined applications; and the technical, organizational, and skill frameworks must be in place.

Every successful transformation into a data-driven company starts with a vision. A target scenario is outlined that not only formulates an overarching target as a business case, but specifies measurable targets for specific applications, from customer retention to production optimization. The vision also includes a transformation path that splits the journey

Overview of sample big data and advanced analytics modules

 Vision

Development of a vision	Strategy development, including new business models that signify a disruption to applications or underlying foundations

 Vision and target

 Data as an asset

 Cloud analytics

 Key insights in real time

 Foundation diagnostics

 Social media listening

 Internet of Things

 Artificial intelligence

 Prioritization of applications and road map

 Agile test-and-learn pilots

 Crowd-sourcing of globally available know-how

 Automation and robotics

 Applications

Commercial levers (sales-specific)		Internal optimization (capex/opex)	

 Assortment optimization

 Dynamic B2C pricing

 Predictive maintenance

 Call center routing

 Cross-/ up-selling

 Value-based B2B pricing

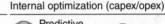 Demand forecast

 Personnel deployment planning

 Customer migration

 Sales area planning

 Debt management

 Supply chain optimization

 Next-best action/ offer

 Marketing mix optimization

 Fraud/ theft identification

 Location/ area planning

 Acquisition

 Income management

 Forecast of risk/ debt losses

 HR

 Foundation

Technological and HR base		New operational model	

 Data

 IT

 Culture and attitudes

 Processes and steering

 Analytics

 Employees

 Performance management

 Organization

through the data landscape into stages, and sets deadlines for achieving these milestones.

At this level, the company defines the points in the business process where it wants to implement data analyses. The most fascinating areas are where companies target the emerging ecosystems and make the decision to enter new territory, from smart homes to digital health. However, dramatic improvements are also possible in standard areas. Big data analysis can be used to optimize customer contact (e.g., to avoid contract terminations), in direct customer communications, and in cross-selling. Internal processes also benefit in ways such as optimizing machine utilization, predictive maintenance measures, and employee retention.

Ideally, the implementation of the big data strategy will start with a manageable but complex application, and one that promises high returns. If results are achieved quickly here, the entire transformation project is given fresh impetus. And once several such subprojects start delivering results quickly, the entire project funds itself.

The Foundations

These partial successes can be achieved, however, only if the company has already laid a stable foundation of technology, processes, and talent. At first, only the basics are needed. Expertise and skills will grow with implementation. Five factors are important to ensure a successful transformation.

Data. In the digital economy, data is the new gold. Google is the perfect example of what is possible. The more data a company collects, the more reliable its data-driven decisions will be. For many years now, companies have been collecting data on a large scale, but they lack the methods to bring it all together and analyze it as a whole. In some cases, the reasons are technical where highly ramified corporations store data in different IT systems. In other cases, the reasons are organizational, where marketing, production, logistics, and HR all operate their own silos.

Analytics. After data collection comes the analysis. Analytical approaches are required with differing perspectives: these are known as descriptive, predictive, and prescriptive analytics. The first explains what happened in the past, the second predicts what will happen in the future, and the third recommends decisions that can shape the future development of the company. New algorithms in machine learning systems with artificial intelligence open up new opportunities.

Pioneers like Amazon and Google make their algorithms publicly available. Tensorflow, which Google originally used to improve its search results, can now be used for image recognition and automated responses for call centers. No one, however, is allowed access to their treasure troves of data, an indicator of how these companies like to differentiate themselves and what they see as a general commodity.

Tools. Data analysts need professional programs that help them manage and structure the data volumes. This can be software such as SAS or IBM Modeler that enable them to quickly integrate machine learning components with the help of graphical interfaces. More companies, however, are using public, open-source software like R or Python for these tasks because they develop so quickly with the active members of their large communities. Also, they contain all the advanced algorithms required. In turn, the users, as the target group of the analyses and recommendations, need simple-to-use software that visualizes the results. Companies buy programs like Tableau to do this, or develop software themselves as decision-making aids.

Translators. In addition to management as the recipient of the analyses and the technical talent that processes them, companies on the transformation journey also need a third group of employees, translators. They need to be able to translate the business requirements to the data scientists and data engineers, and also explain to the decision makers which analyses are possible with which statements. The job requirements for this are high. People who take on the role of translator need to understand the digital space just as well as the business world. In general, companies often underestimate just how much expertise their employees need to successfully use big data and advanced analytics. Instead they turn their attention to strengthening their IT systems, which is also important, but much easier to solve.

Processes. Data, analytics, tools, and employees are all united by processes. It's worth remembering that the value chain is only as strong as its weakest link. If incorrect or poor data is collected, even the best analytics are worth nothing. The results will be nonsensical. As the early computer scientists put it, garbage in, garbage out. Even if the data and analytics are top quality, things can still go wrong if the process isn't foolproof. For example, if an agent in the call center of a wireless provider does not follow a recommendation provided by the virtual assistant based on customer data during the course of the call (the next best action) because he or she finds the recommendation difficult to understand, the data, analytics, and tools remain useless.

When used correctly, however, big data and advanced analytics can solve the trickiest of problems. Take an example from the world of consulting. A supermarket was considering expanding its range to include organic products and sugar-free, gluten-free, and lactose-free items. The problem was limited shelf space. Which products should give way? The obvious, simple solution was fundamentally wrong: if stores kept only their most profitable items, important anchor products would be lost, which are vital for retaining customers. Using entropy models and hierarchical clustering, the company developed a model that enabled the retailer to accurately predict the migration effect of an item being removed from sale, as well as the increase in margins following the inclusion of new products. The supermarket chain now uses this model to calculate its optimum range, and is growing twice as fast as its rivals.

Artificial Intelligence: The Next Disruptor

If Google and Amazon are proved right, companies will soon no longer be able to differentiate through smart algorithms; instead, these clever formulas will be shared as general commodities. All the same, the data scientists who create these algorithms needn't fear for their jobs. They will just see a change in the way they work. Instead, their work will involve selecting the best algorithms for the company and combining them in the best way to mine the data.

The next great leap in development is expected to come from artificial intelligence. Machines and their algorithms will increasingly be assigned tasks that are too complex for humans to manage or that the machines can perform more efficiently. Even today, machine learning systems are being used in industrial pilot projects. In 2016, a Google algorithm, AlphaGo, beat the world champion of the board game Go—and that's just the beginning.

6.3 CYBER SECURITY: THE ART OF THE SECURE DIGITAL ECONOMY

James Kaplan on the seven steps toward effective safeguards against hacking.

In 2016, resourceful hackers removed $81 million from Bangladesh's central bank after it joined the global banking communication network Swift; the hackers deployed malware to redirect the money transfers of Bangladeshis. A year earlier, hackers had gained access to the servers of the Sony film studios. They published the salaries of the executive directors, revealed the personal details of employees, and attempted unsuccessfully to blackmail the film studio into canceling the release of a film that made fun of North Korean dictator Kim Jong-un. And in 2014, a talented group of digital natives stole the code that the transponders in the electronic keys of Volkswagen cars use to open doors and start engines, the perfect tool for car thieves.

These are just three examples from a flood of incidents, but they illustrate how vulnerable the digital economy is. The risk is considerable: a McKinsey study estimates that if companies and governments do not take effective measures to combat cyber risks, global losses could run to around $3 billion worldwide by 2020. As the economy becomes increasingly digital, attackers are finding ever more entry points.

They attack from different sides and have completely different interests. Sometimes nation-states are behind the attacks, either to steal information to boost their own economies or to weaken political opponents. Sometimes competitors launch the attacks to steal a rival's technology and use it themselves, or simply to demonstrate how poorly their rival protects sensitive data and to inflict serious damage on its reputation. Other groups have an ideological agenda. These "hacktivists" may want to uncover injustices carried out by the target company against others, or to promote an ideology, be it anticapitalism, nationalism, or ecological policies. Some simply want to show they can do it. Attacks can also come from inside by frustrated or bribed employees or workers driven by their conscience.

Seven Steps toward Cyber Resilience

In a worldwide survey of managers, two-thirds agreed that cyber attacks posed a serious problem, and could result in significant strategic implications. Only 5 percent believed that their company was truly competent in six of the methods listed for preventing attacks. And 80 percent were worried that the hackers were learning faster than their company.

The countermeasures even have a negative knock-on effect on business. Security measures, for example, can delay the launch of new mobile features by an average of six months. Three-quarters of the managers surveyed stated that the productivity of their customer-facing employees had fallen because security requirements had slowed the sharing of data.

There is widespread agreement that the previous security models are overwhelmed. After a time of carelessness until around 2007, IT departments established a type of security network with strict processes and secure technical infrastructures. But these are now increasingly full of holes. To meet today's risks, it's time for a solution that focuses on security even at the process design stage. The best way for companies at risk to respond is with a program aimed at cyber resilience. *Resilience* is a term that business science has borrowed from evolutionary biology. It describes the ability of a system to absorb disruptions and shocks, and to carry on working successfully despite them. Companies can achieve cyber resilience in seven steps.

Companies now see cyber security as an integral business component based on seven practices

		Lever
1	Prioritize **data inventories and business risks**, and involve management level	
2	Mobilize **frontline employees** by demonstrating the value of data inventories	
3	Integrate resistance to cyber attacks in cross-company processes	Business
4	Integrate **incident response** mechanisms in all business functions, and improve with realistic tests	
5	Integrate **security functions in the technology** to increase scalability	General IT
6	Differentiated protection of the most important assets	
7	Deploy **active protection systems** to enable real-time response to attacks	Cyber security

With the right IT security structure and by applying the seven principles, companies can build strong resistance to cyber attacks

Priority Lists: Which Data Represent the Greatest Business Risk?

Very few companies have a clear idea of which business data is the most important. Security teams therefore need to work with management in the first step to examine the entire value chain and assess where the greatest risks lie. Is it the data for the design of a new product, a self-learning manufacturing process, or sensitive customer data, the loss of which would lead to a maximum credible accident?

Banks and insurers have assessed their risks in this way for years. They call the approach the "crown jewels" program, and it could be used as a model for many other industries.

Customer-Facing Managers Must Be Part of the Team, and Recognize That Data Is an Asset

Only those people who work with data truly understand its value and will take the topic of security seriously, which is why employees need to be trained on the subject.

At Microsoft, founder Bill Gates personally took this upon himself early on, in 2002. The security of products is the absolute top priority, he wrote in an urgent reminder to all employees. If it comes to the choice of whether a new product should be given additional features or be made more secure, he wrote, security must always be the choice. In 2003, Gates introduced Patch Tuesday at Microsoft, an initiative to continuously patch security gaps in the software.

Cyber Resilience as Part of Risk Management

Cyber security forms part of the company's risk, and must be managed as such. Risk assessments of online attacks must be integrated into the company's other risk assessments, presented to the relevant members of management, and discussed at executive levels.

To ensure resilience, prevention of online attacks must form part of the planning of all processes. Even in the early days of Industry 4.0 and the industrial Internet in 2012, GE stated its intention to make security components an integral element of the design of its machines, software, and networks. And in 2014, the group acquired the security specialists Wurdtech to bring additional skills into the firm.

Cyber War Games: Continuously Testing Prevention Systems

Why sit around waiting for ill-intentioned hackers when you can have someone else perform an attack to expose weaknesses before malicious hackers do? United Airlines took exactly this approach, and offered free air miles to clever hackers who could discover weak points in its programs as part of its "bug bounty" initiative. Barclays Bank went so far as to hire an entire department of in-house hackers who attack the bank's IT systems and then immediately repair any weaknesses. The CEO of a European electronics group even stepped down for two days to take part in a cyber war game to simulate online attacks on his organization.

Companies that understand the reality of the situation also practice their response to a successful cyber attack. If data breaches become public knowledge, the wrong statements can have serious consequences. The correct responses must be prepared, not just for IT managers, but also for marketing, customer service, and of course for PR.

Security Technology: An Integral Element of the IT Architecture

Operating systems, communication logs, and applications are established elements of the IT architecture. Each of them can become a security risk if it offers access points for possible attacks because of poor configuration, testing, and maintenance. Security elements must be built into all components, whether hardware, middleware, or application software, and their resilience must be continuously tested and refined during the development process. Together, all of these components mean a huge volume of potential security problems that can be identified only through persistent testing and ongoing maintenance.

With the trend toward rapid digitization, many companies in recent times have hastily introduced new technologies for which they lack the necessary administrative skills, and are unable to understand the technologies' interaction with the existing architecture. Budgets are reallocated from the maintenance of the old IT systems to the establishment of new digital skills, which makes sense from a business perspective but often has serious consequences for the medium-term security of the IT architecture.

One important step is to introduce different security zones. A European sports apparel manufacturer, for example, introduced a "play zone" in which online campaigns can quickly be created and implemented. The play zone is isolated from the existing systems with its own security zone. This means if security problems occur, the campaign can be quickly stopped or even deleted without the other systems being affected.

Another key element is ownership of the security elements. Often, the enemy is internal, with responsibility disputes among IT, the security organization, and product development tying up resources and budgets. Security technology, however, should be given top priority in the governance of each company. For example, GE firmly anchored an IT security function on its board of directors. Business units and the firm's head office are regularly and systematically subjected to security audits. According to Bill Ruh, head of the GE software division: "At GE, we focus on software platform security, protect critical infrastructure elements, and help our customers to perform reliable and secure transactions online."

Protection Levels: Not All Data Needs the Same Level of Protection

"He who defends everything defends nothing," said Frederick the Great, who knew a thing or two about attack and defense. Likewise, different processes can be given different levels of protection according to their position in the list of priorities, by employing greater or lesser encryption or requiring passwords of different strengths.

Banks, for example, only employ standard verification procedures for their online banking customers when it comes to routine queries. However, if customers want to transfer larger amounts or make unusual transactions, the banks often require additional codes sent to the customer by text message.

Active Defense, Preferably Before an Attack

In most cases, plenty of information is available about potential attacks, from both external and internal sources. Companies must in the future develop the ability to combine all the available information into a single risk profile, and then construct targeted firewalls that protect their systems from intruders. Once these protection measures are in place, the company will be well fortified and able to fend off attacks. In 2011, for example, defense group Lockheed Martin initiated the Nexgen alliance for the early detection of cyber threats. Network partner EMC, a cloud-computing firm, strengthened the alliance with its acquisition of NetWitness, a specialist in real-time web tracking, automatic threat analysis, and measures to combat illegal hacking into computer networks.

To establish greater security against cyber attacks, positions of responsibility throughout the entire company must be involved: operational managers when it comes to assessing which data is the most valuable, compliance officers when it's about assessing the possible risks associated with losing customer data, HR when it's about deciding which employees have access to which data, and the purchasing department when it's about negotiating security requirements with suppliers that need to connect to the company's IT system. To coordinate such a complex effort, top management must take sole responsibility.

Just like the World War II Enigma encryption machines, it's a perpetual battle between coding and decoding, ciphering and deciphering. The race continues, faster, more skillfully, more shrewdly, and more uncompromisingly than ever before. As the value chain makes its inexorable shift to the digital world, the potential gains for attackers grow.

6.4 EMBEDDED SOFTWARE: MACHINES AND EQUIPMENT GO DIGITAL

Mark Patel on the five guiding principles that can help traditional hardware manufacturers develop a software strategy.

In October 2016, Ford hired 400 employees from BlackBerry, doubling the connectivity talent dedicated to delivering more software and services to Ford customers.[1]

With the transition to Industry 4.0 with its connected machines and sensors that continuously collect data and transmit it to central servers over Wi-Fi, even machinery and equipment manufacturers need to upgrade their products to digital. Other industries that were strictly analog have already made the switch. Today, the average car, for example, has more lines of software code than an Apple MacBook. By 2012, smartphone makers already employed twice as many software developers as hardware developers. And a good two-thirds of all machinery and equipment manufacturers now also offer their customers software solutions.

So how do companies successfully tread the path from analog products to digitally ready products? How do they equip their machines with the right software? They need to bring in new skills and talent, as well as new organizational structures and processes. Ten steps lead the way toward

[1] www.ottawasun.com/2017/03/30/ford-plans-3379m-rd-centre-in-ottawa-for-self-driving-car-technology

embedded software, five of which center on strategy and implementation. We address these next.

Strategy: Focusing on What Creates Value

Companies that previously specialized in the mechanics of their machinery will find it extremely difficult to suddenly develop a convincing strategy for installing software from a standing start. What do customers want? How much are they prepared to pay? What are competitors doing? Unfortunately, many companies lack the experience to answer these questions. The following five principles can help develop a software strategy that really delivers value:

1. *Develop a detailed plan for the transformation that fits the company strategy.* Software requires far more frequent updates and ongoing support than traditional mechanical products, which is why the company needs its own software strategy. This strategy must outline the software-specific capabilities that will differentiate the machines from rival products in the future, what type of software is needed, and the deadlines for achieving this. First, however, market research needs to identify which problems or inefficiencies customers encounter that could be solved by software.

   Intel, for example, developed a range of digital assistants for its high-performance chips used in advanced analytics. In its market research, Intel discovered that customers often feel they are on their own when they run into problems. The strategic plan for software development is based strictly on the company's overall strategy and its quantitative targets for the most important products. And if brand image is a crucial component of the strategy, this must be supported with particularly advanced and powerful software. Automaker Mercedes plowed extensive resources into establishing digital capabilities, from entertainment and navigation systems to autonomous driving. Cars everywhere are full of software, and as a premium brand Mercedes must lead the way here just as much as on the mechanical side.

2. *Top management must be involved in the development of the strategy.* As with the other transformation projects in this book, the same

thing applies here: without the chief executives, nothing will work. Without the impetus that only the top management can provide, transformation efforts will generally focus only on smaller projects, and never fully realize the potential that a full-scale rollout throughout the organization can deliver. And only top management can make the strategic decisions necessary in the event of target conflicts. For example, does the company want to develop software primarily to boost sales of hardware products, or does it want to achieve additional revenues through software sales?

3. *Focus on the company's strengths rather than trying to emulate the strategy of a start-up.* For most traditional manufacturers, it makes little sense to go into direct competition with start-ups, which have the advantage of speed, agility, and specialist skills. Instead, they should concentrate on products where their strengths can help: their customer base, brand appeal, and industry knowledge. Aggressive new market entrants can even be combated by forming alliances with competitors to help develop better software. Audi, BMW, and Daimler, for example, work together as partners in the mapping service Here, which they acquired from Nokia. Here delivers the accurate, automotive-grade maps needed for autonomous driving. Because it also supplies other automakers, it keeps mapping service providers from outside the industry at a distance.

4. *Strategic aim: Establish an unassailable position and achieve network effects.* This is an ambitious target, but entirely feasible. Many companies have become indispensable in their particular field because they offer unique products or services. Siemens, for example, succeeded in developing machines and automation software for production lines that are now used by 14 of the world's 15 biggest automakers, while capturing an 80 percent global market share in the industry. Companies that offer a strong product can also invite external software developers to develop apps—the more smart applications a product has, the greater its appeal. After launching the iPhone, for example, Apple set up its own App Store, which delivers very strong revenues.

5. *Develop a pricing strategy.* Customers don't trust free products, and businesses don't like them because they generate no revenue. This

is why strategists should come up with lucrative pricing strategies. One option is the "freemium" model where the basic software is offered free with the purchased device, but a better version with more features costs extra. Another option is a pay-per-use model either for the software alone or for the overall package. And a third option is a subscription system regardless of use—again, either for the software alone or for the machine and programs.

Implementation: Recruiting Talent and Expertise

At first, traditional industrial companies wouldn't appear to be at the top of the list of potential employers for digital talent, who prefer to head for the Googles of this world or successful start-ups. Industry is perceived as lacking the freedom needed for successful development work or the same levels of technical tools and challenges. How can companies overcome these prejudices?

- *Attract key personnel.* If an industrial company is able to attract a star of the developer world, not only does it demonstrate that it takes its software business seriously, but also gains access to digital talent through that person's network.
- *Participate in the software ecosystem and evaluate potential acquisitions.* The advantage of leveraging an ecosystem or acquiring another firm is that the new team can start working productively from day one, which is important when time is of the essence. If the team has been working together a long time, there's less risk of migration, because most developers don't want to leave a team that collaborates so successfully.
- *Create the conditions that digital talent expects.* This doesn't mean just a high salary. We investigated what digital natives really value. They expect an excellent job. For most, this means working with the very best technology on challenging tasks, in internal networks, and with the necessary freedom. They expect strong top management that has open contact with the developers. And they want to work only for a company that has an excellent reputation in the industry, has dynamic and socially responsible working practices, and offers workplaces where people feel at ease. And, of course, the salary must

be right. On top of the basic salary, there should be short-term performance bonuses and a long-term asset growth plan.

- *Allow groups of developers to work independently.* Software developers are used to working in close collaboration with colleagues on projects that usually need lots of test runs and modifications to programs. Since their style of working tends to differ from the work flows for machine development, it's generally a bad idea to integrate the programmers into the existing organization. Instead, the system works best if the software team forms its own business unit with its own management and its own processes.

- *Employ an integrated communication system.* Many companies still follow a sequential development process in which the programs are only written once the hardware has been built. This wastes time. With new digital tools, software developers today can begin long before machine construction is finished, testing their programs on virtual prototypes. To ensure that the entire development process runs smoothly, hardware and software engineers should provide each other with regular progress updates, develop the requirements profile of the new product together, and coordinate their targets and schedules.

For most companies in the manufacturing sector, there is no choice. Their machines must come with software; otherwise, they won't be competitive. Our recommendations will help on the road toward the digitized product, but are not a magic formula—expect the unexpected along the way.

6.5 THE CHIEF DIGITAL OFFICER: A STEVE JOBS FOR EVERY COMPANY

Steve Van Kuiken discusses the art of the digital transformation with CDOs.

Offense is the best form of defense. We hear it time and again. That's how Bill Ruh, chief digital officer (CDO) of GE, sees it. "If you don't figure out how to get more productivity and efficiency in your products, someone else will. In the end, every major company has to be a software company, because if you don't own this asset, you stand to be disrupted," he says. When Ruh joined GE, he found a heavy focus on analytics on the company's own machines. He described this as a defensive strategy. His focus was to make GE go on the offensive. "GE would help customers be proficient on all machines, not just GE's," he says.

Bill Ruh is one of what is a small but growing group of chief digital officers in businesses today. At Starbucks, Adam Brotman drives digitization forward; at tech giants IBM and SAP, it's Bob Lord and Jonathan Becher; and at elevator maker Schindler, Michael Nilles is in the hot seat.

CDOs must be multitalented. They need to be strategists and digital natives, and have a strong understanding of customers and employees. Developing a digital strategy is just one part of the job description; above all, the CDO must also be a skilled networker, both internally and externally. At an external level, he or she will identify the most exciting technological developments and most promising start-ups, and at an internal level, the CDO will convince the entire organization of the merits of the digital transformation. Just as important as knowing what can be expected of employees in all things digital, the CDO must also understand what customers expect from the company, and what technology they will feel comfortable using.

The chief digital officer is responsible for the overarching digital agenda of the company

Aim

- **Targeted digitization of current business**, and relocation of offline functions to an online platform
- **Introduce new technologies**, foster innovation, understand Internet trends, and present ideas for applying new technologies and their potentials

Main tasks	Position in organization
Drive forward modern technologies	**Reports directly to CEO**
- Observe technology trends	
- Inform department about new technologies	**KPIs**
- Apply new technologies in the development business solutions	**Time-specific KPIs**
Steer demand	- Percentage of software launches by target date
- Provide resources for departmental projects	- Overall time of development
- Driving force in the steering of extensive, cross-departmental demand	**Cost-specific KPIs**
Develop new solutions	- Number of overall transactions accounted for by online transactions (in %)
- Implement new technologies together with providers	- Proportion of budget-compliant projects (in %)
- Manage work volumes of different areas, including outsourcing providers	**Quality KPIs**
	- Proportion of sales completed online
	- Rise in number of online users
	- Rise in conversion rate determined by purchases
	- Fall in migration rate at different purchase phases

The CDO Must Break Up Silos

"Leaving digital in a silo is setting up for failure," says Sean Cornwell, chief digital officer at Travelex.

A good CDO must have the "ability to bring everyone together," says Roland Villinger, CDO at Audi. "Technical developers need their time and space, sales want everything yesterday, legal has to play it safe, the IT guys speak a different language anyway, our external partners have a completely different culture, and it's my job to bring it all together." Villinger is responsible for all digitization projects aimed at the customer, from car features to service offers, and projects that affect internal processes, with the exception of production. As CDO, Villinger is also responsible for attracting sufficient digital talent to Audi. "We look everywhere," he says, describing how Audi searches through all the normal recruitment channels. "But we see our biggest successes when we're able to utilize our network. The best thing is when someone recommends us."

Because his work spans departments, the CDO needs to break down the silo mentality. "We have a laid-back culture where people tend to focus on their own area first," says Villinger. "But we need to ensure that we build an integrated digital ecosystem." For each physical vehicle platform in the company, there's also a virtual digital platform with its own architecture. Villinger holds regular meetings with colleagues from across the Volkswagen empire to discuss which offerings should be developed for the group as a whole, and which should be brand-specific for differentiation purposes. "It's a fine balancing act, because on the one hand, we want to strengthen brand identity, but on the other, we want to leverage our size advantage," says Villinger. "When we get it right, we're untouchable." To make it all click at Audi, he needs to bring together the old world where only the performance and design of the car counted, and the new world where connectivity and digital services have been thrown into the mix. "My role is one of a disruptor, an agent of change," says Villinger, "and it's my job to get everyone on board." This isn't always easy. Those who think digital act fast, try out solutions, and are prepared to accept failure.

"We are building the playbook for the new digital industrial world," says GE CEO Jeffrey Immelt. To execute on this bold strategy, CDO Bill Ruh must establish a digital culture throughout the company and optimize the current business model for the digital age. The cloud-based Predix platform allows GE to break up digital silos. "We connect engineering, manufacturing, supply chain, maintenance, services, which exist in every industrial company, including GE. These had been disconnected. What we're doing is connecting them,"[2] says Ruh.

And when it comes to customer focus, Google and Amazon were the early front-runners. Empowering and meeting the demands of its customers is a strategic focus for CVS Health. According to the CDO of CVS Health, Brian Tilzer, "Digital technologies are ubiquitous and highly configurable—a powerful combination, because it allows us to empower our customers anytime and anywhere. That's why we are doubling our digital investment." Again, this is a key element of the work of a CDO. The CDO needs a precise understanding of the customer decision journey throughout every touch point with the company from first contact to purchase. Which digital offerings throughout this journey do customers appreciate? Where do they exit the journey? Which digital tools are feasible to help customers configure and choose a product? Which are worthwhile? What are the competitors doing, and are there new ones on the horizon—possibly with start-ups in Silicon Valley or Berlin? The CDO must find the answers to all these questions.

Developing Internal Talent

It's an important philosophy for Max Viessmann, who heads up digital at his HVAC and refrigeration company. "You need to invest time to get everyone on board," he says. "It mustn't be about the digital winners and analog losers." Many members of the digital team came from the existing workforce. "The external proportion isn't actually that high," Viessmann says. Anyone who demonstrated an affinity for the topic was able to join one of the project teams, and those who proved themselves had the opportunity to stay permanently. Viessmann wasn't concerned with their qualifications. "We have machine engineers, business administration graduates, social scientists … ultimately, it doesn't matter." What counted was their attitude. "I spend 30 percent of my time explaining to our employees we're not all digital natives—that's what we're working toward," Viessmann says.

Digitization has also long since arrived at elevator manufacturer Schindler. "Three or four years ago, we were discussing things defensively:

[2]https://www.forbes.com/sites/jasonbloomberg/2016/07/25/digital-transformation-at-scale-at-general-electric-digital-influencer-bill-ruh/#228be337a2fe

What can happen to us? Is Uber coming to disrupt our industry?" CDO Michael Nilles said in an interview with the *Wall Street Journal*. "We now ask: Where are the opportunities?" Schindler is connecting its global fleet of elevators to the Internet of Things as part of its digital transformation, with the aim of offering new services to direct customers and their elevator passengers. Schindler has allied with GE and Huawei to develop components for the Internet of Things. According to Nilles, the data collected forms an indispensable platform for developing new services. He believes that in the future, companies will be differentiated by the software offerings they provide for their hardware: "You are not going to distinguish yourselves anymore with a product."

Chief digital officers with the necessary powers are becoming increasingly prevalent, and renowned companies of all sizes and across all industries are adding the role to their management boards. From tech giants like Cisco and IBM continuing through Volkswagen, CVS Health, L'Oréal, Starbucks, Williams Sonoma, and all the way to the city of New York, organizations worldwide are adopting this function.

A CDO with reach and authority—a Steve Jobs for every company— can help to break down the functional silos, and shape the journey toward digitization as a permanent disruptor.

6.6 THE DIGITAL ORGANIZATION: ALL POWER TO THE MULTIFUNCTIONAL TEAMS

Julie Goran on autonomous teams, agile sprints, and product owners.

Is it possible to have an organization model that has no fixed structure, and is constantly evolving? Yes, and it works very well in fact. ING, the Dutch banking group, embarked on a journey to transition from a traditional fixed organization to an agile model. In the headquarters organization, the staff was split into some 300 nine-person squads that are multifunctional teams that work toward a specific goal. The squads are grouped into 13 so-called tribes. Each tribe has a dedicated purpose, which is broken down into subpurposes and deliverables for each squad. Squad members follow a set of agile ceremonies to align and work together. There are no managers; they all learn together, work through problems together, and make decisions together. The successes and failures of all the tribes are shared in quarterly business reviews (QBRs), which also serve as platforms for cascading broader business goals and objectives to each of the tribes, and aligning the priorities, resources, and focus areas of the different tribes. Many core processes such as budgeting, performance management, and procurement processes are now fundamentally different in order to support an agile operating model. The success of this new model is very impressive—software releases are now on a weekly basis rather than five or six times a year, and employee-engagement scores are up multiple points.[3]

Agile companies are almost tailor-made for the digital age with their simple, stable, and effective structures that enable extreme flexibility and fast response times. That is precisely what's needed, because along with its opportunities, digitization also brings with it plenty of challenges. It makes the business world more volatile with its sudden leaps in progress; it makes it more uncertain, more complex, and more ambiguous. The old way of organizing companies is coming under increasing strain. Hierarchies are too slow for the digital pace, rigid budget plans can't keep up with demand, and before a project even starts, the constantly growing complexity overwhelms even the most capable executives. In this new age, innovations can destroy established business models, competitors can form new ecosystems outside the industry, and businesses can grow at incredible speeds. The new age needs new organization structures.

The agile organization combines a stable framework with dynamic skills. Again, top management sets the direction. There's a simple, common reporting structure, and lean processes and values are specified by the head office. Then there are the dynamic components: a culture of fast learning based on trial and error that grasps opportunities and tries them out while willing to accept failure, teams free of hierarchies that work autonomously, and employees who take responsibility.

How Do Agile Organizations Work?

As the first industry to practice the agile method, the software industry laid out three principles in a manifesto. As stated in the Manifesto for Agile Software Development at www.agilemanifesto.org, for development work to succeed, individuals and interactions are more important than processes and tools, just as working software is more important than comprehensive

---

[3] www.mckinsey.com/industries/financial-services/our-insights/ings-agile-transformation

documentation. Collaboration with customers is more effective than any amount of contract negotiations, while responding to change is better than following a plan. It's a manifesto against bureaucracy and in support of creative freedom, born of the experiences of long-drawn-out projects that seemingly never end, and once they do finally end, the market and customers have already moved on.

To become an innovative company, the organization must at its core be dynamic, agile, customer-oriented, data-protected, and fast

		From	To
Customer focus		Focus on processes, procedures and control	Focus on customer benefit
Fast decisions		Gut decisions	**Data-driven** decisions
Fast deployment		Project-specific deployment	**Continuous refinement** based on rapid feedback

Observable behavior

Underlying mind-sets

Fast failure		Fear of failure	**Mentality of fast failure**
Experiments		Nostalgia: preserve tradition and familiarity	**Conscious experimentation to find new solutions**
Transparency		Protectionism	**Openness and transparency**

Agile companies refrain from the quests for perfection that are so time and cost intensive, and base their models on companies from the digital world, which bring products to market that at first often have only limited features. Agile companies use heuristic methods to complement and improve their products with continuous market testing cycles. Products can be launched with only a few core functions, an approach known as the minimum viable product (MVP). A prime example of a company that takes this approach is U.S. automaker Tesla, which constantly improves the performance and features of its cars even after purchase by offering software updates. This generates revenue because customers want to use these new functions.

It's a real paradigm shift for many companies, because from now on, products are never truly complete; they're continuously updated.

To work in agile mode, companies need a new organizational structure. In the future, the core of the organization will be formed by stable, product-based teams working toward their set targets largely autonomously. Depending on the task at hand, these teams will comprise employees from across all functions—including IT, design, marketing, controlling, right through to production, as required. The product owner plays a key role in the team. He or she represents the customer and the customer's interests, sets priorities, allocates tasks across the team, and coordinates the remaining players, but has no managerial function.

The teams work in sprints that generally last one to four weeks, and always follow the same process. At the outset, the product owner explains the goal. The team then estimates the time and effort needed and what can be delivered by when, and then gets to work. Each day, the team members meet to organize the day's work, resolve problems, and discuss progress. At the end of the sprint, the team presents the results to the product owner and all other parties with an interest in the product. Sprints always end with a review session: What went well? What went wrong? What can we learn? As a result, each individual team learns continuously, and so too does the organization, from the efforts of all teams.

Organizing product development into cross-functional teams is so successful because the teams are responsible for their products and services right from the beginning. Since the team is already made up of all the important functions, it doesn't rely on other departments that could jeopardize delivery. This responsibility and autonomy are excellent motivators for the team members.

Many Employees Have to Take on New Roles

When companies adopt this type of organization, many employees have to learn new skills and take on new roles. Also, fewer managers are needed because the teams take on more responsibility. As a result, many of those managers who remain in the organization have to give up their familiar managerial roles and develop into coaches who pass on their knowledge. Managers who retain their managerial positions then lead through visions and values, acting as catalysts that bring together the mind-sets and actions of all stakeholders. And of course, they continue to manage the organization through the most important financial and performance KPIs, coordinate cross-team initiatives, and communicate with all key players, both those inside the company and those with an interest in it: employees, owners, and society in general. Many IT employees also find they have new roles. Whereas earlier their work was far removed from the customer in the back office, many now have to find solutions for customer requirements as the product technology managers of their teams.

The agile organization also redefines relationships with suppliers. Data analysis and software development will be considered core strategic areas for many companies. Instead of outsourcing this work, companies will attempt to do much of it themselves, often in partnerships or with flexible freelancers forming a network that needs to be built up and maintained. Budget planning will also become more dynamic, and will no longer be performed once a year, but instead will follow the methods of venture capitalists. First there will be a manageable budget for the development of a simple product that can be tested in the market. If this product is successful, more funds are gradually assigned. Conversely, if the product fails, the budget is very quickly reduced.

The biggest change, however, relates to the corporate culture. Instead of employing a top-down hierarchy and imposing regulations, the agile organization relies on trust. Self-organizing teams agree to defined targets, work without directives from above, and justify the trust placed in them by delivering results. At Netflix, for example, employee freedoms go so far that workers are allowed to decide for themselves how much vacation time they take. Management doesn't get involved; instead, the individual just needs the approval of the team.

The trend toward more responsibility rather than control will increase in the coming years. As larger sections of the workforce form into self-governing teams, the traditional management structures will be rendered obsolete. For the employees in the teams, however, it means greater freedom than ever. Together, they will decide on working hours, training requirements, new hires, dismissals, and possibly even salaries. This leads to a better experience for customers and employees. At the same time, the company grows and is successful in the market.

6.7 TALENT MANAGEMENT: EVERYONE WANTS DIGITAL NATIVES

Hugo Sarrazin and Satty Bhens on the upheavals in the labor market and the strategies deployed in the battle for scarce talent.

Digitization of tasks in the form of production robots, chatbots, and digital assistants has sparked fear among many employees, who are wondering if they will still have a job tomorrow. In 2013, for example, economists Carl Benedikt Frey and Michael Osborne caused a sensation when they analyzed 702 occupations in the United States and assessed the likelihood of these jobs being performed by robots or computer programs in the near future. They concluded that almost half of U.S. employees could lose their jobs in the next 20 years.

However, a different picture emerges if we focus on individual activities rather than occupations as a whole. A study by the McKinsey Global Institute shows that with current foreseeable technology, full automation will be possible in less than 5 percent of jobs. It does confirm, however, that automation will be possible for no less than 45 percent of individual activities currently performed by employees across various professions. This percentage could further rise to 58 percent if machine processing and analysis of natural language reaches an average human level. The Center for European Economic Research also estimates that 20 to 30 percent of academic activities could be automated. Although this ultimately means a similar volume of work becoming automated as predicted by Frey and Osborne, the prospects are quite different. Ideally, machines will assume the monotonous side of people's jobs, leaving them more time to get on with more creative and fulfilling work.

However, not everyone can do that work. In view of recent findings, economists and social researchers predict a polarization of the labor market. They anticipate that creative, highly qualified labor will become more sought-after than ever before, and that people who provide personal services will retain their positions, but employees with average qualifications who perform mostly routine activities will gradually be replaced by powerful computers and robots.

Companies Fighting for Digital Talent

The battle for young, highly qualified, tech-savvy talent—the digital natives—has already begun. And it's not just fought with high salaries. Companies are having to change their entire organizations to accommodate digital natives' high expectations of flexibility and independence, triggering fundamental cultural change throughout the world of employment.

Digital talent is scarce. In the McKinsey Global Survey of almost a thousand top executives, a lack of suitable managers and expertise was cited as the biggest obstacle to the digital transformation of their companies, with 31 percent citing this concern.

Recruiting and developing digital talent is therefore at the very top of the agenda in many companies. It's not just about hiring IT specialists. Digitization has long been more than just an IT matter. It even goes beyond experts who specialize in the development and marketing of digital products and services, beyond data scientists, and beyond social media experts. Instead, it's about a new generation of employees who are fully conversant with digital technologies, who think like entrepreneurs, who are flexible, and who act fast. And it's also not just about simple recruitment, either, but about hiring digital experts and incorporating them into teams of experienced employees, where the analog-minded can learn the skills they need for the digital economy.

To find and retain this treasured talent, much needs to change in organizations, particularly in HR departments. Recruitment can no longer be left to the HR department. Instead managers with digital experience need to take responsibility for the process. Potential candidates are approached at conferences or online communities, and rather than holding traditional interviews, candidates program against each other. Once they are successfully recruited, their skills are regularly assessed and development opportunities are discussed. And to retain digital talent in the long term, their remuneration must be based on the kinds of salaries partner companies pay to their top performers.

What Can Established Companies Do to Become Attractive for Digital Talent?

Traditional companies don't normally possess the sex appeal that start-ups do. How can they make up for this deficit? As experience shows, higher salaries aren't the answer. So if remuneration is at the same level as at other competitors, then other factors count more, such as an inspirational mission and challenging and interesting work. Some large firms turn their disadvantage into an advantage, and tell potential candidates that they want to reinvent their entire organization to be ready for the digital age—just the job for new talent. And this is precisely the approach taken by GE when it explains its mission to digital natives: GE wants to become one of the world's top 10 software companies by 2020. It's all about storytelling. Companies that are able to outline their vision in an authentic and stimulating story can win the hearts and minds of talent.

Because birds of a feather flock together, some companies sign up well-known players in the digital scene who are sure to attract other talent.

Other companies take it even further, and, rather than recruiting big names, they simply buy the entire start-up—it's known as "acqui-hiring." In 2011, for example, Amazon acquired software developer Quorus, a company that brings together social media and online retail, and develops apps that allow users to get advice from friends before making a purchase. Amazon incorporated the entire team into its development structure.

New Ways to Search for Talent

HR departments often feel helpless when it comes to assessing digital talent, because their normal measures don't work. Software developer Catalyst DevWorks analyzed the resumes of hundreds of thousands of IT systems administrators, and found no correlation between the quality of university degree and career success. So rather than concentrating on qualifications, the HR managers of the software firm developed their own tests, using clever algorithms to identify the IT expertise and skills of an applicant.

Since then, many HR departments now use online tests, games, and analyses to improve their recruiting methods, sometimes even using psychometric tests to determine how well a potential recruit will fit into the company's culture. Often, really simple ideas work: one corporation uses a 30-minute test to compare the profiles of applicants with profiles of people who have been especially successful in the relevant field. Its number of bad hires has fallen significantly.

But how can companies track down digital talent? A good starting point is online platforms like GitHub, the biggest online repository of open-source software, where proud programmers upload their software along with their names. If a company identifies a particularly clever solution, it can contact the author—it's already clear the programmer can do his or her job. Companies searching for talent regularly hold programming competitions on platforms like TopCoder, Kaggle, or HireIQ.

And if the talent can't come to the company, the company can go to the talent. Many companies are establishing their own digital laboratories near leading universities or in cities that attract digital natives. Walmart, the world's largest retailer, for example, based its WalmartLabs close to Stanford University.

How Can Companies Retain Digital Talent?

Since digital talent is in short supply, people with the right skills are constantly being targeted by HR consultants across all channels from LinkedIn to Facebook in an attempt to attract them to new pastures. This makes it all the more important for companies to bind their freshly acquired talent with a clear incentive program from day one. Tailored programs put together by specialists like the U.S. company LearnUp are now available to help ensure a smooth onboarding process. Google, for example, was able to increase productivity by 15 percent using this type of systematic training.

Digital technology even makes it possible to identify dissatisfaction among employees and thoughts of leaving. Predictive analytics examine social interaction in teams and raise the alarm if any relevant indicators are identified. HR can then step in and offer the employee a mentor, a new position, and perhaps even a promotion. Once again, Google leads the way when it comes to using digital technology in HR. The search engine giant established a People Analytics Unit, which examines how team dynamics and harmony affect output, and how to best stimulate the creativity of software engineers. The company boasts that its software has enabled it to significantly increase not only the productivity of individual employees, but also the productivity of entire development teams.

Attract and retain top talent: taking a leaf out of the Silicon Valley book

* Small teams work best
* Roles in the team should be fluid
* Collaboration and knowledge sharing are indispensable
* Allow experimentation and failure
* Measure performance on business impact, not on costs
* Use flexible targets and performance assessments
* Reward makers, not managers

6.8 PARTNER MANAGEMENT: STRONGER TOGETHER
Anand Swaminathan on the art of managing a collaborative network.

Apple knows how to do it: Its HealthKit platform brings together players from across the world of medicine. Physicians, researchers, hospitals, and patients, as well as a wide array of clever app developers, all connect to its open platform. And just like a spider in the middle of its web, Apple occupies the central position, connecting the various players such as doctors who want to research illnesses like asthma or Parkinson's disease, or offering Apple customers the chance to manage their conditions better using apps developed by the company or its partners. The commission that Apple receives from the sale of these apps is just a side revenue stream. What the company really wants is hardware sales and data, which is the new gold of the digital age.

HealthKit is a prototype of a functioning partner network. All players benefit—doctors and researchers because they no longer have to spend time organizing and managing a research network, iPhone owners because their smartphones offer even more useful lifestyle functions, and Apple itself, with increased sales and data. Apple is the pioneer of partner management; after all, it's thanks to the ideas and apps of external programmers that the company has risen to being the most valuable company in the world.

And Apple's digital example has now spread to the analog world: The complexity and pace of digitization has rendered the old tried-and-tested principle of do-it-yourself obsolete. In the rapidly emerging new ecosystems that are appearing in every industry, it's impossible for a single company to take on all roles. A company that wants to break into the digital world needs to be open-minded enough to work with partners.

In the auto industry, there has long been collaboration between multiple partners. What is new, however, is digital thinking. The car of the future will exist in an ecosystem that includes not only traditional suppliers, but also completely new digital companies. The real innovation is the new interaction between numerous partners who present the car as a system consisting of hardware, software, and services. Vehicle developers work with start-ups, large digital companies, high-tech firms, and other digital service providers.

Siemens, for example, has allied with IBM and a small start-up named Local Motors, and is experimenting with an open network. Based on a crowdsourcing concept, numerous independent programmers and engineers designed a vehicle that was almost entirely produced using 3D printers at the customer location, making good on the start-up's name. It took just two months from the decision phase and product design to final production of the first prototype—a fraction of the normal time it takes in the auto industry.

Finding and Managing the Right Partners

In partnerships, a company can essentially choose one of three roles: it can be an initiator and coordinator of an ecosystem, it can be a member of a partnership, or it can establish its own ecosystem as part of a greater whole. Companies that choose to act as the coordinator at the heart of an ecosystem must be attractive to the partners they hope will connect to the ecosystem. A strong brand attracts other partners because they can expect good sales under the banner of the brand. Equally attractive is a coordinator or aggregator that already has a good customer base such as Apple. Other sought-after partners are those whose digital technologies differentiate their ecosystems from the competition, or those that have succeeded in establishing a market standard. Once a market standard has been established, it makes sense for any company that hopes to generate revenue in the area to adopt that standard. Otherwise, they're out of the game.

If a company plans to establish a subecosystem as part of the overarching system, it must ensure that its subsystem interacts perfectly with the surrounding ecosystem. For example, if a company wants to offer a smart system that controls heating and climate control, it must ensure its system can work equally well with other vertical systems in the overarching smart home ecosystem—such as digital entertainment or smart lighting—as with established aggregators like Apple's HomeKit.

For traditional companies assessing whether a large high-tech firm or a start-up is a suitable network partner, a four-step assessment can help. The first consideration is the market in which the potential partner operates, and its level of competition. Naturally, the ideal situation is a dynamic market and a strong competitive position. Next comes the business model. Is it viable and future-proof? What are the company's products and services like? How innovative are they, and how customer-focused is the offering? Next is the human factor. What is the company's management team like, and how good are its personnel? And finally, is the company's culture? Does the potential partner and its methods of doing business fit in with your own company's culture? The answers to these questions offer a reliable indication as to whether cooperation in the same ecosystem is worthwhile.

To manage the collaborative network, the participating companies require four skills:

1. *Methodological partner management*, from defining the objectives of the network and the manner in which the individual collaborators work on the products and ideas, through to the underlying business agreements.
2. *An internal organization* that ensures trouble-free collaboration at the interface between business and ecosystem.
3. *New management processes* that integrate partner management as a function in the organization of the digitized company. At the top management level in particular, many will need to move away from a mind-set of "us against the world" to "stronger together."
4. *The establishment of a culture* that promotes partnerships and encourages the company to see others as partners rather than competitors.

Several aspects need to be managed for a partnership to succeed. Everything starts with reaching agreement on measurable targets. To leverage its full potential, the partners should examine the entire value chain, and determine those points where collaboration will be the most rewarding. In most cases, achieving as much as possible together is the main priority. So that the ecosystem functions as efficiently and cost-effectively as possible, regular checks are important to ensure budget compliance and achievement of milestones. Partners' ideas for new products and services should also be continuously evaluated. All the network partners should also deploy the right people for the ecosystem. Without the talent, the partnership can't succeed. Finally, the people assuming these new partner management roles must be given extra training.

Coopetition: When Competitors Collaborate

There will always be things to negotiate where the interests of the network partners clash. In the digital world, this is especially true when it comes to sharing data. As such, each partner must decide for itself which data or elements of its data model it wishes to share with the other partners, and which data it believes is so sensitive that it can't be shared. The partners also need to discuss how to distribute the profits. How will a company profit when its customers purchase products from a partner through the shared platform? How much commission will be paid to the network coordinator from revenue generated by a partner's app in the ecosystem?

The collaboration not competition philosophy hasn't quite reached all sections of management just yet, but companies appear much more open to the idea. With the pressures of digitization, attitudes are changing. Direct competitors are bundling their expertise. Take the premium auto brands Audi, BMW, and Mercedes, for example, which jointly acquired the mapping service provider Here from Nokia. Extremely precise maps are a prerequisite for autonomous driving, which is being developed in the industry. Here is the world leader for the very data that all three partners need, and which they even sell on to other interested parties. These types of alliances are known as "coopetition," a portmanteau of cooperation and competition, And we are likely to hear about many more of them in the coming years.

Over the next few years, the emerging digital mega-ecosystems centered on mobility, smart homes, digital finance, and digital health care, for example, will turn many companies that operate in isolation into network partners. The vision paints a picture of a business world that resembles a model of neural pathways, each connected to countless synapses and all connected to each other.

QUESTIONS MANAGERS SHOULD ASK THEMSELVES: WHERE ARE YOU?

In Chapter 3, we explained why all businesses need a digital concept. In Chapters 4 through 6, we outlined what needs to be done. We presented the most important emerging economic ecosystems, explained how business architectures need to change, and described how the foundation must be built on technology and organization. The ideas, concepts, and examples of digital pioneers show how others do it.

Now it's up to you as a manager. Where are new ecosystems emerging in your industry? Does your business architecture also conceal efficiency potential that could be leveraged through digitization and advanced analytics? Are you already using state-of-the-art technologies and secure, agile IT systems? Do you have the right talent on board? Are you investing in the establishment of targeted strategic partnerships? Take the time to perform a self-diagnosis. Your answers will reveal your shortcomings, and prepare you for the next chapter, the How of digitization: how to create a transformation plan, how to oversee a successful switch to digital mode, and how to roll this out to the entire organization—Digital@Scale.

What? Key self-appraisal questions for management
Level of agreement from 1 (very low) to 5 (very high)

			1	2	3	4	5
Building new ecosystems	1	Are competitors attacking our business model with new technologies?					
	2	Are we leveraging the potential of digital technologies to reinvent ourselves?					
	3	Are new profit pools emerging at the boundaries between traditional industries?					
Developing the business architecture	4	Are we fully grasping digitization to fundamentally improve the customer experience?					
	5	Are we developing new products quickly and radically enough to get ahead?					
	6	Are we fully leveraging the efficiency potential of digitization and advanced analytics?					
Strengthening the foundation	7	Are we using state-of-the-art technologies and IT?					
	8	Do we have an agile and flat organization, and do we promote entrepreneurial thinking?					
	9	Are we attracting digital talent to the company, and are we building targeted partnerships?					

□-□-⑦-□-□

HOW? DECISIVE, HOLISTIC, AND RAPID IMPLEMENTATION

NOW THAT WE'VE *covered the Why and the What of the transformation process, it's time to look at the concrete implementation. In the next three chapters, Anand Swaminathan and Jürgen Meffert describe the How—the heart of the transformation into a digital company.*

The learning is over; now it's about action. We've learned why digitization is not an option but a necessity, and we've seen the possibilities, from the new ecosystems and digitized company functions to new technological and organizational foundations. Now it's about putting it into action, and actually transforming the company. Just as in the What chapters, there are many questions: How do we set our priorities? Where do we start our transformation into a digital company? How should a digital company be managed? How do we make it agile, and how do we convince the doubters? Again, a three-step structure helps to sort these questions, find the right answers, and approach the transformation.

First, we need a plan that defines the stages of a transformation program often lasting years—our blueprint. This chapter explains where to start, what's important, and which course needs to be set right from the outset.

Test, fail, learn, profit: the digital company operates very differently from its analog predecessors. The organization, its management functions, and its processes need to be set to digital. Chapter 8 explains how to actuate the digital operating system, successfully launch your first pilot projects, and how to change the culture.

How? Key questions for management

Creating a plan	1 Do we have a plan for the digitization of our entire enterprise?	2 How do we place the customer at the center of change?	3 What structure will support the required change?
Actuating the digital company	4 Digital natives think in weeks, not years: how agile is our company?	5 Market success: how can we correctly measure the success of digitization?	6 How do we assemble a team with digital experience and industry insight, and how do we manage it?
Scaling forcefully	7 How do we scale quickly, systematically, and forcefully?	8 How can our IT make our business faster?	9 How do we get the organization on board, and do we have a concept for handling concerns?

What succeeds in the tests will quickly be rolled out across the board—which always means the entire enterprise. And that takes courage. Chapter 9 explains how IT competence will become a key weapon, how start-ups can help you, and how speed will become your new creed.

On the long road toward becoming a digital company, it often helps to take a look at companies that were born digital. They all share characteristics that are worth emulating: pace before perfection, experiment and learn from failure, start with small budgets and ramp up after success, make data-driven decisions rather than using gut instinct, and always consider what the customer really wants, because all too often that's not initially clear.

For the digital company to succeed, it needs its own management philosophy. Niklas Östberg, cofounder and CEO of Delivery Hero, knows what this means: With presence in 33 countries and valuation of $3 billion after the last financing round, his company offers a platform that brings hungry customers and restaurants together. Meals are ordered online and delivered to the front door.

Both sides win, Östberg argues in an interview with *McKinsey Quarterly*. Customers can choose from a wide range of offers, view quality and taste ratings, pay quickly and easily, and save money through a loyalty program. The restaurants benefit from the additional demand, the lower operating costs, and the valuable information they get back, such as which meals sell best where, what's missing in a region, and which price barriers slow demand. There's plenty to learn from this data.

As is typical in the digital economy, Östberg operates a highly federated management structure across his international empire. "We give local CEOs autonomy and authority to encourage entrepreneurship. But you have to set the rules of the game. And you have to set the culture of your company." Technology can help to strike that balance. "We're a data-driven culture," says Östberg, "which means a local manager can't simply argue 'we should do it this way because that's how we do it in our country.' Arguments must be based on data." It's a typical digital model. Delegate, yes, but trust must be earned through fact-based arguments—pure gut decisions are the way of the old economy.

To realize the opportunities of digital, companies need tailored, individual digital strategies in which targets are formulated, projects launched, and even partnerships considered. Such a strategy requires a shift in culture: the digital economy is fast-moving and demands rapid scalability, with far more focus on short-termism than in the analog world. For many CEOs, the balancing act between having a clearly structured road map and the ability to adapt quickly is a major challenge.

To see how this can be overcome, a good place to start is to examine the methods used by venture capitalists (VCs). When deciding whether or not to invest in a start-up, they always look very specifically at three factors: the management team, the business concept, and the milestones of the business. They limit their risk by initially releasing only small budgets, tying these to milestones, and then determining whether predetermined quantitative or qualitative targets have been hit. If the targets have been hit, fresh money is injected for further development. If things aren't so certain, it then depends on how the management team responds, how they change the business plan, whether they bring in new skills, and whether they can convince their VC. If they fail, the venture is promptly ended.

What can we learn from these methods? To break into the digital world, we must copy the first principle of the venture capitalist: invest only if you're convinced by the team and its experience. The next principle, a good business plan, comes more easily to companies: after all, they have plenty of experience of making plans. The third principle, budgets and linking them to targets, is a real challenge for businesses. Large companies typically have a cyclical strategy and planning processes where decisions are made and budgets approved, usually once a year. In the digital world, this type of periodic planning plays less of a role—venture capitalists even regard it as irrelevant. For them, it's about hitting targets at agreed milestones when new money can be invested. This logic should be built into your organization. The journey into the digital new economy is guided by 11 principles, which we will look at in greater depth in this chapter and the next two chapters.

How? Eleven principles: what they really mean

	Principles	What they really mean
Creating a plan	1 Think big—digitize the entire enterprise	• Holistic thinking • Prioritize by value contribution • Close the gaps
	2 Surprise—it's about the customer	• Optimize critical processes across all business units • Iterate the concept—learn with the customer • Introduce digitization across the company by value contribution
	3 Break down functional silos	• Determine the digital maturity of the company • Establish a new digital business unit • Establish a digital competence center • Assign a mandate and build digital talent
Actuating the digital enterprise	4 Switch to the digital operating system	• Recruit and expand the team • Establish fast concept iteration • Establish steering by milestones
	5 Change the culture	• Further develop the work environment • Transform the culture—working on four dimensions at the same time • Communicate—talk digital and act digital
	6 Steer change	• Deploy steering team like a venture capitalist would • Manage like a VC: link budgets to milestones • Resolute application of new steering systems
	7 Encourage leadership—at all levels	• Lead by example • "License to kill"
Scaling forcefully	8 It's about the whole	• The plan's alive • Turbocharged digital build-operate-transfer (DBOT)
	9 Turn IT into a weapon	• The method depends on the starting point • Success factors for two speeds • Establish an agile system
	10 Collaborate closely with start-ups	• New business ideas stimulate the organization and deliver fresh impulse • Start-ups accelerate the transformation
	11 Be fast	• Act decisively, not hesitantly

7.1 CREATING A PLAN

How to Create a Blueprint for the Digital Transformation

In 1964, Canadian media analyst Marshall McLuhan noted the dangers of newspaper publishers being so reliant on classified advertising. "As soon as another medium comes along for this information, the business model of the press will collapse." That's precisely what happened at the turn of the new millennium. Since then ads for property, automobiles, and jobs have all moved online, and newspaper publishers are experiencing their worst-ever crisis.

However, this is not true for all of them. In a powerful show of strength, publisher Axel Springer reinvented itself as a digital company. Since 2005, the newspaper group has followed a meticulous plan, and has acquired a stake in some 70 digital companies—including successful online advertising portals that are the new home of classified advertising—and has launched around 90 of its own initiatives.

How to Make a Digital Transformation Work

Springer's 10-year transformation process focused on change at all three levels. By acquiring digital companies, the publishing house ventured into completely new ecosystems, while dramatically reshaping its business architecture. It strengthened its foundations by overhauling its technical infrastructure and setting the corporate culture to digital. Springer went on the offensive in five areas:

1. *Subscription offensive:* By offering the subscription service BILDplus, the publisher destroyed the belief that journalistic content should be offered online for free. In 2016, more than 300,000 subscribers paid between €4.99 and €14.99 a month to read the best articles and view videos.

2. *Integration offensive:* Launched in 2013, WeltN24 is the group's first offering across the three platforms of print, TV, and online. The heart is the newsroom, where the journalistic content is written for *Welt* online and the various print editions of *Die Welt*, and where the videos for news broadcaster N24 are filmed, all according to the motto "online first." As is the trend, the website has an increasing emphasis on video content from N24.

3. *Early-stage offensive:* In 2013, Springer founded Axel Springer Plug and Play, an incubator for new digital start-ups. The start-ups received €25,000 for their initial costs, office space for three months, mentors, and technical support from the publisher. If business went well, further funding was provided. By 2016, the publisher had a stake in more than 70 promising young start-ups.
4. *U.S. offensive:* In 2016, Springer acquired the business portal Business Insider, often referred to as the *Wall Street Journal* for the digital generation. With 200 million users a month, *Springer* is now one of the world's six biggest media groups in terms of reach.
5. *Collaborative offensive:* Digital companies deliberately seek out alliances. Thus, Springer partnered with Samsung to offer South Korean smartphone customers an attractive news portal. The UpDay app delivers important need-to-know news, as well as updates from personal areas of interest. As a tailored news service for the mobile generation, it offers a playground for the journalism of tomorrow.

Springer needed a decade to reinvent itself for the digital age. As this example shows, just as with any complex transformation, a digitization program needs a structure and a plan. Short-term thinking and simply optimizing isolated solutions are not enough.

7.2 THINK BIG: DIGITIZING THE ENTIRE ENTERPRISE

By the end of the transformation process, digitization will have touched and changed every aspect of the business. We already know this, which is why you need to think holistically, identify key gaps early, and prioritize the issues according to value contribution and impact.

Holistic Thinking

When it comes to getting the company in shape for the digital future, piecemeal thinking isn't enough. By the time the impact of an isolated digital project has spread throughout the organization, the traditional competitors will have overtaken you and new players may even have conquered the market. The digitization plan must take an overarching view of the company and be implemented at all three levels, spread across several years. It must lead the business into new ecosystems, modernize its business architecture, and equip the technical and organizational base for the digital challenges ahead.

A modern strategy process is the best starting point: but what does *modern* mean? A modern strategy isn't drafted on a desk or conjured up in an ivory tower. New ideas are needed. The business must dive in and explore new thinking right from the start. Whereas the 1990s and early 2000s were marked by innovative benchmarking approaches, today there are other sources of inspiration. New ecosystems are emerging between the traditional industries, taking flight with new technologies, and being driven forward by real entrepreneurs. They are everywhere, along with their start-ups from Silicon Valley to Israel, from South Korea to Japan and increasingly China, and sometimes even not too far away from home. Seek them out, contact them, and maybe even arrange a visit.

It's easy to find exciting new companies. Take a look at the finalists in the start-up competitions run by McKinsey, for example. They include the Digital Top 50 (across Europe, and in conjunction with Google and Rocket Internet) and "The Spark." Three start-ups—Relayr, Konux, and NavVis—were chosen as winners of "The Spark" from almost 100 high-quality applicants with incredible ideas, 10 of which made it into the final round. Some of these start-ups have the potential to change your ecosystem, and perhaps one of these could be a potential partner, a source of top talent, or even an attractive acquisition.

The changes needed to the business architecture are much easier to identify, as the importance of a multichannel offering is clear. The best indication of what customers really expect is their behavior. The same is true for product innovations. However, changes to the supply chain, production, and service require a little more groundwork, where typical questions include: Which algorithm offers the greatest potential for predictive maintenance? Which sensors will improve the supply chain?

A digital walk-through, studying and evaluating available digital technology, is no longer enough to appreciate the full impact of these new technologies. Instead, a feasibility study or a proof of concept (POC) is needed, usually with the construction and testing of a prototype of the product or process to be improved. The digital transformation is no trivial undertaking. To ensure its success, two considerations are vital right at the planning stage.

Prioritize by Value Contribution

Once the overarching plan is in place, it's no longer about the What, but about the When. Which area will we tackle first? To decide, management must assess what value contribution is generated using which measures at which point in the value chain, and with how much effort over what period. Will the most potential be gained from diving into the new ecosystems? Or will there be better returns from an improved understanding of customer needs using big data and advanced analytics? Perhaps the fastest value contribution will be realized from a digital restructuring of production or logistics.

It's not an easy decision. After all, companies are often entering new territory here, and they lack experience. It's also important to determine whether the organization in its current form is capable of handling the transformation. In many cases, the schedule is ultimately determined by the talent available. Once the list of priorities has been set, the digital transformers define their timetable. This often spans several years, and includes milestones for achieving targets.

Close the Gaps

After considering the positives, the greatest value contributions, we now consider the negatives. Wherever a capability analysis reveals dangerous shortfalls, fast action is required. Most companies find they come up short when it comes to handling big data and using advanced analytics to analyze it. In 2016, a global survey conducted by McKinsey on the topic revealed that 86 percent of CEOs felt their companies were at best only partially successful in the area, and 25 percent even rated their businesses as complete failures in their big data and advanced analytics operations.

However, intelligent analysis of big data is the primary way to optimize digital products and services, and companies that lack the necessary expertise must decisively invest in building the required skills fast. This is where partnerships can help. When Michael Nilles, chief digital officer at elevator manufacturer Schindler, wanted to speed up his company's capabilities in data analysis, artificial intelligence, and self-learning machines, he targeted partnerships with GE and Huawei. The partners even established a shared office for their teams in Silicon Valley.

A lack of agility in production was the first gap that jewelry maker Swarovski sought to close on its journey into the digital world. The

Austrians invested almost €5 million and 50,000 engineering hours in a production line that cost-effectively processes even small order volumes. Their digital product palette now includes assortments that can satisfy ever more individual customer needs.

However, today's customers also want a multichannel offering with payment options across all channels, and this is another area where Swarovski set about closing its other expensive gap. Today, Swarovski not only runs brick-and-mortar stores in cities around the world, but also operates a digital sales platform that sells its own products and even acts as a marketplace for luxury accessories of other manufacturers.

To shore up another weakness, the jewelry maker invested a further €5 million. Swarovski had been unable to form partnerships to help leverage ideas and technology, so the company renovated an old factory and transformed it into loft offices where new high-tech companies work alongside Swarovski developers. Those businesses with the most promising ideas are rewarded with investment from the Austrian crystal specialist, and several successful partnerships have already been formed. One example is a partnership with fitness band manufacturer Misfit. To power the display and tracking instruments in the bands, Swarovski engineers supply tiny solar cells, which they developed for decorative crystals that convert solar energy into colorful displays. Misfit and Swarovski are already looking at further collaboration in the field.

Siemens also saw potential for improvement in its partnership management, at least where start-ups are concerned. In 2016, the firm founded next47 as part of its digitization program. The Start-up Unit, as Siemens calls the department, has been given €1 billion over the next five years to support young and innovative companies and to buy a stake in them. The unit focuses on the areas of artificial intelligence, autonomous machines, decentralized electrification, connected mobility, and blockchain applications.

The transformation into a digital company is a marathon, not a sprint. A road map lasting several years should be planned that addresses all three levels covered in our What chapters: Which new ecosystems does the company want to break into, and what role will it play there? How will digitization change the business architecture from marketing through to production? And how should the organizational and technological foundations be strengthened to achieve this?

7.3 SURPRISE! IT'S ABOUT THE CUSTOMER

All successful digital companies like Apple, Google, and Amazon have one thing in common: without exception, they design their products and processes firmly from the point of view of the customer, end to end. Customer desires and needs determine what they offer and how. So what do customers expect? And what are the pitfalls that can allow a product or service to fall below customer expectations?

Answers differ, of course, depending on the industry, but moving away from the actual product properties, customers always expect seamless and smooth processes from ordering through to delivery and after-sales service. However, that's still the exception rather than the norm in many companies. Anyone who has ever called a wireless provider's technical support line knows all about it. First you wait an eternity on hold, then there's a long-drawn-out process of identifying the problem, and then you're forwarded through endless agents until the problem is finally resolved, or until you slam the phone down in frustration.

Optimizing Critical Processes

Thus, successful digital companies all prioritize processes that are targeted at the customer. It's generally a manageable number. A telecom firm that analyzed its interaction with customers identified five key processes: contract selection and signing, the payment process, contract management (adding or canceling services), customer communication in the event of disruptions or problems, and contract termination.

Customers who place an order today no longer tolerate their order slowly making its way through the various organizational functions until it's eventually dispatched and completed. Instead, they expect streamlined, seamless processes across all functions—an end-to-end process. They expect it to be digital and possible in just a few clicks, regardless of whether they have a query, want to change a contract, or are submitting a complaint. Companies that can offer this will have a competitive edge.

In digitizing and restructuring their processes, companies should focus on the customer journey and their touch points with the customer—an idea shaped by the successful online retailers. Each point along the journey from first contact to final purchase is planned to make the process as easy and as convenient as possible for the customer, and to provide excellent support. The customer experience is at the heart of the process. The concept can also easily be applied to the B2B space, and even to internal customers.

When digitizing processes, ask yourself at each touch point: What does the customer expect? What does the process depend on, and where are the pain points if something goes wrong? As obvious as these questions may be, the philosophy is still far from standard. Conventional organizations tend to focus on efficiency rather than customers. So what really is important to customers? Which customer journeys are relevant? Which customer journey should I start with? How do I move from the first customer journey to the next? And how can I generate digital momentum throughout the organization?

Direct banks like ING-DiBa have clearly correctly identified their customer pain points. They have reduced the time it takes to open a bank account from weeks to minutes. With user-friendly digitized processes they have successfully captured large numbers of customers from traditional banks.

ING-DiBa digitized all of its central customer journeys over the last 10 years—for example, in opening an account

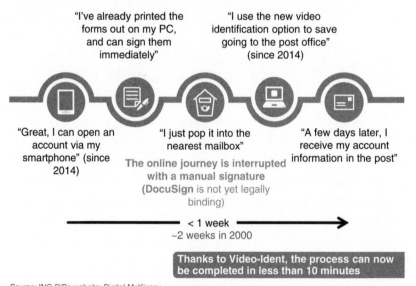

"I've already printed the forms out on my PC, and can sign them immediately"

"I use the new video identification option to save going to the post office" (since 2014)

"Great, I can open an account via my smartphone" (since 2014)

"I just pop it into the nearest mailbox"

The online journey is interrupted with a manual signature (DocuSign is not yet legally binding)

"A few days later, I receive my account information in the post"

< 1 week
~2 weeks in 2000

Thanks to Video-Ident, the process can now be completed in less than 10 minutes

Source: ING-DiBa website; Digital McKinsey

Processes related to investment products all focus on a smooth experience for the customer, and in the event of problems the pain point is quickly identified. Elevator manufacturer Schindler, whose elevators carry one billion passengers globally each day, has shifted its focus to predictive maintenance in its digitization efforts. "We fix problems before our customers even know there is one," according to Michael Nilles, CDO at Schindler.

The Swiss firm has partnered with Apple to drive the strategy forward. Using the iOS operating system and apps specifically developed for Schindler, the firm's service technicians now receive meticulous plans for their service deployments. Sensors in the elevators enable remote monitoring, and continuously measure critical data such as elevator routes, speed, and temperature. No fewer than 200 million units of information are transmitted each day, which are then transmitted to a computer platform where the information is analyzed and translated into service jobs. Each morning, Schindler field technicians then receive a work list on their FieldLink app together with suggestions for the most efficient routes between the service deployments, and a list of spare parts that will likely be needed for the work. The technicians can even order these spare parts on the app to ensure they are ready and waiting before they arrive at the service location. Once at the location, the engineers can check the FieldWiki app to read through repair instructions or view videos. "Our customer service is now faster and more efficient," according to CDO Nilles.

For some customers, simply not having the right information is a pain point. Maersk, the world's biggest container shipping group, developed an app for its customers that allows them to track their containers in real time. The app can send notifications if delays are likely or if early delivery is expected. Customers can also view information about Maersk schedules or find the address of the nearest shipping office.

Concept Iteration: Learning with the Customer

Since digitization makes product and service offerings possible that never before existed, there is no way of knowing what customers really appreciate and what they don't use. Companies have few options, then, but to look once again at how the digital companies do it.

To save time and costs, they first develop a product that only meets basic requirements and offers core essential functions. This is known as the minimum viable product (MVP). Rapid improvements are then implemented based on customer reactions. Tesla and iPhone were initially launched with limited features, but effectively addressed a customer pain point. Tesla offered the world's first luxury electric car, while the iPhone did away with clumsy number pads and keyboards. Both products were then continuously improved with the help of customers and their feedback. Until a new hardware product is released, the manufacturers keep their existing products fresh by releasing new software solutions in rapid cycles.

Driving Digitization According to Value Contribution

Of course, it's not just the positives that are revealed by customer feedback. By carefully analyzing customer behavior, pain points can be identified where customers migrate and revenues are damaged. In retail and gastronomy, long lines are certainly one of these weak points.

In 2015, Starbucks added mobile ordering and payment to its app. This allows customers to order their coffee from the nearest store on the go, prepared to their precise preferences. It's also linked to the Starbucks loyalty scheme, and since it allows payment, customers can simply walk into the branch, stroll past the lines, grab their coffee, and go. The app has been a real success and is well used, resulting in increasing revenues. However, the company also gains something equally valuable, if not more so—a treasure trove of data on the buying habits of its customers. This gives it a direct route into that most difficult of fields, one-to-one marketing. Starbucks can now send its customers tailored offers through its app based on their preferences.

Amazon identified the more mundane aspects of shopping, such as buying household supplies like washing detergent, as a pain point for its customers. The online retailer therefore introduced a Wi-Fi-enabled replenishment device for customers, Dash Button. Now, when customers notice their detergent is running out, they can simply press the button, which sends a replenishment order to Amazon via Wi-Fi. No further steps are necessary because the delivery address and credit card number are already stored in the customer's Amazon account.

While the traditional analog companies largely rely on conjecture when it comes to ascertaining customer desires or pain points, digital companies are able to draw on a vast pool of data. They can precisely analyze which product variant is well received or poorly received, by whom, at what time, and where. They also know the exact point of the customer journey where potential customers leave the process after experiencing a pain point. This knowledge enables data-driven decisions on customer targeting, giving a huge advantage to digital companies.

7.4 BREAKING UP FUNCTIONAL SILOS

The transformation into a digital company is a huge task. New skills and capabilities need to be established throughout the organization. Processes need to be rethought, and structures rebuilt. Pilot projects are initiated. And finally, digital talent needs to be integrated with a completely different working style. The traditional, highly compartmentalized organization is unable to handle all of these challenges, often lacking the agility to keep up with the scope and pace of change. The first task, then, is to equip the organization with the skills it needs to break up its functional silos, but how?

How Digitally Advanced Is the Company?

There's no one-size-fits-all policy toward becoming a digital company. The road depends on the company's current level of digital experience. From a pragmatic perspective, we distinguish three levels:

- *Level 1:* Companies with very little experience of digital and whose core business rarely enters digital territory. This segment includes many traditional machinery manufacturers such as makers of turbines, transmission systems, clutches, powertrains, and so on.
- *Level 2:* Companies that have already confronted the subject of digital, and whose business is attacked by digital companies. These include insurers, telecom companies, energy suppliers, and automakers. They all face the challenge of systematically restructuring their large organizations.
- *Level 3:* This is the fully digital company. It already possesses all the critical capabilities needed for the digital age, and decisively seeks to expand its business.

Naturally, all manner of in-between stages is possible, but for our purposes we will use these classifications. This book deals with Level 1 and Level 2 companies. Where are you? A quick stocktaking exercise and external benchmarking helps to find out. The Digital Quotient (DQ) that we briefly introduced in Chapter 3.1 enables very precise stocktaking. If you are interested and want to know where your own company stands, read more at www.mckinsey.com/business-functions/digital-mckinsey/how-we-help-clients/digital-quotient.

Organizational maturity

Maturity	Level 1	Level 2	Level 3
	New digital business unit	Digital competence center	Fully digital company
Descrip-tion	• New unit, separated from core business • Managed largely autonomously • Often attacks existing business models of other business units	• Overarching scope • Digital competence center as driver of the change process • Systematic end-to-end digitization of all processes in the company	• Company built or rebuilt according to digital principles • Typically a start-up
Talent	• Internal digital talent bundled into new unit • External talent hired • Often with start-up acquisition	• CDO • Digital natives systematically integrated into end-to-end processes	• Digital natives build the business
IT	• Greenfield	• Two-speed IT architecture	• DevOps ready
Example	• Swarovski	• ING	• Spotify

In general, Level 1 companies making the break into digital should first focus on establishing a digital business unit. This unit is typically autonomous and has its own mandate, often separate from the core business. It needs a team with digital experience to develop an ambitious business plan, and initiate its own pilot projects while being strictly managed with milestones. Level 2 companies, in contrast, are aiming to restructure their entire organization in stages. To this end, a digital competence center should be established that dovetails with the operations of the business units.

Establishing a New Digital Business Unit
The first step is always the most difficult, and this is certainly the case when establishing the first digital business unit in a traditional company. These

early pioneers have to start almost from scratch, and have no structured processes on which to build digital capabilities or develop digital products and services. They find themselves isolated in a traditional organization, and often don't even have their own budget. But one thing they do have is freedom. They can establish fast decision paths, they don't need to worry about the existing IT systems, and they can employ modern methods such as agile scrum development that breaks down complex development projects into short sprints on the road to developing a final product. The people involved should include freshly recruited talent, the best people from the core business of the parent company, and sometimes a recently acquired start-up form the crystallizing core from which the pioneers can grow.

A wealth of experience on what is most important for digital business units reveals four factors that clearly determine the success or failure of companies that have introduced agile methods:

1. The organizational structure must be specifically geared toward products for which fixed teams have autonomous responsibility.
2. The product owners and their teams must collaborate as closely as possible with IT.
3. Managers must see themselves more as coaches and coordinators as part of an overarching strategy, and transfer responsibility to their teams.
4. Just as with start-ups, budgets start off low at first for products offering the minimum necessary features. This budget is then increased for further development if the product is a success.

The fourth point is critical: this is where the old and new worlds collide. Can the existing management team productively manage such a business unit? In many cases, the answer is no. Traditional organizations often lack the crucial digital skills and experience. Instead, the management team should hire an experienced expert, or alternatively invite a venture capitalist whose network of experts would greatly increase the chances of success, to invest with them in their digital business unit.

Establishing a Digital Competence Center
Level 2 companies face a myriad of very different paths, and it's vital that they choose the one that best suits their needs. Much can be learned from

those companies that broke into the digital world early, starting off with successful pilot projects, and then firmly digitizing their core processes. The next step is now about switching the entire organization to digital, which is where the digital competence center comes in.

Digital competence center: Example for organizational embedding

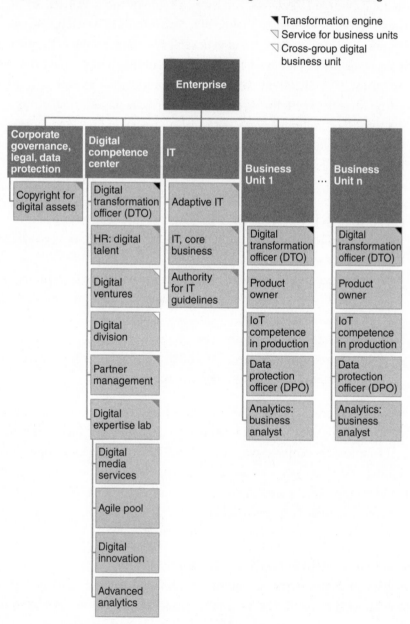

Under this concept, the digital competence center primarily acts as a service provider to the business units. The digital transformation office (DTO) sets the pace, and coordinates and manages the transformation as an engine of change, working closely with the DTOs of the individual business units. The competence center is responsible for recruiting digital talent and for their career development. A digital ventures unit helps to identify acquisition targets and prepare for the purchase. If these new acquisitions can't immediately be integrated into one of the existing business units, a digital division could be established to accommodate them. The partner management function helps establish the new digital ecosystem.

Now we need a digital expertise lab that brings together all the experts with their new skills. This includes agile coaches, user experience/user interface (UX/UI) designers responsible for the user interfaces of the apps and websites, and project managers for the upcoming innovations. It also includes data analysts and employees with experience in digital media. The digital expertise lab and its assorted team will drive the first wave of digitization through the company.

This means the IT department also needs to be ready. To establish the two-speed IT architecture that we looked at earlier in the book, we now need to strengthen its systems and ability to process data and information. Three capabilities are particularly important: adaptive IT, data processing for the core business, and authority for IT guidelines. Adaptive IT processes the data collected by the apps, and builds the infrastructure for processing big data as well as the software tools and interfaces. Adaptive IT also consolidates and runs the IT environments of desktop computers, mobile devices, and servers. Another team looks after shared network elements and platforms such as Skype, the cloud, and identity management. Finally, an overarching team ensures that the intellectual property rights (IPR) of all digital products are clearly and consistently managed according to common guidelines.

The competence center and IT support the business units through the digitization process, and each unit has its own DTO to liaise with the competence center and drive the transformation forward. Product owners manage the cross-functional teams for digitizing the customer-facing processes, and initiate corresponding pilot projects by drawing on the central resources of the competence center. In most cases, business-specific skills are also needed—for example, the deployment of sensors for the Internet of Things, or data analysis capabilities to analyze the data delivered by those sensors.

Granted, establishing a functioning competence center and digitizing the relevant business units are complex tasks. This is why some companies use the digital build-operate-transfer (DBOT) approach, especially when time is of the essence. DBOT aims to significantly accelerate the establishment of digital skills and digital business units. Companies employing this approach use temporary external expert teams, and first establish their new business models in a separate business unit. This approach means that experts who are well-connected in the digital world can provide valuable services, such as helping in the recruitment of digital talent and establishing new business units. The managers of the unit build up their core team and then get to work. Once the team is fully assembled, the first positive results can be expected in just a few months, after which time the external experts can gradually be replaced with in-house talent.

Assigning a Mandate and Building Digital Talent

The digital competence center as the driving force of digitization and as a service provider to the business units can start work with around 15 employees. This includes a manager, perhaps two employees for the central digital transformation office, and one person each for HR and participating units. The digital expertise lab should be staffed with around 10 experts who are familiar with agile methods and analytics. Another two employees in IT are responsible for the area of adaptive IT. First, the back-end systems of the apps, the infrastructure for big data, the software tools, and the interfaces need to work. Depending on the company size and its level of digitization, additional resources may be needed to operate the systems for desktop PCs, mobile devices, and servers.

A large technology firm gradually switched its organization to digital by first training five teams in agile methodologies, and then sending them to work. The experiences they gained from their training and work deployments were fed back into the training material, which was then used to benefit the next wave of 20 teams. In turn, their experiences were used to train the next teams. At the same time, the company assigned fixed, cross-functional teams to the products, moved IT closer to the customer, and reduced not only the time for developments, but also the error rate.

The term *digital natives* doesn't necessarily apply only to people, but can also refer to companies that were born digital. Google and Amazon are the best examples, but there are many others such as Spotify that have long moved on from the start-up phase. In terms of their digitization processes, only a little optimization work remains, but they serve as a good example to all the rest. Digital companies share many commonalities, the most important of which is the fact that decisions are data-driven and never based on gut instinct. Their employees form hypotheses from this often incomplete data and translate it into a product that is also often incomplete. This product is then tested on the market, and its success or failure is quickly analyzed. Google, for example, tests several thousand ideas each year, and fosters a culture that celebrates failure, because that's where we learn most. Another thing that digital natives have in common is speed. Agile teams quickly develop prototypes, test them on the market, and either ditch them quickly or improve them based on collected data. This is a huge challenge for traditional firms.

In the next chapter, we describe how Level 2 companies—those that have already confronted the issue of digital and gained some initial experiences—lay the foundations in terms of personnel and organization required to implement the digitization plan outlined in this chapter. Chapter 9 then explains how to scale up the plan throughout the organization.

☐-☐-⑧-☐-☐

HOW? RAMPING UP THE DIGITAL COMPANY

NOW THAT THE *plan is ready, it's time to get the organization in shape for digitization: the leap from theory to practice.*

At the end of 2016, Facebook founder Mark Zuckerberg wrote on his Facebook page what had been keeping him busy over the past few months. He had been writing control software for the many unconnected smart systems in his home, controlling heating and air-conditioning, door and window locks, music, and TV. And while the social media mogul humorously described the difficulties he encountered during his programming, he also delivered three serious messages to his employees and all competitors. First message: The topic is so important to me personally that I'm investing a lot of time in it as CEO. Second message: Hey, look! I'm technically skilled enough to do the programming myself. Third message: Dear competitors, we're going to fight in this highly competitive area and realize our own vision.

This is how managers of successful digital companies lead. Storytelling is one of the most effective management instruments. There are a lot of things they do differently from the managers of traditional analog companies. And when it comes to digital transformations, the latter managers could learn a thing or two from Facebook, Google, and Amazon.

This chapter describes how companies can apply the most important digital methods and philosophies. What does a digital operating system look like? Where can I find the right team? What role does the customer play? What does agility mean, or permanent testing and learning? What role does cultural change play, and how do I drive it forward successfully? What form does authority take in a digital company? Which team is responsible, and which key performance indicators (KPIs) and principles are used? And how is the digital company managed—what role does management play? And where do I find digital talent?

Companies face different challenges depending on their level of digitization. As we recall, digital novices at Level 1 first establish an autonomous digital unit. However, they don't have to perfect their efforts by first making sure they've completed all the points laid out in this chapter. It's speed that counts. Instead, they are free to pick and choose which sections of the chapter to study. For the more digitally advanced Level 2 companies that are gradually digitizing the processes of all their business units, this chapter can serve as a road map. What companies at both levels have in common is that they need to act more "digital," with the ultimate aim of emulating those companies that were born digital. The journey follows four principles: the switch to a digital operating system, anchoring cultural change, steering by KPIs and milestones, and managing like a digital native. The next section will look at what that means, and how the first pilot projects can be started.

8.1   SWITCHING TO THE DIGITAL OPERATING SYSTEM

To switch your business to digital, three fundamentals are needed: (1) recruit a team that's as enthusiastic as it is technically proficient and (2) that values speed above perfection, and (3) introduce milestone-based project management in the style of the venture capitalist.

Recruiting and Expanding the Team

Data Scientist, IoT Software Developer, User Experience Design Expert, Product Owner, Scrum Master. These are job titles from the digital world. But do you know what the job titles actually mean, or what drives these people? Two things are certain: they're needed and there aren't enough suitable candidates. Where can they be found, and how can they be recruited?

Job fairs have only limited success. Above all, digital natives need to be lured by exciting and meaningful work through the channels where these new, mostly young stars of the future spend most of their time. Social media, blogs, and start-up conferences are good places to start. Use the new formats like hackathons and start-up competitions to get to know digital natives. Be present at the leading digital events and conferences such as the Consumer Electronics Show (CES), Disrupt SF Hackathon, South by Southwest (SXSW) Interactive, Launch Festival, or competitions within academic institutions such as HackMIT and the UC Berkeley start-up competition.

These are all good opportunities for traditional enterprises. Digital talent isn't put off by a big corporate name, but by a dull job profile or the lack of concrete challenges. Recruiters need to weave interesting stories and stoke enthusiasm for the new work ahead. Potential candidates are generally attracted by authentic values and strong corporate stories. Interviews should be conducted by top-level managers, even as high as the CEO, with people who exude the passion needed to attract talent and build the fledgling employer brand. Finally, the company must strive at least as hard as the candidates to present itself as an appealing prospect, and to fend off the attractive employers who top all the relevant rankings.

Skilled digital natives love ambitious projects and big ideas. They want to rewrite the future of industrial robotics and automation rather than simply optimize the logistics processes in a plant. For recruiters, that's often only a matter of tone. The recruiters themselves should also be part of the digital community, and not come across as people from a distant planet. This is a challenge that many HR departments often find overwhelming. There are specialist agencies and freelancers who can step in to fill in this gap, at least for the early setup phase. An experienced digital recruiter, then, must be right at the top of the list of recruitment targets.

If, despite all the good advice, companies still fail to put together a digital team, they can just go ahead and buy one instead by acquiring a start-up with all the necessary talent. One prominent example is Walmart. In 2011, the retailer paid $300 million to acquire the social media company Kosmix.

And since it's so difficult to find talent, it's even more important to retain it. Work must be challenging and future-focused, and the working environment must be appealing with open working areas in attractive locations. Creativity is directly proportional to the number of restrictive walls. Training and one-to-one coaching must also be on the table, as well as intensive mentoring and personal development plans for each individual.

However, it's wrong to assume that all open positions must be filled with experienced digital talent only. Companies need to learn to develop talent themselves. They need to be open to young people, and, more than ever, to recruit by potential rather than references and reputation. Companies should be able to give everyone in their organization the opportunity to experience and learn the new digital technologies, and this includes providing the space for talent to develop naturally. Google, for example, gives its employees the freedom to spend up to 20 percent of their time working on their own chosen tasks, and 3M introduced a similar measure years ago.

Ability to Establish Fast Concept Iteration

Fast concept iteration is something that Steve Jobs believed in. When the Apple founder launched the first iPhone in 2007, it still only used the slow Global System for Mobile (GSM) transmission standard even though his rivals were using the faster Universal Mobile Telecommunications Service (UMTS). The early iPhone couldn't even receive GPS signals for satellite navigation. Digital natives refer to it as the minimum viable product (MVP), a product that offers only the minimum possible number of essential features. For the product to be a success, it needs to address a pain point, a place in the market where customers encounter problems. With its touch screen design, Apple displaced number pads and keyboards and hit on one such pain point. With Apple's open interface, a rapidly growing range of apps soon followed that could be downloaded to the device, thus greatly increasing the appeal of the iPhone. Customers did the rest: the Apple engineers fed reactions and comments of customers back into development virtually in real time, and before long they had the most popular smartphone in the world.

Companies pursuing a digital transformation should adopt the MVP approach even if it means their engineers and designers will need to rein in their quests for perfection. It prevents expensive and protracted product development based purely on assumption. U.S. innovation guru Steve Blank even goes so far as to encourage businesses to see the customer as a partner in the product development process. Early adopters in particular should be seen as kindred visionaries, and should be utilized. However, companies still have to identify a particular pain point for the first version of the product, which is no easy task.

Even Lufthansa followed the MVP route when it digitized its check-in process. This critical core process was adapted to the technological possibilities and customer needs over several stages, following a continuous and iterative method. Time and time again, a crucial question had to be answered: How much change are passengers willing to accept? Nonetheless, the airline had identified a real pain point—standing in line in front of a check-in counter has always been one of the downsides of flying.

As a first step, Lufthansa installed check-in machines, where friendly employees were on hand to help passengers with any problems. Customers welcomed the service. In the next stage, the airline offered customers the option of checking in at home on a PC and printing out the boarding card themselves. The move promised more convenience, and was only one step removed from using the check-in machines. Again, customers welcomed it. It also meant that Lufthansa was able to significantly reduce costs since the customer now provided the necessary hardware. And as the process went mobile with the spread of smartphones and apps, the digitally attuned Lufthansa customers could now free themselves of the PC and printer altogether, and now simply scan the boarding passes on their smartphones.

The process is far from over, however. Just as with lean production in the past, continuous improvement is the order of the day. Lufthansa rival KLM, for example, as one of the first partners of Facebook, uses a chatbot on Facebook Messenger as a new channel for communication and interaction. KLM customers can now call up their digital boarding cards on Messenger. The service also means that KLM can provide its passengers a far more personalized offering via Facebook. Just like WhatsApp, travelers receive a push notification telling them they can now check in or notifying them of any changes. The development has personalized the check-in process.

A key component of the digital operating system is its specific ways of resolving problems. If digital companies want to redevelop or improve products or processes, they tend to rely on design thinking. This is where cross-disciplinary teams tackle problems by using the classic methods of designers: observe, understand, develop ideas, translate quickly into prototypes (rapid prototyping), test on the market, and immediately feed customer reactions back into product improvements. The aim is to produce a simple solution that is also simple from the point of view of the customer. After all, the solution is ultimately being developed from the customer's perspective and for the customer's benefit.

Above all, the customer interfaces must be as simple and intuitive as possible. The mobile apps of today will likely become the voice-based interfaces of tomorrow. Voice assistants like Alexa from Amazon, Google Home, or Apple's Siri provide simple and intuitive input options that are much easier than screens and keyboards. Online retailers are developing check-out processes that enable the customer to complete purchases in a single click rather than running through multiple steps. Digital natives like PayPal and Amazon already offer this. There are other examples of innovative design concepts that are focused on the needs of the customer, and that radically simplify the buying process. One of these is Amazon's Dash Button, which allows customers to order replenishments for frequently used items like laundry detergent with just the push of a button.

To anchor design thinking in the innovation and product development process, management itself must understand these technologies, and ideally have experience of them. Participating in hackathons—team events geared toward the shared improvement of a digital process—is a good starting point. An effective exercise is for a team member, for example the manager, to play the role of the customer, and always argue from the customer's point of view. Although all companies claim to focus on the customer, too often the customer's voice is overheard or taken into consideration only at the end of the process.

Establish Steering by Milestones

What marks a digital enterprise? The fact that it forms fact-based hypotheses and takes data-driven decisions. To come by these facts, new data needs to be collected, whether self-generated or acquired from third parties. Companies should therefore ensure they always follow measurable targets—for example, reducing process costs or increasing customer acceptance, conversion rates, or process speed. Naturally, multiple targets can be pursued at the same time.

These targets must be anchored with KPIs with meaningful metrics defined for each process to be digitized. The targets for the milestones to be achieved can be derived either from the company's business targets or from benchmarking. The targets and the actual results on the given dates are then reconciled to determine whether the milestones have been hit. The third section of this chapter explains how this is done in practice.

8.2 ANCHORING THE CULTURE CHANGE

According to management theorist Peter Drucker: "Culture eats strategy for breakfast." We are only too happy to underestimate the importance of corporate culture, yet it plays a crucial role in digitization: with a traditional culture, a digital transformation won't succeed. It's up to top management to trigger the change—from me to we, from control to trust, from directives to autonomy, from risk-averse to risk taker, from perfectionist to trial and error, and from just enough to reach for the stars. Such cultural change is far more important than superficial niceties like trendy loft offices or buddy-buddy managers who entertain the team.

Developing a Work Environment

How does a business develop a corporate culture that fits with the digital world? The transformation starts with the work environment. That includes flexible working hours, an office landscape in which teams feel at ease, and technical equipment that not only is up to the task, but is fun to use.

The office of the digital age is as flexible as its employees. Very few people will always sit at the same desk in the same room. Instead, most will sometimes work from home, on the way to the customer, or even in a different branch office. Whenever they come into the office, they simply look around for a free desk. There are work cafés as well as standard conference rooms for the frequent work involving teams. If quiet contemplation is needed, rooms are available with comfortable seating. And of course, everyone is always available online and on the firm's network wherever they are.

Cultural Transformation: Addressing Four Dimensions at the Same Time

At least as important as the hardware are the immaterial assets. Do the values and standards of the company foster the new spirit, from collaboration and open communication to cross-hierarchy togetherness? Do the management principles fit with the target culture? Do employees feel empowered by their managers in the cultural change? And have managers been offered the right incentives to drive the change forward? To align your corporate culture with the needs of digitization, four dimensions must be addressed: generate understanding, create formal structures, build skills, and act as a role model.

Rapid and long-term cultural change requires work on four dimensions at the same time

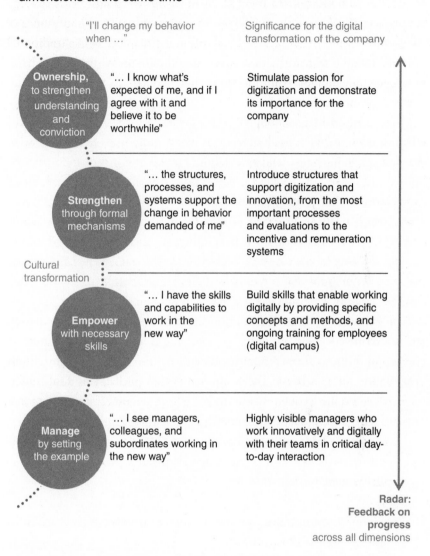

"I'll change my behavior when ..."

Significance for the digital transformation of the company

Ownership, to strengthen understanding and conviction

"... I know what's expected of me, and if I agree with it and believe it to be worthwhile"

Stimulate passion for digitization and demonstrate its importance for the company

Strengthen through formal mechanisms

"... the structures, processes, and systems support the change in behavior demanded of me"

Introduce structures that support digitization and innovation, from the most important processes and evaluations to the incentive and remuneration systems

Cultural transformation

Empower with necessary skills

"... I have the skills and capabilities to work in the new way"

Build skills that enable working digitally by providing specific concepts and methods, and ongoing training for employees (digital campus)

Manage by setting the example

"... I see managers, colleagues, and subordinates working in the new way"

Highly visible managers who work innovatively and digitally with their teams in critical day-to-day interaction

Radar:
Feedback on progress
across all dimensions

Communication: Talk Digital and Act Digital

Without effective communication, both internal and external, there can be no cultural change, and the digital transformation will fail. Although it could be argued that this applies to all companies whatever their current state, when it comes to digital transformation, the importance of communication is taken to a whole new level. It's not just about informing employees, but about motivating them to get involved and be passionate about the change. This is possible only by overhauling the old, traditional values. Other players in and around the business also need to be convinced—most importantly, customers, shareholders, suppliers, and partners. Clear and active communication is needed that takes into account the needs of all target groups.

Today, the traditional communication channels are supplemented with effective new media. Town hall sessions where employees can engage with the management, blogs, and newsletters replace the in-house journal or holiday message, while external communication now takes the form of tweets and YouTube videos. With digitization, the frequency of messages increases all the time. Instead of scheduled annual or quarterly cycles, employees and external parties expect information on tap. Firms exhibiting at major events like the Consumer Electronics Show (CES) in Las Vegas or the Auto Show in Detroit accompany their exhibits with live streams and a constant stream of tweets, blogs, and Facebook posts.

Unlike in the past, good communication today is no longer a one-way street. Town hall meetings give employees and managers the chance to connect and discuss issues. Comments and replies can be posted to blogs and Twitter and Facebook posts. Companies that find all this a little awkward haven't quite arrived in the digital world, where all comments and criticisms from employees and outsiders are opportunities to improve.

The most important thing is that all communications and messages follow a well-thought-out and orchestrated communication strategy. Three factors are crucial:

1. General communication should focus on brief, clear core messages—less is often more.
2. A clear communication plan and process should be followed, with the key questions being: who provides the content, which subjects are covered and which media are used, what are the best occasions, and which external and internal channels are used?
3. A communication product owner is needed who keeps the content up to date, analyzes measurable findings, and delivers improvements in communications.

And yet, despite all the enthusiasm for the new communication channels, the traditional media can still be an important strategic weapon in the digital transformation. Once again, GE sets the standards. Its 2015 annual report was simply titled "Digital Industrial," demonstrating above all else the importance of digitization at GE.

8.3 STEERING CHANGE

Back to our role models, the venture capitalists. We need a steering committee for our transformation based on the venture capitalist model linking cash injection to milestones, and defining the right, meaningful KPIs that are constantly monitored and analyzed.

CDO: Hero or Fig Leaf?

The digital transformation needs more than just a pacesetter; it needs proper management in the team, from an open-minded supervisory committee and an involved executive management that includes a modern chief financial officer who dynamically adjusts budgets and management instruments, to a chief digital officer (CDO) with comprehensive authority. Take the difference between rowing and white-water rafting: while rowing involves constant, predictable conditions, rafting throws up unexpected challenges at all times. This is why the helmsman in the white-water rafting of.digitization must be more like a coach and a team leader rather than just a pacesetter.

The CDO plays a key role, demonstrating passion for digital and igniting this passion in all employees. The CDO is a strategist, customer analyst, product innovator, technical expert ... the role demands everything. The CDO links organizational departments, establishes cross-functional teams, uses networking skills to recruit external talent, motivates people, and represents them effectively at board level.

Bill Ruh, CDO at GE, is one of the best in the business. He's not only responsible for the cross-divisional development of GE's industrial Internet strategy and for software development in all business units, but he's also the CEO of GE Digital, which in 2016 turned over $6 billion delivering software and services to industry. This combination of responsibilities ensures that Ruh has an important voice in all decisions. In short, the CDO must not be seen just as a digital expert, but must also have executive responsibility. CDOs must be assigned their own budget with sufficient funds, over which they have full control for talent recruitment and so on. Siemens assigned its new unit next47, established in October 2016 to seek out investment opportunities, a budget of $1.1 billion over the next five years.

In organizations with multiple independent divisions, the CDO needs support. Internal digital transformation officers (DTOs) are therefore assigned to each division, but remain part of the cross-company digital transformation office. The DTO is the engine of change in his or her business unit. The job demands confident and independent people who understand their business model and who think and act digital.

Manage Like a VC: Link Budgets to Milestones

When it comes to budgets, managers should take a page out of the venture capitalist playbook. They need to move away from their mentality of deterministic budgets set for a number of years, and instead adopt a strategy of releasing smaller, more manageable tranches when investing in innovative products and businesses. Once a development has reached a defined milestone—for example, the production of the first minimum viable product (MVP) or the successful capture of the first customers—subsequent funding is quickly and nonbureaucratically approved. It is equally important to take appropriate measures—reducing the budget or even ending the venture—if key milestones such as receiving positive customer feedback are not achieved. The most important milestones are defined across the innovation process, from the concept and the first MVP through to market launch and scaling.

Traditional companies find it particularly difficult to scrap projects, and often keep failing initiatives alive to save the reputations of those responsible. Not only does this cost financial and human resources, but it also wastes valuable time in the race to find truly standout innovations. It's irrational behavior. Why would a product that fails even with the early adopters suddenly become a roaring success later? Companies need a body similar to the investment board of a start-up that continuously asks critical questions.

Measure, Analyze, Optimize: Resolute Application of New Steering Systems

To enable data-driven decisions, the company must establish continuously monitored KPIs in all functions, measuring indicators that go beyond order entry, revenue, and profit. Cosmetics group L'Oréal even uses them for strategy, and steers its digital transformation according to three KPIs. The company calls it the 20-50-100 program: by 2020, L'Oréal wants to realize 20 percent of its revenue through digital channels, have a direct relationship with 50 percent of its customers, and enjoy an approval rating of 100 percent in its internally defined "brand love score." It provides management and employees with a clear target and measurable success.

The day-to-day management of digitization, however, tends not to be about strategy; instead, KPIs are set for digital processes. These should meet two criteria: first, the KPIs should be simple, and second, the person who is measured by the KPI should be able to influence it. For example, in Amazon's premium service Prime, the performance of the responsible product manager is assessed based on two KPIs: the growth rate of Prime customers and the churn rate—the number of customers who cancel their Prime membership. Other KPIs such as the profitability of Prime customers are not a measure of performance because they depend on many other factors such as the gross product margin, which can't be directly influenced by the Prime product manager.

Google operates a simple KPI system to assess the performance of its employees and their projects. One of its early investors, John Doerr, brought in objectives and key results (OKR) from Intel. Everyone in the company sets their own targets—from the executive management and department heads, all the way down to individual employees. These targets are quantified as multiple KPIs for a maximum of five projects. Those who manage more must prioritize. Web designers, for example, don't set themselves the target of "the website must improve," but instead state the improvement needed: "30 percent faster site building." Digital natives assess each KPI by a zero-or-one logic, and an average is formed from the KPIs for each project. Target achievement of 75 percent is considered adequate, while a higher value indicates the targets were set too low. A lower value suggests the project should be reviewed to determine whether it should be continued. The projects and their OKR values are published at Google, including those of the CEO. This isn't so much to find the employee of the month, the company says, but rather to ensure that everyone knows what everyone else is working on. Many start-ups such as Spotify, Splunk, and Slack use OKR. However, the methods are equally applicable to large enterprises, Google being the perfect example.

The chart shows how a team that wants to optimize a website for online retail chooses meaningful KPIs for the site. Moving from left to right, we see every point in the customer journey from visiting the website to delivery of the ordered goods. From top to bottom, we see the performance to be measured: the conversion rate, the number and duration of site visits, and technical performance. Possible metrics are then listed for each line. Much can be measured; the art is in knowing which figures are the most meaningful.

Customer-specific KPIs aren't useful just in the end consumer space; industrial companies can also apply them to the classic B2B space. These companies often show glaring weaknesses when it comes to digital communication with the customer, starting with their websites. Employing the right KPIs makes the performance of digital communication easy to measure. And once a company recognizes its weaknesses, it can take targeted steps to resolve them, which will be greatly appreciated by enterprise customers, who, just like end consumers, want things to be clear and simple.

Intelligently applied KPIs are critical to the successful digitization of processes. Metrics need to be measurable, quantified, and relevant. In some ways, it's an evolution of lean management—lean on steroids.

8.4 ENCOURAGING LEADERSHIP AT ALL LEVELS

It doesn't get any easier: management in digital companies works by completely different rules, the first of which is to get involved. Perhaps managers even need a "license to kill."

Top Management Must Lead by Example

The advent of digitization brings challenging times for the top management and middle management of traditional firms. Even before this, these companies were a dying breed with their rigid hierarchies and subordinate foot

KPIs for steering the customer journey

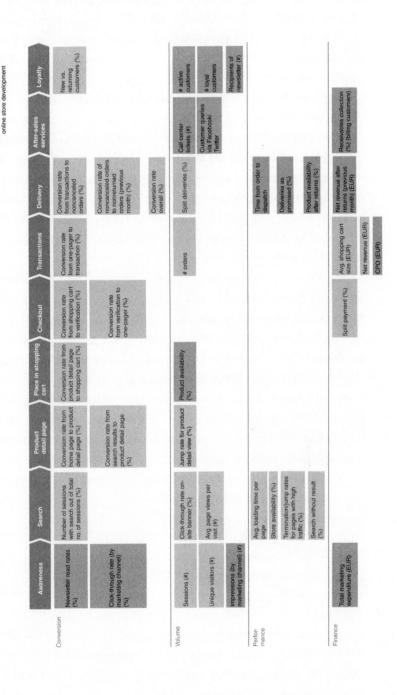

Direct relationship
with online store development

No direct relationship with
online store development

	Awareness	Search	Product detail page	Place in shopping cart	Checkout	Transactions	Delivery	After-sales services	Loyalty
Conversion	Newsletter read rates (%)	Number of sessions with search out of total no. of sessions (%)	Conversion rate from home page to product detail page (%)	Conversion rate from product detail page to shopping cart (%)	Conversion rate from shopping cart to verification (%)	Conversion rate from one-pager to transaction (%)	Conversion rate from transactions to noncanceled orders (%)		New vs. returning customers (%)
	Click-through rate (by marketing channel) (%)		Conversion rate from search results to product detail page (%)		Conversion rate from verification to one-pager (%)		Conversion rate of noncanceled orders to nonreturned orders (previous month) (%)		
							Conversion rate overall (%)		
Volume	Sessions (#)	Click-through rate on-site banner (%)	Jump rate for product detail view (%)	Product availability (%)		# orders	Split deliveries (%)	Call center tickets (#)	# active customers
	Unique visitors (#)	Avg. page views per visit (#)						Customer queries via Facebook/Twitter	# loyal customers
	Impressions (by marketing channel) (#)								Recipients of newsletter (#)
Perfor-mance		Avg. loading time per page					Time from order to dispatch		
		Store availability (%)					Deliveries as promised (%)		
		Termination/jump rates for pages with high traffic (%)					Product availability after returns (%)		
		Search without result (%)							
Finance	Total marketing expenditure (EUR)				Split payment (%)	Avg. shopping cart size (EUR)	Net revenue after returns (previous month) (EUR)	Receivables collection (%) (billing customers)	
						Net revenue (EUR)			
						CPO (EUR)			

soldiers. Digitization, however, demands a significant downward transfer of responsibility, and therefore power. The digital transformation starts with the person at the top, and it's the CEO who must trigger the change in the corporate culture. It's up to the executive board and top management to take responsibility for the digital change.

Authenticity and conviction are vital. And while a new, more casual dress code may play a role, creative, inspiring, and authentic communication is far more effective than allowing sneakers and ditching ties. Managers who have others print off their e-mails or delegate the task of replying in their name are neither inspiring nor authentic. Not everyone can blog like Facebook founder Mark Zuckerberg or tweet quite as often as venture capitalist Ben Horowitz or Tesla owner Elon Musk, but today's CEO should at least be confident with the latest social media, be able to use it, and, most importantly, want to use it.

Digital companies are masters of storytelling, usually on social media, wrapping their messages up in witty and inspiring stories, This is a key motivational and management tool. Jeffrey Immelt, CEO of GE, has made this management tool his own. For five years and across all channels he has been relating his often emotional, always engaging story about how GE wants to become the number one company in the industrial Internet. Immelt impresses customers and business partners not only with his stories, but also with his commitment. Each month, he meets with the pilot partners of Predix, GE's central data and analysis platform, to understand which system functions are really relevant, and how the partners can improve their production and maintenance using big data analyses. Such commitment sends a strong signal: these partnerships are of critical strategic importance, and a matter for the CEO.

License to Kill

Digital natives are on first-name terms. When the successful founder of a large retail group got to know his recently appointed CDO, he left the meeting with the words: "James, if you're going to complete your mission successfully, you're going to need a 'license to kill'; otherwise all the stand-patters and skeptics will leave you to rot." But of course it isn't really about getting rid of the stallers; it's about having the authority and backing to make decisions without having to worry about doing things the traditional way. A new digital unit, for example, mustn't be hindered by restrictive IT guidelines and directives; otherwise, conflict between the new CDO and the head of IT can quickly occur even over basic things like choosing a modern e-mail system. And again, the new unit mustn't be restricted by the group's HR department when it comes to approaching and recruiting new digital talent.

CDOs need to prove their worth in all of these battles. They must recognize when it's better to fight and when it's better to retreat for the sake of the firm, which is no simple task. A CDO must not be left to fight alone. This special agent needs the CEO to watch his or her back. It's the job of the company's leadership to strengthen its transformation agents, and support unpopular decisions that do away with the old.

Starbucks is a perfect example of why it's so important to back the CDO: since 2012, Adam Brotman has led the firm's digitization, reporting directly to the CEO. Brotman has masterminded a digital success story at Starbucks: Wi-Fi in all coffeeshops, mobile apps that allow customers to order on the go, the successful MyRewards loyalty scheme, and much more. The Starbucks digital team played a large part in the massive revenue growth of recent years, the higher customer satisfaction scores, and the increased operational efficiency of the shops. Within five years, the market valuation of Starbucks rose from $19 billion to over $50 billion.

▢–▢–⑨–▢–▢

HOW? SCALING FORCEFULLY

LAST, BUT NOT *least, we look at rolling digitization out to the organization as a whole—Digital@Scale.*

When Max Viessmann took up his position as chief digital officer (CDO) at heating systems manufacturer Viessmann in the summer of 2016, the digitization of the family-run firm moved into its second phase. "The first thing I did was to freeze 80 percent of initiatives," says Viessmann. "Once we had thoroughly analyzed and understood all aspects of digitization in the first phase, it was about concentrating all our resources into growth drivers." So what became of this theoretically brilliant plan that Viessmann followed to launch its digital transformation? "Every day, we learn something new because things change so quickly, including the target scenario," says Viessmann. "It puts the organization under huge pressure to derive new targets from the findings—but it also does it good."

The Viessmann experience is nothing new for companies that are going digital. They create a transformation plan, adapt their organization and processes, and get going. When they come to ramp up the digitization process and roll it out across the organization, they find that events in the real world cause them to change their plans. For example, new digital products and processes are needed following customer feedback. Companies hoping to install a digital mind-set and working methods throughout their organizations can't simply follow the plan laid out in Chapter 7 deterministically. Instead, the organization will need to be continuously adjusted and readjusted after having completed the boot camp of Chapter 8 and adopting a venture capitalist mentality—Digital@Scale demands high flexibility.

9.1 IT'S ABOUT THE WHOLE

Now that we've actuated the digital enterprise, put together the elements for the first pilot projects, and even collected results from those pilot projects, it's about rapid rollout. The first place to start is with a manageable number of customer-facing processes. As we learned, the customer must be at the heart of all considerations in the digital company, and the customers' feedback and data virtually make them the most important "employees." Only then can we start looking at internal processes, from production and supply chain to sales, marketing, and administration.

The Plan Is Alive!

Just as with the individual projects, we also set milestones for the digitization of the entire enterprise. Once a milestone has been achieved, the process gets the green light, and fresh money can be injected for the next steps, because, as we remember, budgets in digital companies are only released on a milestone-to-milestone basis. If our target hasn't been reached by the specified time, we need to ask why: Do we need to change our approach to the plan? Is something wrong with the plan? Does it need to be revised or improved?

Digitization is a journey into the unknown. The transformation plan sets the direction, but will always have to be revisited and adjusted following new findings and experiences. The more processes we digitize, the more their unusualness in the organization recedes, and the new digital system becomes the norm.

Turbocharging with Digital Build-Operate-Transfer

If more speed is needed, we can borrow an approach born in the auto industry: build-operate-transfer (BOT). Automakers commissioned their suppliers to build and operate facilities on their factory premises. Once the specialist firm had brought the facility to full working order, control of the equipment was transferred to the automaker as previously agreed. With digital BOT (DBOT) it's no longer about plants, but it's certainly about specialists. To speed up digitization, companies on the transformation journey can call on the services of digital specialists to rapidly digitize the initial processes. After a given period, usually six to nine months, these specialists can then be gradually replaced by the companies' own employees.

Scaling forcefully

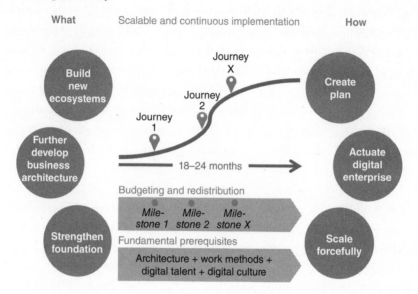

DBOT is far superior to other methods of accelerating the transformation. Permanently outsourcing the digital work to a third-party service provider, for example, means that the business always lacks the necessary expertise in digital, and becomes dangerously reliant on the service provider. Forming a spin-off company with a digitally experienced partner is also fraught with risk: it uncouples the digital future from the traditional business; it transfers out important pillars like the customer relationship, technology, and products; and it limits the company's ability to feed positive impulses back into the existing organization.

Walmart, the world's biggest retailer, is a perfect example of how a large corporation can move from the analog world and take the digital world by storm. WalmartLabs grew from a small core of 60 digital experts and now has offices in India, Brazil, and the United States. In 2016, the organization employed 3,500 specialists, all working on ways to redefine the shopping experience of Walmart customers, whether in the physical stores, on the website, or on mobile devices. The aim was bold: "Redefining e-commerce globally."

9.2 HOW TO TURN IT INTO A WEAPON

IT is critical to the success of the digital transformation. The manner, scope, and timing of measures differ depending on the starting position. Common to all measures, however, is the aim of turning IT into a weapon.

The Method Greatly Depends on the Starting Point

The digital level of the company, as defined in Chapter 7.4, determines which approach is needed when it comes to IT. Level 1 organizations have a clear task: regardless of the installed IT base, they need to form an agile IT team for their new digital unit that responds flexibly to the needs of the unit. For them, it's about immediately applying best practice concepts in their digital unit, and not reverting back to the approaches of the old analog world. Companies at Level 3 have already done much of the work. They are either born digital or digitally transformed, and all work according to agile methods, whether in customer-facing areas, in collaboration with suppliers, or in the back office.

Once again, the people with the most to do are companies at Level 2. In most cases, they have an IT organization that only has isolated agile teams. The majority of their IT operations work according to the old waterfall philosophy—a linear development model originating in industry. Requirements from a list of product specifications are ticked off step-by-step in a laborious process that offers little learning.

Although digital natives like Google are good role models for Level 2 companies because of the way they use IT as a weapon rather than just an administration tool, the ambition of making a big-enough leap to set themselves at a similar level is misguided, because the risk is too high. The traditional IT world still has plenty of life left in it. The data integrity and data relevance maintained by most traditional IT systems are extremely good and should be protected. As such, investment in data integrity must remain a top priority.

The transformation starts with processes that are critical to success and usually customer-facing. All the experiences gained in the areas of agile organization and agile working must now be rolled out to these processes. Think back to the cross-functional teams that develop the first solutions (minimum viable products [MVPs]) in two-week sprints, test them on the market, and quickly incorporate customer feedback into further development. Pace and flexibility mean a real competitive edge here. Lufthansa discovered just that when it came to digitizing its check-in process. Instead of needing the normal six to 12 months to translate findings from customer surveys into a new, improved process, it now only needed two to six weeks. Companies that are able to respond to customer needs in just a matter of weeks can turn their IT into a real weapon.

Success Factors for Two-Speed Companies

Companies that have broken into the digital world from the analog world on the back of a two-speed IT architecture should adopt the DevOps paradigm as practiced by digital natives. DevOps is a contraction of development and operations, and means just that: development and business operations are not separated.

DevOps uses shared incentives and processes for developers and operational personnel, and provides them with shared tools. Software solutions are developed faster and at a higher quality if teams, tools, and IT infrastructure are optimally tailored to one another. To make this possible, companies must be prepared to make extensive investment in technology and personnel.

Rob Alexander, chief information officer (CIO) at the U.S. bank Capital One, oversaw a successful transformation process. Capital One began with a recruitment offensive. The bank had found that while outsourcing work solved short-term problems, in the long term it meant the organization lacked key skills. No sooner were the new recruits on board than they adopted the philosophy of agile development and DevOps. Following the first pilot projects using agile methods, Alexander and his teams discovered that this agile philosophy needn't be of benefit just to specific areas. Today, Capital One's entire IT is agile.

Alexander is a big fan, describing it as a "universal method involving continuous learning where results are tested in the market so that products can be constantly improved until you have a really strong offering that can conquer the market." Capital One is so passionate about driving its digital transformation because it is certain that the victors in the financial industry will be those that operate like the big high-tech firms. That, Alexander says, is where the future of the banking industry lies.

Transforming Agile into the Leading System

In the early stages of the journey toward becoming a two-speed business, the traditional, or legacy, IT dominates the architecture, with the new, agile IT resting on top as an overlay. With the introduction of agility, IT for the first time becomes a weapon because the business can finally act fast, albeit in isolated areas at first.

Gradually, however, agile IT spreads through the legacy IT. For example, if a certain section of customer master data that's managed in the legacy system in customer-facing processes is no longer important, then the underlying databases can and must be adapted.

After some time and following various waves of process transformations, an architectural question arises: how and when should the agile structures be made into the dominant axis, and how should the legacy systems be adapted without jeopardizing data relevance and integrity? It's a critical moment. At some point, the high-speed architecture—the overlay—will come to define the entire system architecture. To ensure the transition succeeds, our experience has taught us that the management of IT should be transferred to a new team so that the old warhorses don't try to rescue their beloved system.

If IT really is to become a corporate weapon, it's not enough simply to inject talent in the respective departments. Digital competence must also be present at management levels, most importantly at the executive board and supervisory board levels, and at the second management level. IT must become regarded as a new core competency of the company, and the CDO should have an influential voice on management committees. Only then can digitization succeed.

9.3   COLLABORATING CLOSELY WITH START-UPS

If companies strive to do everything themselves, it can become an arduous task to scale up digital approaches throughout the organization. Start-ups can deliver new stimulus, be it in the form of a collaboration or as an acquisition. Young digitization professionals help to develop new business ideas, accelerate the transformation, and provide fresh impetus.

New Business Ideas Stimulate the Organization and Deliver Fresh Impulse

Under Armour, ING, and General Motors had the same idea: they all acquired or took a stake in fast-growing start-ups that support their digital goals. Under Armour acquired MapMyFitness, MyFitnessPal, and Edmondo, all fast-growing sports and fitness apps. With these acquisitions, Under Armour now controls the world's largest digital health platform, giving it access to massive data sets on its consumer base.[1] ING operates an

[1] https://www.forbes.com/sites/parmyolson/2015/09/30/kevin-plank-under-armour-apps-technology/#551575f319a9

online mortgage broker platform in the form of Interhyp. General Motors has invested $500 million in Lyft, has bought autonomous vehicle start-up Cruise Automation for $1 billion, and has launched its own car sharing service start-up called Maven.[2] All of these give GM a route to future markets, but also provide a hedge against current trends that are affecting the automotive industry.

However, aside from the strategic benefits of these acquisitions, it's almost as important that, in working with the digital natives of the acquired companies, the employees and managers of the traditional companies learn to think and act digital. For example, Robin Thurston, the former CEO of MapMyFitness, was made chief digital officer of Under Armour after the acquisition. Thurston led the company's connected fitness business—which included the aforementioned acquisitions—and a platform called Record, a hub for health where users could also get updates from popular athletes. Start-ups accelerate the transformation.

Naturally, start-ups can't assume responsibility for implementing the digital transformation in large corporations, but simply working and dealing with fast-growing, young companies can give the decision makers a feel for fast and agile development methods.

Large companies often institutionalize their stakeholdings and transform them into business units. Under Armour and its connected fitness business is a good example of this.

Many companies are setting up corporate venture capital/investment funds. For example, Toyota as of the beginning of 2017 had invested in 15 tech start-ups through a $310 million fund. Perhaps the most significant example in this category is the Japanese telecommunications and Internet corporation SoftBank, which has established one of the world's biggest investment funds. The $100 billion SoftBank Vision Fund has investment from the Saudi Arabia government, but also more recently from Apple. In an interview with Reuters, Apple director of communications Josh Rosenstock outlined the importance of the investment: "We believe their

---

[2] http://media.gm.com/media/us/en/gm/home.detail.html/content/Pages/news/us/en/2016/Jan/0104-lyft .html; http://media.gm.com/media/us/en/gm/news.detail.html/content/Pages/news/us/en/2016/Jan/ 0121-maven.html; http://fortune.com/2016/03/11/gm-buying-self-driving-tech-startup-for-more-than- 1-billion/

new fund will speed the development of technologies which may be strate-gically important to Apple."

9.4 SPEED AS A GUIDING PRINCIPLE

Speed is infectious: an organization that uses agile methods, develops fast, quickly tests products in the market, and immediately incorporates market feedback into further developments no longer has anything in common with the customary, ponderous methods of the traditional enterprise.

Acting Decisively, Not Hesitantly

To ensure that the doubters don't slow down the pacesetters in a complex and comprehensive transformation, speed is absolutely critical. By employ-ing agile methods and concentrating on the rapid rollout of MVPs—those basic starter products that are continuously improved—classic develop-ment times can be reduced by up to 90 percent.

Development teams at a major energy utility used dynamic sprint methods to test an initial MVP in just six weeks, fully covering the process stages of discover, define, design, and deliver. The product was an app that helps field engineers detect gas leaks, evaluate the importance of the leak, and trigger the relevant actions in order of urgency.

During the initial discover phase, the developers accompanied the engineers on their site visits, learned which information they needed in what order and context, assessed whether they had one or two hands free to hold a tablet in the specific situations, and when and how they needed and received support from the back office. They also noted the many pain points, such as missing or incorrect data, and the amount of manual list entries that had to be completed on paper. Experts call it ethnographic research, and it's part of the design thinking development process.

After six weeks and a number of rigorous hackathons, a prototype of the app was ready for field testing. And after various iterative cycles, the final product was ready for market launch another six weeks later. In the past, these types of projects could have lasted up to six years, and might not have even seen the light of day at the end. The rapid market launch of the app triggered a snowball effect: the organization and management were both surprised and delighted, which further cemented their belief in digitization, and in turn further accelerated the transformation.

Speed as a guiding principle requires a complete rethink: energy supplier example

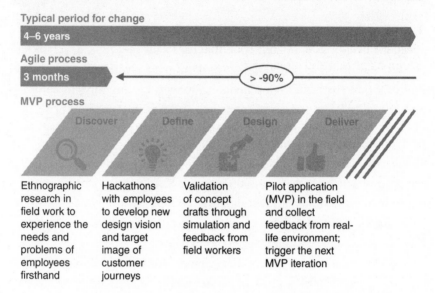

Typical period for change

4–6 years

Agile process

3 months ⟵————— > -90% —————

MVP process

Discover	Define	Design	Deliver

| Ethnographic research in field work to experience the needs and problems of employees firsthand | Hackathons with employees to develop new design vision and target image of customer journeys | Validation of concept drafts through simulation and feedback from field workers | Pilot application (MVP) in the field and collect feedback from real-life environment; trigger the next MVP iteration |

9.5 RAPID SCALING: DIGITIZING THE ENTIRE ENTERPRISE

Using the example of the energy utility and its rapid MVP development described in the preceding section, we will now show how digitization is rolled out across an entire enterprise. The utility company plans to digitize all key processes as part of a three-year program.

An Energy Utility Shows the Way

In the first step of the transformation, the energy supplier analyzed its most important processes, and assessed where digitization could offer the most benefit. In terms of production, for example, the aim was to reconcile supply and demand curves using big data. This is no simple task considering fluctuations in supply caused by renewable sources of energy. In terms of transport, a key area is maintenance, which could be made considerably more efficient with predictive analytics. Smart pipeline networks are an option for optimizing distribution. In terms of service, field engineers need constant access to maps, data, and all the necessary software tools. In sales, data analyses and segmentation optimize customer interaction. Other applications include the establishment of a platform on which energy supply, including from third-party suppliers, can be traded in real time, and an automated back office. A wide range of options therefore needs to be prioritized.

Forceful scaling of a digital transformation follows a clean diagnosis and a plan

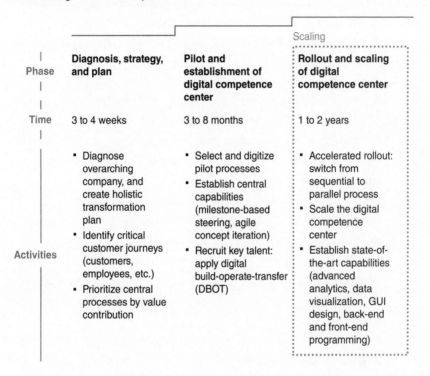

Phase	Diagnosis, strategy, and plan	Pilot and establishment of digital competence center	Rollout and scaling of digital competence center
Time	3 to 4 weeks	3 to 8 months	1 to 2 years
Activities	• Diagnose overarching company, and create holistic transformation plan • Identify critical customer journeys (customers, employees, etc.) • Prioritize central processes by value contribution	• Select and digitize pilot processes • Establish central capabilities (milestone-based steering, agile concept iteration) • Recruit key talent: apply digital build-operate-transfer (DBOT)	• Accelerated rollout: switch from sequential to parallel process • Scale the digital competence center • Establish state-of-the-art capabilities (advanced analytics, data visualization, GUI design, back-end and front-end programming)

To meet these expectations, IT faces various challenges at every stage—a perfect illustration of the need for a two-speed IT architecture. For the management and billing of energy supply at the production stage of the value chain, IT needs unprecedented access to business processes, both as an adviser and as a partner to the many decentralized energy producers. In terms of transport, IT needs to ensure standardization, which is a routine task, but it also needs agile capabilities to intelligently analyze data from sensors in the smart pipeline networks and translate this into actions for field engineers. These engineers, in turn, need real-time access to plans, data, and software tools via mobile apps, which again demands agile IT methods as well as the more routine work with cloud-based solutions. The ultimate aim is predictive maintenance where equipment is serviced before it goes wrong, and this requires a new mind-set in machine management. The closer the company moves toward customer communication with user-friendly information and offers, the more agile the relevant IT team must be. Only in administration at the very end of the process does the stable, traditional IT architecture dominate again.

The energy utility wanted the digital transformation to trigger improvement in five areas especially:

1. *Safety.* The teams wanted to develop efficient processes without workarounds or temporary solutions to ensure that all involved in the process always had the right data in the right context to enable correct decisions right from the start, and to protect customers and employees from risks.
2. *Reliability.* The teams were to develop joint standards and structures that could be used throughout the company, and establish instruments for effective communication and collaboration.
3. *Customer satisfaction.* Customers were to receive fast and effective support, and have apps and software programs to hand that enabled simple management of contract issues and easy communication with the company.
4. *Compliance.* Strict compliance with legal requirements is particularly important for energy suppliers, as any infringement can be costly. Control and monitoring of all safety-related work was therefore to be improved.
5. *Economy.* The methods needed to avoid duplicate work, to apply solutions to adjacent areas, and to ensure streamlined processes were well known. It was just a matter of applying them consistently.

True to the logic that you can improve only what you can measure, the transformation teams defined meaningful metrics for each area. Safety, for example, was assessed based on sickness levels, the number of work accidents, energy outages, damage to pipelines, and incidents in production.

Reliability was assessed by the average outage time per customer. Customer satisfaction was evaluated based on the results of a survey by a renowned market research institute. Economy was assessed by cost, revenue, and profit curves. To assess compliance, the teams simply counted the number of infringements. These examples demonstrate how the company defined simple yet insightful metrics by which progress could be quantified.

To achieve the targeted improvements, the transformation teams examined the various digital technologies available, starting of course with customer-facing processes. Much has changed in recent years. Customers today pay by smartphone, research prices and service offerings on online forums and blogs, complain about outages or long call-waiting times on Twitter, book service appointments from an avatar with an automated voice dialogue system, check their account balances by text, and use smart meters and smart-home systems like Nest to manage their energy consumption. If an energy company leverages all the technological possibilities for customer interaction, costs for normal customer support can be reduced by up to 95 percent, while also offering customers better service.

All of the young challengers to the big energy utilities show that most processes can indeed be digitized. On average, 90 percent of customer interaction is digital, compared to just 20 percent in many traditional companies. Costs for online customer support are also much lower, comprising just one-sixth of the costs incurred for postal communication, and half that of call center support. Best of all, customers using digital channels are much more satisfied, with surveys revealing that 76 percent of customers are satisfied with digital communication. Only 57 percent of customers contacted through traditional channels were satisfied. All of these metrics are just part of a group of KPIs that are continuously measured.

Now That We Have the Tools, It's Time for Action

The targets and metrics have been defined, and the tools are ready. The next step is implementation. The energy utility defined four areas to start first: processes relevant to the customer, suppliers, field engineers, and administration.

Numerous processes of an energy supplier can be improved with apps

Target group	Value creation stage	Examples
Customer processes	**Transport and distribution**	• Information about outages and bottlenecks in real time
	Sales and service	• Consumer dashboard showing consumption, bills, payments, savings suggestions, etc.
	Corporate center	• Support for call centers with machine learning systems, avatars, etc. • Big data and advanced analytics to optimize segmentation, customer journeys, etc.
Supplier processes	**Production**	• Interactive digital trading platforms
	Transport and distribution	• Disruption notifications in real time
Field service processes	**Production**	• Optimized maintenance and servicing (e.g., interactive planning tools for maintenance and predictive maintenance) • Knowledge management (e.g., codification of tricks and tips)
	Transport and distribution	• Team management and communication in real time • Planning of teams and their deployments for team leads/supervisors • Safety checklists
Internal processes	**Production**	• Real-time forecasting of supply and demand
	Transport and distribution	• Support for scheduling and connection activations • Analytics to identify theft and fraud
	Sales and service	• Optimized CRM, cross-/up-selling with analytics and machine learning systems • Digitization of dunning notices

1. *Customers.* The company identified customer-facing processes on the customer journey as those offering the greatest potential. Opportunities exist throughout the value chain to digitize customer contact, and thus reduce costs while improving the service. It starts with production with apps that allow customers who produce and

supply green energy to stay up to date with their sold quantities. In the areas of transport and distribution, the energy supplier can install digital alarm systems that notify customers of outages and bottlenecks in real time. In terms of customer contact and service, the company can provide its customers with an app that shows key data at a glance.

Acting as a consumer dashboard, the app not only shows customers how much energy they are consuming and how this compares to their historical consumption, but it can also suggest ways to save energy, such as running the washing machine during off-peak hours. Such services offer customers genuine added value, while also encouraging more balanced energy consumption during the day when off-peak prices are available due to low demand. And on the corporate side, call centers can be supported or even fully replaced by digital assistants and machine-learning systems that are capable of answering the vast majority of questions, and can forward the call to the right person for the trickier questions. The company can also use advanced analytics to form the millions of customer data points into a detailed customer profile. The smarter the household becomes, the more data it generates, meaning the ability to handle big data became a vital core competency for the energy supplier.

2. *Suppliers.* The second area on the path toward digitization relates to supplier-facing processes or the supplier journey. At the production stage, it's about providing digital trading platforms for excess supply. In transport and distribution, it's about real-time data on deliveries and disruptions. In sales and customer contact, it's about paperless billing. And in administration, it's about integrating data on suppliers and energy companies.

3. *Field engineers.* At the production level, field engineers are provided with apps for safety checks, predictive maintenance, and repair tips. In transport and distribution, two apps for tablets were created. The first is team management in real time, which provides managers with a constant overview of where their engineers are working, what problems they're working on, and the progress of their work. This app was a great success, helping engineers increase

the number of repairs by around 50 percent. The app was developed using textbook agile development practices: programmers and the later users of the app were in constant dialogue on the team, a rapid pilot version was tested by engineers in the field, and the feedback was quickly incorporated into further development, which all led to an attractive app that's easy to use and has vastly increased productivity. The second is a complementary app that was developed in the same way and helps schedulers plan and prepare their service teams and deployments. Both apps have significantly increased the productivity of field engineers.

4. *Administration.* At the production stage of the value chain, an app was developed for the real-time forecasting of supply and demand. At the transport and distribution level, an app was created for customer service advisers that shows the customer's service request and provides the data they need to evaluate the request and provide the customer with a quote. Required services can also be activated and billed, covering the end-to-end process.

While digitization efforts are still ongoing, complete, concrete improvements have already been made. In the customer satisfaction rankings of a leading market research institute, the company moved up three places in just the first year, while year-on-year revenues rose by an impressive 20 percent.

CONCLUSION: THE DIGITAL WORLD DEMANDS A NEW WAY OF THINKING

We have now covered the whole spectrum of establishing, piloting, and scaling a digital transformation. At every phase, speed is of the essence. Three to four weeks are sufficient for clear diagnostics and a plan; three to eight months for a pilot; and one to two years to implement the plan itself throughout the organization. This is integrated digitization—Digital@Scale.

But digitization isn't just about restructuring the organization. Above all, it's about establishing a new mind-set: teams instead of hierarchies, networks instead of silos, pace over perfection, and learning from customers, not lecturing them. The digital world demands a new way of thinking. While it may not be easy for everyone to say good-bye to their old systems, it is necessary. As we demonstrated at the start of this book: digitization isn't an option; it's a necessity if your business is to survive. It also presents an incredible opportunity—for your company, for your team, and for you as an employee or manager.

QUESTIONS MANAGERS SHOULD ASK THEMSELVES: WHERE ARE YOU?

In Chapter 3, we explained why all companies need a digital concept. In Chapters 4 to 6, we outlined what is to be done. In Chapters 7 to 9, we explained how to implement the digital transformation in your organization decisively, holistically, and rapidly. After that, it's about going live with the digital enterprise.

Everything starts with a good plan that encompasses the entire business, thinks of the customer first, and systematically breaks down organizational silos. It's essential to make a decisive switch to the digital operating system, proactively steer change, and systematically motivate managers to lead, at every level. Finally, the transformation must be scaled purposefully and unhesitatingly throughout the enterprise. In the process, it's vital to heed three key philosophies: make your IT a weapon, work closely with start-ups, and let speed be your new guiding principle. That's Digital@Scale.

How? Key self-appraisal questions for management
Level of agreement from 1 (very low) to 5 (very high)

		1 2 3 4 5
Creating a plan	1 Do we have a plan for the digitization of our entire enterprise?	▪ ▪ ▪ ▪
	2 Do we place the customer at the center of change?	▪ ▪ ▪ ▪
	3 Does our organizational structure support the required change?	▪ ▪ ▪ ▪
Ramping up the digital company	4 Digital natives think in weeks, not years—how agile is our company?	▪ ▪ ▪ ▪
	5 Market success—how can we correctly measure the success of digitization?	▪ ▪ ▪ ▪
	6 Have we put together a team with digital experience and industry insight?	▪ ▪ ▪ ▪
Scaling forcefully	7 Do we scale rapidly, systematically, and forcefully?	▪ ▪ ▪ ▪ ▪
	8 Can our IT make our business faster?	▪ ▪ ▪ ▪ ▪
	9 Do we have worthwhile partnerships with start-ups?	▪ ▪ ▪ ▪ ▪
	10 How do we get the organization on board, and do we have a concept for handling concerns?	▪ ▪ ▪ ▪ ▪

□-□-🔟-□-□

ARE WE IN GOOD SHAPE FOR THE TRANSFORMATION?

INNOVATION CYCLES RUN ever faster, *with each of us experiencing ever more discontinuity. Anand Swaminathan and Jürgen Meffert discuss the markets and technology of the digital age, examining and putting forward proposals on what is needed to successfully negotiate the upheavals of the future.*

Jürgen Meffert: Many people feel unsettled by the rapid pace of change brought about by digitization. To overcome these anxieties, it helps to understand a little of the context. Ever since the days of Adam Smith, the frameworks in which businesses trade have continued to evolve. The economist Nikolai Kondratiev was the first to describe the long waves in economic life that followed technical innovation, from steam power and railways to the automobile and information technology. New technologies always drive innovation cycles—the only difference being that today those cycles are ever shorter, with each innovation being overtaken by the next at exponentially increasing speed. The early industrial landscape delighted in progress: it saw how each new technology further liberated the individual, from physical work, from restrictive working hours, and from danger. Living standards blossomed for millions of people, and life expectancy rapidly increased. People in today's industrial nations live to almost twice the age as their ancestors 100 years ago.

Anand Swaminathan: What are the consequences? Whereas in the past an innovation cycle would span a generation, it is by no means unusual today for a generation to experience several innovation cycles. Upheaval has become the norm, and the trend is rising.

Jürgen Meffert: I've experienced it firsthand when we launched the first word processing computer at Nixdorf, which was set to replace the trusty old typeball typewriter. Barely had it been launched, however, than it was rendered obsolete by the introduction of the personal computer. The rapid spread of the PC changed the rules, and established completely new price points. A computer for every home was born—and very quickly we found ourselves in the next S curve. Since then, the pace of development has intensified even more dramatically, and I find myself wondering what this will mean for the managers of the future and their education.

Anand Swaminathan: Managers in existing companies like linear ways of thinking. But that didn't go too well in the past: whenever a new S curve appeared, technology was the trigger, and the traditional managers found they weren't up to the challenge. The protagonists of each of these technologies would ring in the changes, heralding the age of the new S curve. Innovation cycles accelerate, and discontinuities follow each other in ever greater succession. This is something Joseph Schumpeter recognized almost 100 years ago, describing it as creative destruction in his book *Capitalism, Socialism and Democracy*. Such accelerated innovation also has an impact on the length of office of business leaders. It's been radically reduced. Thirty-five percent of all CEOs in S&P 500 listed companies had been in office for 10 or more years in 1984. This figure had fallen to just 15 percent in 2000. In 2009, CEOs on average remained at the top for just six years, and the trend is falling.

Jürgen Meffert: And the demise of business leaders has also seen many previously leading companies become irrelevant. Again, we just have to take a look at the S&P 500: in 1958, the companies listed on the index had been there for an average of 61 years; by 1980, the average time on the list had fallen to 25 years, and in 2011, it was just 18 years. Big names like Kodak, RadioShack, Sears, and even *The New York Times* dropped out of the index. Once again, we see accelerating trends. *Companies* overtake each other in the index with increasing frequency, thus proving Schumpeter's dictum of creative destruction: the old gives way to the new, the improved. Companies that lack the ability to translate innovation into new products, and that are unable to extricate themselves from their old ways of business because they are so steeped in emotion and tradition, will have no long-term future, and will fall by the wayside. Those that want to remain at the top must carefully manage the moments they launch new technologies. The latest research is working on ways to determine the best time for market entry, on the one hand to prevent competitors stealing a decisive lead, and on the other to ensure the new technology is launched when customers are ready for it, and when its benefits will trigger strong demand.

Anand Swaminathan: What I like about the climbers in the digital world is just how resolute they are in placing the customers' needs at the center of their actions. Marketing is once again playing a key role.

Marketing was originally established as market-oriented company management: a holistic, strategic view of the market, the customer, and customer benefits. Over time, marketing has branched into a whole range of different disciplines. A vast number of new tools and constructs have been developed in classic marketing, further driving fields of specialization. The past 10 years in particular have seen what was once an all-encompassing function become increasingly heterogeneous. As a result, marketing has now lost its importance as a management function, and in many cases has been reduced to simple communication and other functional roles.

Jürgen Meffert: Thanks to digitization, there's now a lot to be said for a renaissance of marketing as part of market-focused business leadership. Holistic customer-to-customer approaches are needed again. And big data and advanced analytics provide marketing with a new platform for truly data-driven decisions. Never before have we been able to ascertain so quickly and so precisely what the customer really wants and doesn't want.

Anand Swaminathan: As division of labor and specialization reach their limits in today's organizations, we may see a renaissance of market-focused business leadership as it was originally defined: that is, the need to understand the customers, their changing needs, and their journey across every touch point in the company. Today, this means quickly redeveloping products based on customer feedback and establishing agile methods throughout the organization from development to production, and from sales to administration.

Jürgen Meffert: Managers and employees can expect a great many changes: cross-functional teams instead of hierarchical silos, digital technology driving change throughout the company at lightning pace, and unprecedented volumes of data requiring intelligent analysis. How can we shape education and skills, and propel society into the new S curve to ensure that digitized enterprises are able to find the employees they need in the new digital age?

Anand Swaminathan: And which central elements of these digital companies will ultimately decide their success or failure? Isn't that worth rolling up our sleeves to find out? Let's draw on our collective experience and see if we can lay down some key proposals for the digital age.

Jürgen Meffert: So let's start with the individual. Our first proposal would be: every person should learn at least the basic minimum in technical skills. It's not such an absurd idea. Everyone today, whether young or old, well-educated or less well-educated, can use a smartphone. It's up to schools to ensure that every child in the country learns basic technical skills. In the United Kingdom, for example, programming is already a mandatory subject. That's entirely feasible for us here in Germany, too, to make sure as many children as possible are digitally literate. In the future, a basic understanding of digital technology will be regarded as being as important as reading, writing, and arithmetic—for everyone, not just for those who use it in their work.

Anand Swaminathan: So now let's move on to the customer. Our second proposal: the customer must be at the heart of all considerations. The digital companies show us how it's done successfully—Google with its ever-improving search engine, Amazon with its personalized recommendations, and of course Apple. With the iPod and iPhone, Steve Jobs satisfied latent customer desires that customers hadn't even articulated yet. He realized that even among their tech-savvy customer base, there was a desire to connect with the products on an emotional level, hence the supremely cool designs of Apple products. They also established an international community of Apple users, and cultivated them on a massive scale. Those who used an Apple for work, study, or play felt part of a global avant-garde.

Jürgen Meffert: Okay, well, let's stay with technology, and formulate our third proposal: consistently use technology for the things that it does well. We humans should welcome robots and computers as liberators. People are designed to think, and to be creative and empathetic. We can happily leave the heavy, physical work, the mundane, monotonous tasks, and anything to do with efficiency to robots and technology. We could let our talents flourish and focus on real added value, on what we humans do best.

Of course, it's important that society also looks at the technological discontinuities constructively and positively, and comes to regard the digital innovations as a liberation rather than a threat. That doyen of economics, Schumpeter, described it as a matter of course in functioning competitive economies: as the old occupations and roles disappear, new, usually better, less hazardous, less taxing, and more interesting jobs emerge. Such retrospection shows that technical innovations have helped us and eased our workloads. They have given us longer, healthier lives and an unprecedented standard of living. It should also be remembered that neither the steam engine, the assembly line, nor the computer led to mass unemployment—the fears are overblown.

Anand Swaminathan: Where does progress come from? Time for our fourth proposal: promote innovation through openness and open standards. The basic premise is simple: markets are always more innovative than any single business can ever be. Once again, the digital companies show us how open interfaces allow the brunt of innovation work to be transferred to external developers. The benchmark is set by the open development conferences of Apple, where thousands of external developers collaborate, sometimes for free. And customers also play an increasingly active role. In the past, businesses protected their technology and innovations; outsiders were to have no knowledge of them, let alone collaborate. Today, things have changed in many companies, and textbooks also take a different stance. Open standards are becoming increasingly important.

Jürgen Meffert: Which brings me on to proposal number five: embrace change as something positive. It's something that today's society finds difficult as people instinctively strive to preserve the status quo for their own good—from where they live and how they work to the corporate landscape in general. I remember very clearly how, many years ago, Siemens dominated the global telecommunications market with its EWSD digital switching system. Then in the 1990s, at the very height of EWSD, a new technology concept entered the market—the router. Although Siemens also offered competitive products in the area, it was Cisco—at that time, just a start-up—that came to dominate the market as the Siemens hierarchy feared the cannibalization of its market-leading EWSD product. So we should abide by the following maxim, at least where business is concerned: allow destruction, let control give way to openness, and be willing to allow cannibalization—better that you do it rather than your competitors. It's something that Volkswagen recognized early on. As part of its platform and multibrand strategy, the company manages its product portfolio to optimize efficiency on the one hand, and to limit the bulk of cannibalization to the confines of its own group on the other.

Anand Swaminathan: Change must be mastered—but you have to practice, which leads me to our sixth proposal: train for the big disruptions. Someone who regularly tries out new things avoids decision patterns becoming embedded. If conditions change, an embedded/reflexive decision pattern may no longer be enough. Take driving on an icy road, for example: if you lose your grip, unlike on a dry road, you have to open the steering angle. By the same logic, when work starts becoming routine, it's time to change. Job rotation—preferably every three to five years—maintains dynamism. Continuous training should be established as a fixed component of corporate policy. I never understand why employee representatives don't argue more strongly for it—after all, it's ultimately about improving people's employability. Perhaps it's even more important than seeking further reductions in working hours. …

Jürgen Meffert: That's a very good point. For our seventh proposal, cultivate networks for more ideas and creativity, we need to take a look inside the company. We've seen how hierarchies often stunt innovation and impede entrepreneurship. By restricting their horizons, businesses, schools, universities, and even countries lose sight of new developments. We can find them everywhere—in Israel, South Korea, Japan, Silicon Valley, MIT, our Max Planck Institutes, and in central research laboratories like Bell Labs in the past. That's where we need to be—or at least have an ear. There are plenty of examples of how important such networks are, and how effective they can be in many areas. A large network helped a friend of mine who recently became seriously ill. Within a very short space of time, the world's two leading experts had been identified, and were able to help—one in New York, and one in Switzerland.

Another example is what's currently happening in software development. Software code is shared and published in open communities such as GitHub, where anyone can use it. Any software developer can upload his or her software elements and access other libraries—ushering in a completely new S curve of productivity in the area.

Anand Swaminathan: Our eighth proposal represents a true revolution in business: competence over hierarchy. What do I mean by that? Regardless of age, academic qualifications, or position in the company, one thing is true: you are what you know, not what titles you carry. Which demands a completely new paradigm in management: the obligation to dissent. Take the example of universities: until just a few years ago, the obligation to dissent was unthinkable. Hierarchy was important—the professors saw themselves as the holders of power rather than holders of an academic chair. Strict guidelines governed dissertations; there was no room for discussion. These days, professors are often evaluated by their students—the relationships have completely reversed.

Jürgen Meffert: Which brings me to our ninth proposal—you'll like it: education and further training should be like a playlist. A playlist on Tidal or Spotify is first and foremost personal—it's tailored to me. It reflects what I like and what's relevant to me. It contains the latest music, of course, but also classic hits and new artists—ones that match my music profile. Because I listen to different music today than a year ago, it always has to be updated. It also needs to be maintained and used over a lifetime.

Such a concept means a revolution for every educational establishment, whether at elementary school level or postdoctorate level. Too often, their curricula are retrospective in nature: too many classics and not enough new hits or new entries—typically old-fashioned. Too few students have their fingers on the pulse. More contemporariness and more individual playlists are needed. A new job profile will emerge like that of a DJ, who constantly delivers a tailored blend of classic hits, up-to-date chart music, and promising newcomers. The mix has to fit the profile. Lifelong learning also applies to business: as part of a dual system, trainers need to adjust their training courses to mirror the latest changes, in terms of both form and content. This way, companies can remain young and "steer the curve," switching from a linear to an exponential mind-set. It's an attractive and valuable model, and feasible for every individual, regardless of biological age.

Anand Swaminathan: And so to our tenth proposal: prevent thought silos. I would be in favor of first providing young people with broader training—a kind of general studies. Specialization should only come later, once the individual has developed holistic business judgment. As such, job profiles should be less specific because without interdisciplinary thinking and team skills today's businesses will fail. Employees should have an end-to-end understanding of customers. The super-specialized tasks can be left to the IBM Watsons and Google DeepMinds of this world.

When I look around, I see that technological innovations have contributed to a sustained easing of workloads, which in turn has led to an increased quality of life and greater life expectancy for many. However, I also see that new technologies always lead to greater uncertainty. Do I know what this innovation really means? Will it create or destroy jobs? What will happen to me? Will I still be needed? Innovations demand a completely new quality of trust—and that has to be earned first. That's where management plays a new and crucial role—we could call it ethical responsibility. It's also important that management provides that vital stability to the company, its customers, its employees, and its business partners in these times of turbulent change. Managers need to take time out to reflect. Or, as a colleague of mine says: sometimes you don't need to saw faster; you just need to take the time out to sharpen the saw.

Let's look forward to the next S curve of digitization: artificial intelligence, avatars, robots dashing about. Humans will still be needed, and will be responsible for progress, prosperity, and success. New, exciting roles are emerging—not least when it comes to ensuring the success of your digital transformation.

ABOUT THE AUTHORS

Anand Swaminathan

Anand Swaminathan is a Senior Partner in the McKinsey San Francisco office. He is a leader at the intersection of Digital McKinsey and McKinsey New Ventures and focuses on helping organizations across industries leverage technology and digital capabilities to evolve their operating models, transform their businesses to effectively serve their customers, and scale operations efficiently. For more than 20 years he has focused on serving clients in the financial services, technology, retail, and industrial sectors. In 2015 he was named to *Fortune* magazine's 40-under-40 most influential young people in business.

Jürgen Meffert

Dr. Jürgen Meffert is a Senior Partner in the McKinsey Düsseldorf office. He is both the Director of Digital McKinsey in the area of B2B and founder of McKinsey's initiative for small and midsize enterprise (SME) growth companies. He advises several leading global firms in the telecommunications, high-tech, and media industries, and has overseen extensive transformation programs in various fields: from growth and innovation strategies, marketing and sales, through to processes and organization.

Contributors

Kabir Ahuja

Kabir Ahuja is a Partner in the McKinsey Stamford office, where he is a leader in the Technology & Media practice. He focuses on helping companies find growth—spanning strategy, execution, capability building, and organization design. He is a leader in the IoT practice with a focus on connected homes, vehicles, and wearables, and spends much of his time helping companies understand and execute in a new connected world.

Aamer Baig

Aamer Baig is a Senior Partner at McKinsey in the Advanced Industries, Digital McKinsey, and Public Sector practices. He leads the Digital and Advanced Analytics client service lines for Advanced Industries, which include Aerospace & Defense, Automotive & Assembly, and Advanced Electronics sectors. For the past 20 years, Aamer has helped clients use digital technologies to drive innovation, transform customer experience, and improve productivity, while building organizational capabilities to sustain impact. He is based in Chicago.

Michael Bender

Michael Bender is a Senior Partner in the McKinsey Chicago office and is the global coleader of Digital McKinsey. Digital McKinsey focuses on technology strategy and delivery for global Fortune 2000 companies, as well as leading technology-driven issues like multichannel customer service, mobility, and e-government. He works broadly across industries on leading technology topics and in particular serves several players in the technology provider arena.

Satty Bhens

Satty Bhens is a Partner in the Digital McKinsey Mid-Atlantic office and the cofounder and CTO of McKinsey's Digital Labs. He has recently served clients in insurance, retail, transportation, travel, and banking. He possesses extensive experience in digital and agile transformations, defining and implementing modern technology platforms, and radically redesigning technology functions to improve their capability and velocity.

Adrian Booth

Adrian Booth is a Partner in the McKinsey Global Energy & Materials (GEM) practice, leads the Digital McKinsey West Coast office, and is a leader in the Digital GEM Transformation service line. Adrian serves industrial clients, solution providers, regulators, investors, and others on issues related to upgrading and transforming energy infrastructure. He has extensive experience across the globe in digital transformations.

Gianluca Camplone

Gianluca Camplone is a Senior Partner in the McKinsey Chicago office. He serves as industrial sector leader for the Midwest region. For more than 15 years, his focus has been on operations, performance transformation, growth strategies, marketing, and sales, serving clients in the automotive, industrial equipment, and building solution sectors across the United States, Europe, and China. Gianluca has been a founder of the Digital service line within the McKinsey industrial practice, increasingly focusing on digital and Internet of Things strategies, digital transformations, digital use case development, and go-to-market strategy.

Enno de Boer

Enno de Boer is a Partner in the McKinsey New Jersey office. For the past 17 years Enno has led the operations transformation teams at several Fortune 500 and SME companies, the Global McKinsey Capability Center Network, and the Mid-Atlantic Operations Hub. He has broad cross-industry expertise across automotive areas, advanced electronics, semiconductors, pharmaceuticals, medical technology, and consumer packaged goods. Enno currently leads Digital Manufacturing in North America.

Sumit Dutta

Sumit Dutta is a Partner in McKinsey's Chicago Office and a leader in the Supply Chain practice. Sumit joined McKinsey in 2000 and has led supply chain strategy and operations transformations across industries, including automotive, basic materials, e-commerce, and commodity chemicals.

Alexander Edlich

Alexander Edlich is a Senior Partner in the McKinsey New York office. As one of the senior leaders of the Financial Services, Private Equity, and Technology practices, he serves leading institutions around the world to improve their performance. Since he joined, he has covered a broad range of assignments on corporate strategy, business unit strategy, growth strategies, performance transformation, corporate turnarounds, organizational design, operational improvement, digital and technology enablement, and sourcing.

David Frank

David Frank is a Partner in the McKinsey Atlanta office. David partners with companies in highly competitive industries to help them create best-in-class customer experiences. He has worked extensively with companies in the travel and logistics sectors to improve their customer-facing operations, with particular focus on improvements in situations involving large frontline organizations, and developing sustainable competitive advantages.

Brendan Gaffey

Brendan Gaffey is a Senior Partner in the McKinsey Dallas office. Brendan has extensive experience serving telecom, high-tech, and media clients across the Americas on growth, strategy, operations, and sales and marketing. He developed a five-year growth strategy for a leading wireless provider, prioritizing adjacent markets, identifying specific plays for the operator within each market, and short-listing key acquisition opportunities. He has also supported the development of new organization models (e.g., venture unit) to better support innovation on a go-forward basis.

Julie Goran

Julie Goran is a Partner in the McKinsey New York office. She focuses on serving clients across industries on issues of organization, strategy, marketing, and operations. Julie is a leader in McKinsey's Global Organization practice and leads the firm's Digital Organization service line. Her work in organization spans organizational design, organizational health and change management, and talent and leadership.

Brian Gregg

Brian Gregg is a Partner in the McKinsey San Francisco office and serves clients in consumer-facing industries, with deep experience in retail, e-commerce, consumer technology, and consumer packaged goods. Brian leads the Marketing service line for the Americas and is coleader of the Consumer Digital Excellence initiative. He has functional expertise in a multitude of marketing and sales disciplines, including omnichannel strategy, digital marketing, customer engagement, customer relationship management/loyalty, brand strategy, market entry/expansion, sales force effectiveness, and consumer-centric innovation.

Martin Harrysson

Martin Harrysson is a Partner in the Digital McKinsey Silicon Valley office in Palo Alto, California. He joined the firm in 2007, and since then he has focused on serving clients in high tech, telecommunications, private equity, and industrials on topics including digital sales, digital architecture, and product development. Martin leads McKinsey's Software Product Development service line in North America.

Holger Hürtgen

Holger Hürtgen is a Partner in the McKinsey Düsseldorf office, and an expert on big data and advanced analytics. He works on analytics issues spanning various sectors, focusing on marketing analytics to predict customer behavior such as contract termination and next-purchase decisions. He uses complex machine-learning algorithms, and helps his clients transform their companies into data-driven businesses.

James Kaplan

James Kaplan is a Partner in the McKinsey New York office. He coleads the firm's global practice in cyber security. In his 15 years at McKinsey, James has assisted clients in financial services, health care, and advanced manufacturing set technology strategies, optimize infrastructure operations, adopt cloud capabilities, prioritize technology risks, and manage multiyear cyber security programs. He also assists private equity firms in making investments in the enterprise technology and cyber security markets. He is the coauthor of *Beyond Cybersecurity* (John Wiley & Sons, 2015) and is a coauthor of the 2014 World Economic Forum report *Risk and Responsibility in a Hyperconnected World.*

Basel Kayyali

Basel Kayyali is a Senior Partner in the McKinsey New Jersey office and leads McKinsey's technology practice in the payor subsector in the Americas. In addition, he is the Managing Partner of the Mid-Atlantic office for Digital McKinsey. He has worked primarily at the intersection of operations, technology, and health care serving players across the health care value chain (payors, providers, pharma/biotech) on various topics, including large operations and technology transformations.

Naufal Khan

Naufal Khan is a Partner in the Digital McKinsey Chicago office. He globally coleads McKinsey's Digital Organization cluster and is the global leader of the IT Strategy & Organization service line. Naufal has more than 20 years of experience in technology disciplines, and helps clients with enterprise-scale digital transformations and IT turnarounds.

Somesh Khanna

Somesh Khanna is a Senior Partner in the McKinsey New York office. He leads Digital McKinsey in financial services globally and previously led McKinsey's New York office. He actively serves both banking and insurance clients on topics ranging from digital transformations to digital strategy and organization. Somesh is a leader with 20 years of financial services strategy, business building and operating, and client management experience as a management consultant, entrepreneur, and commercial banker. He has a proven track record of recruiting, managing, and leading high-performing, high-impact individuals and teams.

Martin Lundqvist

Martin Lundqvist is a Partner with Digital McKinsey and is based in Stockholm. Martin leads all of McKinsey & Company's technology strategic work within the public sector in Scandinavia. He also leads McKinsey & Company's global Digital Government service line. His experiences range from developing country-wide infrastructure optimization plans, defining government common architectures, and setting up cross-agency governance structures to leading agency-level work on digitalizing services, optimizing IT delivery, securing large IT programs, and reviewing organization structures. Further, he is a frequent keynote speaker at public sector IT/digitization conferences and CIO roundtables internationally on topics relating to government-wide digitalization, securing large programs, and vendor management. He joined McKinsey in 2001.

Varun Marya

Varun Marya is a Senior Partner in the McKinsey San Francisco office. Since joining the firm in 1998, he has mainly served industrial companies, private equity firms, and their portfolio companies. He is a leader in the private equity practice and coleads McKinsey's Global Manufacturing practice, where he focuses on digital manufacturing.

Mark Patel

Mark Patel is a Partner in the McKinsey San Francisco office. Mark has more than 11 years' experience serving semiconductor, industrial, high-tech, and biotech clients on strategy and operations topics. Mark is a global leader of McKinsey's IoT service line, working with clients across industry verticals, including technology clients, to accelerate the adoption and implementation of the connection between the physical world and the Internet. He is a passionate believer in the impact that IoT will have in improving our lives, work, society, and health.

Hugo Sarrazin

Hugo Sarrazin is a Senior Partner in the McKinsey Silicon Valley office and the global leader of McKinsey's Digital Labs, a 1,000+ team with expertise in experience design, rapid digitization, data engineering, agile methods, and platform architecture. He started in the Canadian practice 22 years ago and was also a member of the Dallas office, where he led the Tech-Media-Telecom (TMT) practice for the Southern region of the United States. He also led the Business Technology practice of McKinsey on the West Coast in the past. He serves technology providers (software, hardware, online services, and IT services), users of technologies (e.g., CIO/CTO, business leaders), and private equity investors who invest in the TMT space.

Naveen Sastry

Naveen Sastry is a Partner in the Digital McKinsey Silicon Valley office. He has led McKinsey's Internet of Things initiatives since 2010. His work is with both adopters of IoT (CIOs and LOBs) as well as IoT vendors across the services, software, and hardware technology value chain. His PhD research was done at UC Berkeley in conjunction with DARPA on sensor networks more than 15 years ago.

Vik Sohoni

Vik Sohoni is a Senior Partner at McKinsey and a leader in its Digital McKinsey practice. He coleads the global Digital Banking service line, focused on using digital capabilities (online/mobile, automation, data) to transform banks' competitive positions. He is a deep banking expert, having served several of the top banks in North America and Latin America, and has led several large turnaround and transformation programs resulting in major strategic and operating model changes to deal with the new economics of banking.

Ramji Sundararajan

Ramji Sundararajan is a Partner in McKinsey's Silicon Valley office and the global coleader of the Digital Dynamic eCommerce pricing service line. Ramji has 11 years of experience helping revenue growth of consumer Internet companies and digital businesses of omnichannel players, from digital marketing to retention and pricing.

Michael Uhl

Michael Uhl is a Partner in the McKinsey Silicon Valley office. He currently leads the global Technology and Operations practice as well as the Fast Growth Tech group. He is also cofounder of McKinsey's 2020 Corporate Venturing and McKinsey Innovation Bootcamp service line, focused on transforming leading-edge corporations and industries leveraging the global and specifically Silicon Valley start-up communities. Michael has more than 20 years of experience driving significant growth and EBITDA improvements across the consumer electronics, electronic and medical equipment, and advanced industries.

Kelly Ungerman

Kelly Ungerman is a Partner in McKinsey's Dallas office. In her 17 years at McKinsey, Kelly has helped global retail and packaged goods clients on a range of strategy, growth, and transformation topics with a focus on digital and commercial transformations covering topics including digital marketing, e-commerce, omnichannel, customer life-cycle management (CLM), marketing return on investment (MROI), category strategy, pricing/promotions, and organization. Kelly has worked across retail formats (big box, specialty, grocery, value/off price) and categories (apparel, beauty, electronics, home, consumables, etc.).

Steve Van Kuiken

Steve Van Kuiken is a Senior Partner in the McKinsey New Jersey office, and he is the North American leader of the Digital McKinsey practice. He focuses on strategy development, organization, operations, and technology. He has led numerous digital transformations for large organizations across sectors. Steve founded and led the firm's digital practice in health care, and is a frequent contributor to leading publications and conferences.

Belkis Vasquez-McCall

Belkis Vasquez-McCall is a Digital Partner in the New York office of McKinsey. Belkis draws on agile methodology to inspire greater levels of performance across the enterprise and accelerate the pace of new product development. She is one of the pioneers of agile thinking at McKinsey. With more than 18 years of experience in delivering robust solutions and coaching teams, she is focused on agile transformation and partners with leaders in banking, health care, and other sectors to engender productivity and launch innovative products.

Sri Velamoor

Sri Velamoor is a Partner in McKinsey's Southern California office. He joined McKinsey in 2011 and is a leader in the firm's Digital McKinsey practice. He also leads the firm's Provider IT and Digital Health capability areas in North America. Sri's work has focused on a variety of topics in health care sectors ranging from strategy and performance to operations and technology.

Florian Weig

Dr. Florian Weig is a Managing Partner of the Munich office of McKinsey, and is responsible for the Product Development practice worldwide. He advises leading firms in the automotive, semiconductor, and machinery construction industries. He focuses on product optimization, the transformation of development organizations, and programs that deliver operational excellence and increase innovation.

Lareina Yee

Lareina Yee is a Senior Partner in the McKinsey San Francisco office, and leads the global Tech Infrastructure and Services sector for McKinsey's High Tech practice, where she is an expert on digital sales transformations, sales excellence, and culture change. Committed to achieving gender parity in business, Lareina is the head of McKinsey's North American Women Program and leads the firm's ongoing research on women in leadership. She developed the McKinsey Academy for Women, a digital training course for managers that has reached thousands of business leaders. She runs McKinsey's knowledge partnership with LeanIn.org, and she regularly publishes articles and speaks about advancing women in business. Lareina also serves as a board member for the International Center for Research on Women in Washington, D.C.

SPECIAL THANKS

To the project team for this book: Mohit Khanna, Sanket Chauhan, Sanchi Gupte, Anirudh Ravi Narayanan, and Jo Ann Miller.

INDEX